Navigating the C-124
Globemaster

Navigating the C-124 Globemaster

In the Cockpit of America's First Strategic Heavy-Lift Aircraft

BILLY D. HIGGINS

McFarland & Company, Inc., Publishers
Jefferson, North Carolina

All photographs are by the author unless otherwise credited.

LIBRARY OF CONGRESS CATALOGUING-IN-PUBLICATION DATA

Names: Higgins, Billy D., 1938– author.
Title: Navigating the C-124 Globemaster : in the cockpit of America's first strategic heavy-lift aircraft / Billy D. Higgins.
Other titles: In the cockpit of America's first strategic heavy-lift aircraft
Description: Jefferson, North Carolina : McFarland & Company, Inc., Publishers, 2019 | Includes bibliographical references and index.
Identifiers: LCCN 2019026994 | ISBN 9781476677637 (paperback : acid free paper) ∞
Subjects: LCSH: C-124 (Transport plane)—History—20th century. | Flight navigators, Military—United States—Biography. | Transport planes—United States—History—20th century. | Aeronautics, Military—United States—History—20th century. | Cold War—Personal narratives, American. | Higgins, Billy D., 1938–
Classification: LCC UG1242.T7 H54 2019 | DDC 358.4/483—dc23
LC record available at https://lccn.loc.gov/2019026994

BRITISH LIBRARY CATALOGUING DATA ARE AVAILABLE

ISBN (print) 978-1-4766-7763-7
ISBN (ebook) 978-1-4766-3711-2

© 2019 Billy D. Higgins. All rights reserved

No part of this book may be reproduced or transmitted in any form or by any means, electronic or mechanical, including photocopying or recording, or by any information storage and retrieval system, without permission in writing from the publisher.

On the cover: Douglas C-124 Globemaster aircraft (photograph © 2019 Shutterstock); *top* navigator wings (photograph from author's collection)

Printed in the United States of America

McFarland & Company, Inc., Publishers
 Box 611, Jefferson, North Carolina 28640
 www.mcfarlandpub.com

Table of Contents

Acknowledgments	vi
Preface	1
Introduction	3
1. "Oh, I have slipped the surly bonds of Earth...": Rolling Takeoffs	11
2. "Rush by air": Building an Aluminum Overcast	23
3. "The West Point of the Air": Undergraduate Navigator Training	43
4. "Ike's Bluff": The Cold War and Civil Wars	67
5. "Hairy conditions": Over the Oceans	83
6. "Birthplace of Winds": From Attu to Zaire	108
7. "The Right Stuff": Crewing Old Shaky	121
8. "Fate Is the Hunter": Mountains and Thunderstorms	141
9. "Sorry 'bout that": Korea and Vietnam	155
10. "The backbone of airlift": Epilogue	177
Appendix: C-124 Globemaster Accidents Involving Loss of Life or Loss of Airplane	181
Chapter Notes	191
Bibliography	202
Index	207

Acknowledgments

People and organizations that keep materials needed to document historical stories that we pursue have earned my deepest appreciation, and for this book those include: Harry Heist, archivist and former navigator at the Military Airlift Museum, Dover AFB, Delaware; Archangelo Difante, Air Force Historical Research Agency, Maxwell AFB, Alabama; Helen Kiss, Air Force Archives, Washington, D.C.; Ellery Wallwork, Office of History, and Denise M. Rodgers, Chief, Information Access Section, Scott AFB, Illinois. Oriana Pawlyk, Randolf Slaughter, David C. Arnold, Jerome V. Martin, George Eaton, Vernon Williams, and Archives and Special Collections at Louisiana State University in Shreveport gladly helped this author gathering essential materials for the narrative.

My guide to the world of publishing, Larry Malley, and author and former C-124 crew member Anthony Tambini gave me encouragement, advice, and insight via letters and email, as did Cal Taylor and Robert C. Owen. We seemed to connect and appreciate each effort in trying to get the airlifter story in full—and it takes all of our publications to do that. Dr. Dan Maher read the manuscript, as did my old friend and Lowell Thomas Award winner Phil Karber of Cambridge, Massachusetts, who offered details and suggestions that coordinated the approach and landing. I thank them both. Carolyn Filippelli, Boreham Library librarian and Shelly Blanton, archivist in the Pebley Center for History and Culture at the University of Arkansas—Fort Smith provided many specs, and their efforts are much appreciated. Around the poker table, my colleagues in the Department of History at UAFS cheerfully listened to my renditions of recent history. One of them, Dr. Bob Willoughby, presented me with a scale model of the Globemaster that he had built, which went on static display overlooking this work.

As I labored over aircraft accident archaeology, John Hille lent me

Acknowledgments

his knowledge and insights with a first-hand account of the aftermath of a tragic and ironic mid-air collision accident in Oklahoma. Jack Wofford, C-124 Aircraft Commander who made a successful gear-up emergency landing with passengers aboard, and Allen Moore of Cooperton, Oklahoma, a wheat farmer and eyewitness as a 31st Air Transport Squadron airplane and crew fell from the sky and six people I served with perished, gave me a look back to that tragic event which I was researching. As we knocked on their doors, they and their wives graciously invited Peggy and me, strangers until then, into their homes, giving us hospitality and crucial conversations about those accidents.

Early in the effort, I had the good fortune to contact Elio Argentati, who generously sent photographs of C-124s at Tachikawa, where he had served during the Korean War. Paul E. Getchell's niece, Leigh Buttermore Lefaivre, corresponded with me about her uncle, whose name is on the Vietnam Wall, and who was my first roommate in the USAF, and in my book, an American hero. Navigators George Price, Pat Knott, Bill Thornton, Paul Edwards, and James Harry Bassham shared photos and stories from their experiences as navigators on the heavy lifters. Their friendship in the flying years literally shaped my life. I have lost contact with others who helped with the shaping, but I thank them now, and they occupy a large part of my memories.

Mike Radowski so well described the thrill of flying Globemasters over the oceans that I was reluctant to summarize his essay, so incorporated it intact. I am especially grateful to Jim Faulkner, who has diligently worked to keep up with the hundreds of graduates of navigator classes that went through James Connally and Harlingen Air Force Bases. He has advised his fellow navs of whereabouts and fates of their brethren over the years and keeps the reunion fires stoked. We navs are fortunate to have that kind of organizer on our side.

To each flight engineer and loadmaster who crewed the Globemaster II and to a legion of maintenance airmen who "kept them flying," I confirm my deepest respect and profound thanks to them and to their spouses.

I dedicate this book to my wife and friend, Peggy, who once again soldiered up to become my invaluable coast-to-coast traveling companion even when asked to leave behind for a little while her beloved grandchildren, Evan, Luke, and Caroline.

Preface

Ironically, I had no inclination during my four-year assignment to the Globemaster II as a transport navigator while on active duty with the USAF or later as a reservist in the Tennessee Air National Guard to write about the airplane in which I accumulated 2,034 flying hours. The idea to write about it came 40 years later, after I had written two books on hard-working, easy-going people whose unsung but crowning achievements came during periods of testing transition in America. Those two books took 11 years to complete. While naturally preoccupied with gathering and organizing those facts about those worthy subjects at the time, on occasion an image would appear in the back reaches of my mind, like a dot in sky that continued to enlarge until I could make out the shape of a C-124 which, of course, made me want to write about this unpretentious working class airplane whose accomplishments peaked at a testing transition period not only for America, but for the world and for the aircraft industry.

The airplane lived up to its Douglas nickname, "the Globemaster." Powered by piston engines which meant moderate air speeds and weather-affected altitudes over long distances, this "last great navigation platform" was linked by stars in the heavens to vessels used by Columbus, Magellan, and Cook and to pre-satellite aviators Earhart and Lindbergh, who likewise depended on celestial navigation to guide their voyages.

C-124 aircrews piloted, engineered, loaded, secured and navigated this heavy lifter, known affectionately and accurately as Old Shaky, into every environment and climate the world had to offer. It gave aircrews an opportunity for hands-on interaction with and a bird's eye view of the globe over which it flew low and slow and served well.

With my wife, Peggy, at my side as she had been in previous research journeys, we traveled across the country, digging into the story of the C-124

Globemaster II, arriving at venues from Long Beach, California, to Dover, Delaware, and from Scott AFB, Illinois, to Maxwell AFB, Alabama, and to museums, archives, flight lines, and private homes in between, calling on places and people I thought relevant to the story of the Globemaster.

Maybe at first I did not realize how singular the plane was, nor did I realize that we who flew it, maintained it, rode in it, jumped out of it, or visited it in the air shows (where it drew record crowds) witnessed first-hand the C-124's role in changing America's strategic role in the world. Over all seven continents and islands from Greenland to Johnson, the bulbous-nosed heavy lifter ranged, carrying passengers, livestock, food and fuel supplies, missiles, a space ship, helicopters, and in many cases hope.

Approach in a C-124 Globemaster to runway 33L, Athens International Airport, 1963.

Introduction

In 1961, wily Soviet Premier Nikita Khrushchev had German Democratic Republic chairman Walter Ulbricht close roads between East and West sectors of Berlin. Thousands of workers swarmed out under cover of darkness on August 16 to start a gigantic task of replacing barbed wire barriers with a concrete block wall that physically separated the great German city. Maybe the Soviet Union and the Warsaw Pact countries would raise the stakes even higher. This hostile action reminded Americans that the Cold War, a term made prominent by Walter Lippmann in 1947, could turn hot in a hurry. The Pentagon approved the U.S. Army Command in Europe plans to deploy three divisions of troops into Germany along with air support, 24 fighter-bomber squadrons from the continental United States using two squadrons of C-124 Globemasters which would be based in the war zone.[1] This crisis raised tensions as in 1948, when Joseph Stalin closed rail and highway access to West Berlin across the Soviet sector in Occupied Germany, necessitating the Berlin Airlift, but this time the allied airlift mobility fleet boasted the C-124, the only airplane specifically mentioned in the top secret planning document.

The mention was appropriate. For 16 Cold War years, 1949–1965, the C-124 Globemaster II was our country's strategic heavy lifter of troops and equipment. Between 1948 and 1953, Douglas Aircraft Company built 447 for the U.S. Air Force. Dubbed C-124 by the company, and an improvement on the previous C-74 design, the first model of the "Globemaster" series, the C-124 Globemaster II enabled United States strategic, foreign policy, and military planners to calculate responses on a global scale to such threats as Berlin had posed. As surely as the Berlin Airlift, the Truman Doctrine, and the Marshall Plan had blocked Stalin's post–World War II ambitions in Europe, formation of the North Atlantic Treaty Organization in 1948 and the capability of a massive airlift led by Globemasters shortened Khrushchev's list of possibilities, too, and in so doing made the world safer in the critical years when the Soviets had a decided military advantage on the continent.

For those 16 crucial years, the Globemaster II, a key piece of equipment for the Military Air Transport Service (MATS), changed global configurations and sped U.S. mastery. The U.S. had spent $341,000,000,000 on winning World War II, but that did not include saving the British Empire, a concept President Roosevelt had expressly denied as a war aim. Indeed, Great Britain emerged from World War II bankrupt with a crumbling empire.[2] Without a mainstay of world order, new ideologies seemed threatening. President Truman had confirmed that this county would provide aid to emerging democracies against the forces of tyranny in faraway places (to many Americans) like Greece and Turkey. Truman, therefore, abandoned isolationism in the flower of what Henry Luce, *Time-Life* publisher, termed "The American Century."[3] In the Big Three conference at Potsdam in July 1945, Truman confided to Winston Churchill the readiness of an atomic bomb. The Prime Minister, aware of the "melancholy position of Great Britain who had spent more than half of its foreign investments" in fighting the war, realized then that Harry Truman, decisive

Globemaster on approach at Tempelhof AB, Berlin, Germany, 1961 (courtesy Air Mobility Command Museum).

and aggressive, would run things in this "American Century."[4] Churchill urged Truman to threaten Stalin with the obliteration of 25 Russian cities if he did not pull back his divisions from Berlin and Eastern Europe. Most likely, Stalin would not have done that, since he had no other place to station or feed his huge army. In 1946, the U.S. and its six atomic bombs (11 by 1947) along with the one and a half divisions that could be mustered by our Western allies hardly matched the 60 Red Army divisions in Eurasia, so no threat was issued nor would it have made Joe Stalin tremble if it had been.[5] A major counter to Russian power in Europe was the Brussels Pact, which became NATO after the U.S. Congress ratified the treaty on July 21, 1949, and President Truman signed it four days later.

The other super power emerging from World War II had its designs for, say, a Russian Century. Left with an overwhelming military advantage after the rapid demobilization of U.S. forces in 1945 and 1946, the Soviets, however, lacked the economic resources of the United States and lacked the capitalist obsession with new and open markets that an American aegis could provide.[6] The Cold War became one-sided. Despite the 1921 formation of the Communist International (the Comintern), which committed Russia to assisting worker revolutions all over the capitalist world, Stalin-led Soviet Union had a few internal priorities of its own interfering with its readiness to finance and support red insurgencies in Africa, Latin America, and Asia. Many Americans, however, thought that global domination was the compulsion of Russia and its leadership. The "loss" of China, the 1949 successful test of an atomic bomb by the Soviet Union, which no one doubted was made possible because of Soviet spies in the United States, McCarthyism, maps showing half the world's land area in red, brutalities in the puppet states, the loss of the "open door" for global capitalism, fear of repeating the appeasement of Munich, and Domino theories gave reasons needed to resist Communism anywhere.

The American Century gained traction with difficulties. Chief Republican spokesman Robert A. Taft of Ohio insisted on an isolationist course. Taft's leadership in his party and large conservative following countered liberal Republicans and moderate Democrats ready to enter into global markets and global decision-making. U.S. foreign policies and actions seemed to agree with the Taft position more than the latter. The shrinking of the U.S. Army and its post-war decline in training presumed a reluctance to fight ground wars, maybe even any kind of a war. Elements of the Truman administration seemed to concede to Soviet spheres of influence in Eastern Europe and maybe even a little bit of Asia. A speech by Secretary of State Dean Acheson before the National Press Club in 1950 ominously omitted the divided Korea peninsula from our vital interests and might have false-carded Communist leaders. Shortly thereafter, on June 26, 1950, North Korean Premier Kim Il Sung, with 230,000 troops, invaded the South. The United States was soon in a land war in Asia, fighting with ground troops, Army and Marines, moving up and down the rugged land. The Korean War, 1950–1953, though, had its aviation breakthroughs. American and Soviet fighter pilots fought air battles in jet planes; helicopters were widely used; for the first time, C-124 Globemasters appeared in a theater of war. It would not be the last time.

Korea provided the gauntlet for the concept of an American Century. The Truman administration thought it worth fighting for even if on Asian soil and across the widest ocean.

Airlift mobility went hand-in-glove with the confrontations of the Cold War, the post-colonial era, and emerging U.S. self-assumed responsibilities to meet fire with fire anywhere. The Globemaster would be an essential part of this concept with its capability to "rush by air, one division of doughfoots," as a Douglas Aircraft Company newspaper advertisement stated on January 1, 1952.[7]

On October 29, 1956, a combined British, French, and Israeli attack on the Suez Canal surprised and angered the Eisenhower administration. The president's demand for a cessation of the invasion prompted an International News Service article assuring Americans that 200 C-124 Globemasters, each of which could carry "74,000 pounds, or 200 armed troops at a speed of 300 mph over distances as great as 4,800 miles, could speedily place enough riflemen on the scene to guarantee a cease-fire in the Suez area."[8]

Another huge flying machine and a Globemaster contemporary, the Boeing-built B-52 Stratofortress, had high-volume, trans-oceanic capabilities, too. Both airplanes were disrupters, in the sense that military strategy would never be the same after them, as in recent times Amazon, eBay, and Netflix disrupted commercial strategies.

The B-52, as a part of the Strategic Air Command, looked like a bristling warrior, and it meant total war if its full capabilities were ever brought to bear on an enemy. Serving as a pilot, navigator, navigator/bombardier, or any other crew position on a Buff, had its charisma, its mystic glory, its romance. Curt LeMay and the SAC clout saw to that. Carrying nuclear weapons was of utmost seriousness and importance, but C-124s assigned to SAC in Strategic Services Squadrons, as well as those in Air Force Logistics Command and MATS at times, carried atomic bomb warheads, too.[9] Both B-52s and C-124s dropped these bombs (over our own country) inadvertently. Like the Globemaster, B-52s never penetrated the Iron Curtain or Soviet air space so far as officially reported. Both served relentlessly in combat or combat support missions. Fifteen B-52s were downed by enemy fire in Vietnam. Globemasters routinely flew over SAM sites and sometimes landed at forward airstrips that were under fire, but none were lost over Vietnam.

To carry out their respective missions, the two giants had to operate over long distances covering uninhabited areas such as oceans, continental land masses, and polar regions. In the years before satellite-derived navigation aids, this meant one crew position in these planes would be filled by a navigator, a rated (flight) non-pilot officer trained in celestial navigation, meteorology, map reading, and budding navigation electronic aids such as Loran (Long Range Navigation). While the B-52 cruised at high altitudes much of the time over familiar routes, the C-124 often was charting new territories on unfamiliar routes, flying over blank zones on the aviation maps. The B-52 navigators had to be proficient in rendezvous plotting for air-to-air refueling, something the C-124 navigators never had to worry about. On the other hand, the

unpressurized Globemaster operated at low altitudes and at speeds half that of the eight jet-engine-powered B-52. With flight time of 12 hours on some oceanic legs, the Globemaster depended on a series of position fixes—one every hour and 20 minutes at a minimum—the most accurate of which were the celestial lines of positions. Once a year, C-124 pilots had to demonstrate some proficiency in shooting the stars and plotting a position on the chart, but it was a perfunctory exercise and pilots, unless trained as navigators, which some had been, were clearly out of their element in this respect, much as a navigator would be when trying to land a C-124 once a year.

> The Air Force, as do other branches of the U.S. Military establishment, prefers the short-cut use of acronyms. In airplane designations, the C in C-124 stands for cargo. B in B-52, of course, stands for bomber, and fighters were F something. SAM means Surface-to-Air-Missiles, and ICBM is short for Intercontinental Ballistic Missile.

Because of its important global operational need in a day before satellites, digitization, or even inertial guidance, the C-124 Globemaster afforded the last great aerial navigation platform. During years of C-124 ascendency in global airlift, U.S. Air Force navigation schools—students were enrolled in what was called "Undergraduate Navigation Training"—turned out hundreds of graduates. Just as U.S. pilots ruled as the best in the world, so, too, the navigators were highly competent. One U.S. Air

8 Introduction

Force officer assigned to intelligence gathering in Korea mentioned that the intel community never had to worry about Soviet bombers getting to targets from Siberian bases and dropping their weapons anywhere in U.S. territories. We had to worry about their ICBMs, of course, but not their long-range bombers, even though they had them. Why not? They had

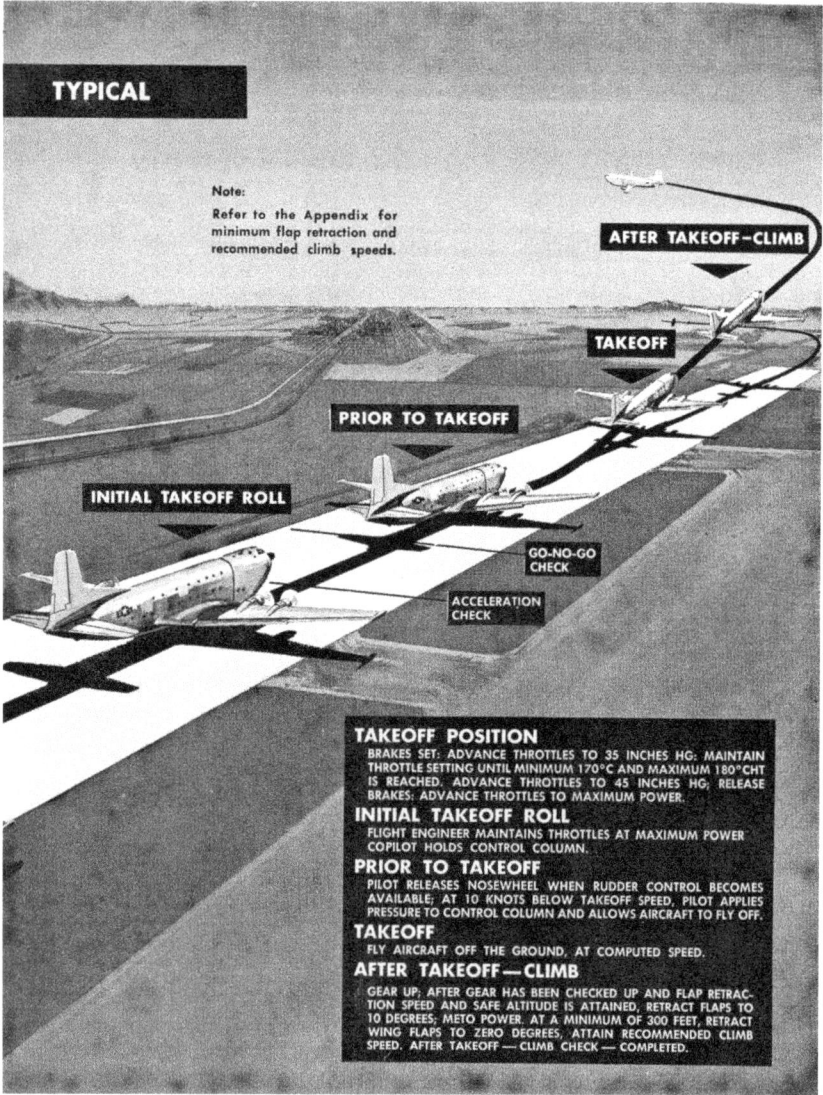

Image scanned from United States Air Force C-124C Flight Manual, 1960, T.O. 1C-124C-1. Subsequent reference use the term Dash 1 for this Flight Manual.

navigational insufficiency. They couldn't find their way to the targets by airplane.[10]

That was not the case in the U.S. Air Force. The art and science of human-computed air navigation peaked with Globemasters and the first B-52s. Examples abound in blogs, short stories, interviews, and reunion conversations about the excitement that could be generated in a long flight in a C-124. That was an old joke, of course, that piloting or navigating a prop plane over the ocean was hours of boredom broken only by moments of sheer terror. In many cases the terror was short, and normalcy soon returned, and the flight or mission was successfully completed. There were exceptions.

An appendix lists the 38 Class A mishaps which destroyed the airplane or in which fatalities occurred: 222 crew members and 367 passengers died in C-124 crashes, 589 people overall taking their last conscious flight in a Globemaster. Yet, the airplane served the Air Force, the nation, and its crew members well and created beloved memories for those people who built, maintained, and operated the Globemaster. Its heyday coincided with a global commitment transition for the United States. The Globemaster lived up to its name.

1

"Oh, I have slipped the surly bonds of Earth..."
Rolling Takeoffs

Major Irv Troske, Aircraft Commander, taxied his C-124 Globemaster smartly at Athens International Airport. Nearing the end of the taxiway, Captain Troske jammed his right foot down on the rudder pedal, making a grand turn onto the active runway while pushing the four throttles forward, signaling his intention for a rolling takeoff.

Behind the bulkhead aft of the pilot's seat, the navigator glanced to his right at the flight engineer panel literally filled with dials. A crusty veteran with seven stripes on his sleeve monitored the rising rpms of each of his four Pratt and Whitneys, checking their temperatures and oil pressures. Irv steadily advanced the throttles and through the headsets growled, "Max power, water on!" The engineer clicked on the ADI switches. As the big plane picked up speed, the copilot kept a watch on his takeoff data card. At the go-no go point, he called out "Go!" and we were committed. Twenty seconds later, the indicated air speed reached 115 knots, some 4,000 feet down the 10,000-foot runway. Irv let the plane fly itself off the ground, pulling the wheel into his lap, rotating the MATS airlifter for climb-out into a clear Greek sky.

John Gillespie Magee, Jr., an American who enlisted with Royal Canadian Air Force and came to Britain in 1941 as a 19-year-old Spitfire pilot, wrote the poem *High Flight*. Magee may have not known how difficult it was for a C-124 Globemaster II to slip the surly bonds of earth.[1] Rolling takeoffs felt smoother without the ludicrous lurch that standard procedure for that aircraft presented. Conventional methods took longer. First there was the slow turn to the active, squaring up, placing the nose wheel on the centerline of the runway, locking brakes, pushing the engines to max power, scanning all the gauges for problems or potential problems, and then and only then releasing the brakes. The nav's job at the time was to mark the departure time in the flight log and check for any loose rivets on the wing or cowling which with the huge vibration generated by four powerful and roaring engines might appear at any time and in any amount. The brake release was invariably followed by a hesitation as if the plane was surprised by the decision. This first timid but rickety movement of the C-124 in breaking the surly bonds brought the concept of mortality even into a 20-something-year-old mind.

So Irv, at the least, was sparing us noise, vibration, and a sense of foreboding that challenging serious odds can bring, and the nav appreciated this dalliance with MATS formalities. Irv was certainly not the only transport commander who stamped his personality onto flight and aircraft operation procedures. But I liked him because he was aircrew first and regs second in the best sense of that perspective. Maybe it was his upbringing in North Dakota, the unpretentious son of Russian emigrants to the North American steppe who brought with them secrets of growing red wheat in a cold climate. He had a deep cleft in his chin and dark wavy hair, a face faintly reminiscent of Orson Welles, and an apple-shaped body that was covered most of our time together by a rarely washed green USAF flight suit. Irv liked cigars, both lit and unlit, the latter handy during take offs and landings, about the only times in the C-124 that crew members with a nicotine habit refrained from smoking. Indeed, the Air Force Food Service kitchen stewards thoughtfully packed a sample pack of Winston right in with the boiled egg and the ham sandwich (always on white bread) common in the crew flight box lunches. Most of us carried a Zippo lighter in one of the flight suit's zippered pockets.

MATS, an acronym that stood for Military Air Transport Service, was a major flying component of the United States Air Force from 1948 to 1966, years when the Cold War zoomed to its tragicomic height.[2] With an inventory of cargo and passenger airplanes, MATS' mission was to fly goods and people all over the free world at the beck and call of not only the Air Force, but the Army and State Department, too, in order to protect democracy and spread U.S. largesse. The U.S. Navy and the Marine Corps did not use MATS much since they did not want to farm out important services to budget rivals and thus developed a separate system for aerial transport of their material.

MATS had books of regulations for operation of their aircraft and for training and retraining of airmen who flew them.[3] MATS was a serious outfit with its way of doing things, making men like Irv appreciated by his

1. "Oh, I have slipped the surly bonds of Earth..."   13

peers, who enjoyed poking a little fun at or sometimes end-running uptight superiors. For the most part, we got away with it and still flew safe, maybe even safer.

MATS constituted one of four major flying commands, along with Strategic Air Command (SAC), Air Defense Command (ADC), and Tactical Air Command (TAC). Two of these commands dripped with glamor, being equipped with fighter planes and fighter pilots. But the SAC, with its massive long-range bombers, was the most prestigious because of its signature boss, General Curtis E. LeMay. Not since Douglas MacArthur did a military office know as much about publicity, public image, and fandom as did LeMay, he of the famous phrase uttered in a National Security Council meeting, "We should bomb them back to the stone age!" Not many peace-time generals become household names—after all, MacArthur was a *theater* commander during World War II and virtual emperor of Japan afterwards who had those platforms to generate the copious attention paid to him—but LeMay did.[4] In fact, so recognizable was Curt LeMay even after his retirement as a four-star general that the American Independent Party recruited him as their vice presidential candidate in 1968.[5] The public seemed fascinated not only by the LeMay legacy, but with SAC's splendid motto—"Peace is our profession"—nuclear bombs and the huge B-52s that carried them, and the mystic command headquarters at Offutt AFB, Omaha, Nebraska, that could launch attacks capable of creating a nuclear winter. Two box office success movies featured SAC: *The Strategic Air Command* (1955) that starred James Stewart and June Allyson, and *Dr. Strangelove: or How I Learned to Stop Worrying and Love the Bomb* (1964) with three characters played by Peter Sellers, which became a black humor film classic by spoofing generals, nuclear war—and SAC.

The USAF maintained three single-engine pilot training bases in 1960.[6] Each base graduated four classes a year, so about 300 superb pilots emerged annually, most of them dreaming about leaping into the cockpit of a Starfighter.[7] Air Defense Command had the responsibility of protecting the skies above America, intercepting all intruders. This, too, was serious business during the Cold War, when a surprise attack from our nuclear opponent might have devastating effects. Any airplane—commercial, military, or privately owned—had to enter the country through a time-space window provided by air controllers. Otherwise, alerted by North American Air Defense (NORAD), nearby air bases scrambled their fighters, who rose to challenge violators.

Fighter pilots longed for air-to-air combat in which they would match their high-performance jets and advanced weaponry against their Soviet bloc counterparts. It was true that in Vietnam the MiGs were a performance match with the U.S. fighter inventory, the F-104 Starfighter, the F-101 Voodoo, the F-102 Delta Dart, the F-106 Delta Dagger, and the F-105 Thunderchief, until the coming of the fantastic F-4 Phantom in 1965. MiGs performance was heightened by Russian notions or lack of notions about insulation and redundancy in designing their craft. Russian pilots had to put up with noise and vibration in their cockpits and had no elaborate back-up if or when primary systems failed. But the savings in weight allowed more speed at higher altitude, a higher service ceiling, and a sharper turn radius.

Multi-engine pilots trained at Vance in Enid, Oklahoma, and at Goodfellow AFB in San Angelo, Texas. Upon graduation, with new pilot wings pinned to the chest, duty assignments were handed out according to the class order, with the highest scoring student receiving first choice and so on down. Pilots going to SAC and TAC had more specialized training at their operational bases, learning skills demanded by their complicated aircraft and weapon systems, while MATS pilots usually got on-the-job training at their destination base and hit the ground running as it were, only having to get good at landing a plane from seat 34 feet above the touch down and 50 feet in front of the main gear.

World War II introduced radar, penicillin, DDT, the Atomic Age, and the Jet Age. Propeller planes in the military inventory had their days numbered, but until 1957, the Air Force trained its pilots using single-engine prop airplanes, especially the T-6 Texan. In 1960s, the Navy deployed the propeller-driven A-1 Skyhawk as a front line fighter-bomber in Vietnam, so for two decades while in transition from the propellers, bases had to store both jet fuel and high octane airplane fuel, and maintenance squadrons still had to work on both kinds of propulsion.

While new pilots might be attracted to SAC bombers because of a desire to fly jet airplanes, because patriotic themes coursed through the programs, and because flying B-47s or B-52s might somehow seem more patriotic than flying cargo, nevertheless many top pilots, like Irv Troske, chose the heavies, going to MATS assignments upon graduation. Navigators, the non-pilot rated officers manning USAF heavy airplanes, did the same.

So, in the spring of 1962, Irv Troske and I, the navigator, happened to be aboard the same piece of machinery at 10 a.m. local time, rumbling down runway 33 at the old Athens International Airport en route to Turkey, where we would off-load more supplies for this neighboring

NATO ally. Athens International was abandoned in 2001 for a new version in the southeast part of the classic city state, along with Sparta the subject of the first scholarly book on war, by Thucydides. The airport built in 1938 had been home to the Luftwaffe during Nazi Germany's occupation of the Balkans during World War II. The USAF followed suit, and MATS planes were greeted by airmen who refueled, supplied, and inspected incoming American aircraft, giving us perfect support at this port of call and ready to continue our North Atlantic Treaty Organization (NATO) mission.

Weighing some 90 tons, our C-124 climbed to 1,500 feet Above Sea Level (ASL) before making a slow turn to the right, and we set in a heading of 077° on the N-1, which would take us directly across the Aegean Sea to Cigli Air Base near Izmir, Turkey. Though it was a clear day and Irv had a preference for flying Visual Flight Rules (VFR) on such short legs, we were instead Instrument Flight Rules (IFR) under control by Athens Center, which had us programmed to fly 9,000 feet above sea level—and so we continued our climb out to assigned altitude, Irv reporting over Very High Frequency when we reached it.[8] Our radios included the VHF and Ultra High Frequency (UHF) short wave frequencies and Single Side Band (SSB), our long-range high frequency radio. With the call numbers set into that crystal, we contacted MATS control at MacDill AFB in Tampa, Florida, to report in. Radio operators had been trained for duty in multi-engine planes during World War II, but were along with aerial observers and foreign language radio operators among the first crew positions to become extinct, their duties being handed over to pilots and navigators by the 1950s.

Flying in Europe, we had available to us airway maps that gave vectors to the VOR stations common in NATO countries, and thus navigation skills were secondary to this radio beam means of establishing position and headings. C-124s, like all post–World War II transports, were equipped with basic navigation aids such as the gyro-assisted N-1 compass displayed on both pilot and navigator instrument panels, the Automatic Direction Finder (ADF), which was a low frequency radio emanating from a tower located at each airfield with a unique frequency and call sign, and the VHR omni-directional range/tactical air navigation system (VOR/TACAN), a reliable sending-receiving radio system that exchanged signals between ground station and airplane and therefore could establish headings and distances. Transponder technology, under a secret code name of "Parrot," was developed during World War II to help identify friend or foe. Pilots rolled in a four-digit code number in the console set, which "squawked" a signal that could be used to identify the plane by ground controllers once they sent the machine an inquiry on a certain radio frequency.

Mounted on the windshield divider bar, visible at a glance from both pilot and co-pilot seats, was the "whiskey compass." This device, forerunners of which were operable by the 16th century and used by Admiral of the Ocean Sea, Cristobal Colon (aka Christopher Columbus and Cristoforo Colombo), on his voyages to the New World, remained important to air navigation. Radios could be subjected to interference or jamming when flying in Europe, and the N-1, not often but occasionally, could go on the blink. In such failing circumstances, the needle floating in alcohol encased in a glass bubble at the most forward spot in the cockpit became as important to finding direction for a C-124 pilot like Irv Troske as it was 500 years ago to a ship captain like Columbus.[9]

Over the nav table behind the pilot seat, I spread the ONC (Operational Navigation Chart) on which I had plotted routes for today. At flight ops before heading out to the plane which had been parked far from the terminal—the usual treatment for a C-124 because of its hulking shape and size—Irv and I had called Air Force Weather Service at Frankfort for a weather (wx) briefing. Light winds and cirrus clouds meant that we should be able to stay on course with our flight planning and have an easy

TACAN station on California coast, 2014.

1. "Oh, I have slipped the surly bonds of Earth..." 17

day in the blue. The night before, three of us dressed in civvies had gone out for drinks and dinner at a harbor café in Piraeus. A platter of fried squid, a bottle of red wine, and excitement generated by a lively band imitating with heavy Greek accents the hits of Little Richard, Ray Charles, and Chuck Berry were having their repercussions the next morning when a fellow crew member nagged me out of bed. So, good that the skies were clear, something had to be. With flight planning and pre-flight check lists complete, Irv called for startup of the Pratt and Whitneys. The C-124 had an engine numbering style like other four-engine airplanes, beginning with #1 the farthest out on the port (left) wing. An electric motor began the rotation of number two engine's three propellers, each blade some eight feet in length. The slow turn of the prop increased in rate with a whining noise and, when it caught, invariably a huge puff of white smoke and a rough, grumpy noise signaled that life had come to our inboard power plant. Irv by then had number three turning and back to number one until we were humming and brimming with all four. The airman on the ground disconnected the ground power unit (GPU), and after throttle and quantities were checked, we cautiously moved forward off our spot, with wing tip clearances and turn ratios closely monitored by the second engineer scanning in the astrodome. Usually, we had a clear path to takeoff without much waiting.

Rising from the runway at Athens into the clear blue sky, aloft and comfortably cool above the sticky heat, the flight crew reset altimeters to 29.92, and Irv leveled us out at 9,000 feet. The flight engineer smoothed out the engines, checked plug firings on the diagnostic screen, switched fuel tanks, and set the throttles for the standard 185 knot air speed. We were in our element. A few tokes from the oxygen mask, with the regulator turned to 100 percent, helped refresh the nerve endings in my eyes, and with the operational navigation chart (ONC), a glance at the Tacan read out, and my Weems air computer, I figured that with a slight tail wind giving us a ground speed of 190 knots we should reach Cigli, some 380 nautical miles to the east, after two hours flying time.

With the plane's electronics working normally and a clear day, I left the D-1 periscopic sextant in its case and map read across the beautiful body of water below, and over islands mentioned by Homer, an easy day for the nav. Being 24 years old had its advantages in the area of quick recovery.

After a smooth landing—Irv was good at that—his voice on the headset confirmed that we were on the ground (implying that since his landing was so smooth, we might not have noticed), and I logged the time as 1500

Greenwich Mean Time. It being 1:00 p.m. local (Eastern European Time), we hopped a ride into town from the airport to find lunch. At the outdoor café where we sat eating soup, a blacktop highway ran by, and the direct and intense sun had softened the surface. Along came a group of workmen with shovels and picks over their shoulders. These muscular men with big ears in light, soiled shirts and ragged trousers that came down just below the knees strode along in the soft tar of the roadway. They marched on, evidently unaware of the impression they were making on the bitumen roadway, and on us, not showing any discomfort from bare feet trudging on hot asphalt, these tough, unflinching laborers, our NATO allies and the sworn enemy of our enemy, the Russians. We couldn't help but compare the stoicism of these men with the hedonism of the slender, gregarious, gold-necklaced Greeks we had encountered on the street the night before. Greeks and Turks! Hellenes and Trojans!! How differently turned men. How different their worlds.

Turkish determinism during the Gallipoli campaign of World War I undid Winston Churchill's strategy of opening a second front in the Balkans against the German Empire and instead brought about the fame of Mustafa Kemal Ataturk and his subsequent rise to power. Winning the battle but losing the war cost Turkey at the 1919 Paris peace conferences. The Turks' vast imperial domain that had stretched from the Persian Gulf in the east to the Strait of Gibraltar in the west was then just one of the chips on the table. Stripped of that empire and the feudal income it produced, Ataturk set about modernizing Turkey, a step, he thought, in the right direction toward restoring Turkey's former status as a peer and sometimes a feared peer to the European nation-states. His government decreed mandatory Western dress codes for the 20th century, unveiling women and de-fezing men. Islam was anything but a unifying religion, and Ataturk gave a cold shoulder to the Arab states that emerged after the 1919–1921 Treaties of Paris from territories that had been under Turkish (or Iranian) control and had paid tribute to Istanbul (or Tehran) throughout the 19th century.

Armenian Christians felt the merciless ethnic hostility, too, as Turkish forces exterminated over a million of them. Ataturk cut off the Soviet Union from full and free access to the Mediterranean via the Strait of Marmara, and agitated Greece over territorial disputes from Macedonia to Cyprus. Ataturk died in 1938, but his anti–Russian legacy led to Turkey becoming an ally of the United States and a NATO member, and to our landing a C-124 at Izmir in 1963. "An enemy of mine enemy is my friend" is an expression that dates to ancient Sanskrit texts. The verse must ring true in the U.S. State Department who liked the part that Turkey stood up to the Russians and was a moderate Islamic nation-state among its devout and theocratic neighbors.

Turkey was such a friend of the U.S. that the Globemaster flew unimpeded through her skies, from Izmir to Ankara, landing at Esenboga Airport. Kemal Ataturk had set up his resistance headquarters in this ancient Hittite village during the tumultuous years of post–World War I treaty-making. Ataturk succeeded in holding together the core of modern Turkey despite Western plans to divide it up. The 1923 Treaty of Lausanne recognized the reality created by Ataturk, who in 1923 made Ankara the Turkish capital, replacing the more populous, better situated, awesomely monumental, Ottoman Empire capital, and famous city 250 miles north, Istanbul (once known as Byzantium and then Constantinople). In 1963, far from being byzantine, i.e., not bound by bureaucratic red tape, about a request from an American pilot, Turkish air controllers consented for Irv Troske to fly his Globemaster VFR to the next stop, Incirlik Air Base, near Adana, Turkey, a permission for a foreign military airplane rarely obtained anywhere in this century.

Not only did Irv fly visual rules in the crystal-clear weather we had, he dropped the plane down to 500 feet AGL (above ground level) so that we could all share in the thrill and the view of those dry, sparsely vegetated

Anatolian hills from a C-124 in 1963.

Anatolian hills as we skimmed the landscape en route to the Mediterranean. Irv had offered a young American school teacher a space-available ride to her destination, Incirlik Air Base, where she would be employed at the dependents' elementary school. At takeoff, she was seat-belted into a passenger seat in the cargo compartment. A little into the flight, the loadmaster brought the teacher up the aluminum ladder that had 23 steps leading to the crew cabin, giving her this aerial view of the Anatolian plains. It was the first time she had had that kind of a vantage point in an airplane, a memorable experience that no doubt from then on informed her lessons on geography. She seemed proud of her countrymen and we of her. I had to hand it to Irv.

Landing at Incirlik, we saw gleaming F-106s parked in rows, ready to protect our interest in the eastern Mediterranean against Soviet indiscretions. The Cold War had its borders, and we were on one. When John F. Kennedy was president, MATS was flying into Libya, but not into Egypt. We flew into Ethiopia, but not the Sudan; Iran, but not Syria; Israel, but not Saudi Arabia. Political specialists broke up the globe thusly: Free World, Soviet-Sino bloc, and Third World, or as they called themselves, the Non-Aligned Countries.

Not landing in the bloc nations but overflying the U.S.S.R were the U-2s. Evan Thomas, in his book, *Ike's Bluff*, documented and interpreted President Dwight D. Eisenhower's fear of a burgeoning military-industrial complex in the United States. To keep military expenses down to balance the budget, Eisenhower and his Secretary of State, John Foster Dulles, relied on *the bomb* to deter wars between us, the first world, and them, the second world. The policy succeeded, but then Ike knew well the military's tendencies to build ever-increasing inventories and empires within the services. In Thomas' telling, the U-2 flights kept an eagle's eye on the Soviet Union's *lack* of ICBM and long-range bomber capabilities. The U-2s were effective in that regard, and the president knew that his country was in no real danger of a pre-emptive strike by the Russians. American intelligence from these flights and other sources estimated that when Francis Gary Powers was shot down in 1959 and a détente summit scheduled in Paris with Nikita Khrushchev was canceled by the infuriated Soviet Premier, the Soviets had exactly four ICBMs and fewer than 200 long range bombers. On the other hand, the U.S. nuclear weapons numbered in the hundreds for missiles and thousands for bombers.[10]

Eisenhower could not run for a third term because in 1951, the states had ratified the XXII Amendment, limiting the president to two terms. Even if that amendment had failed, Ike was 70 and had two heart attacks while he was president.¹¹ In 1960, John F. Kennedy, a practicing Roman Catholic, won election over Eisenhower's former vice president, Richard Milhous Nixon, a non-practicing Quaker. Religion was an issue, if a minor one, among the voters. The victory was unusually narrow, and Kennedy was unusually young. Joseph Kennedy, John's father, was a very rich man who used his resources where needed, notably in Chicago, which provided the slim margin of votes by which JFK won the election. Harry Truman, no stranger to big city bosses and ward politics himself, once remarked, with wry Midwestern humor, that where influences on Kennedy were concerned, "It's not the Pope I'm afraid of. It's the pop."¹²

Brush fire wars spread as national liberation movements rocked the European colonial empires. Urged by Maxwell Taylor and the Joint Chiefs of Staff, the grand military strategy of the United States to combat aggression and to limit Communist expansion turned increasingly away from the Eisenhower-Dulles foreign policy of threatened massive retaliation toward use of ground forces: counter-insurgency, instant, cavalry-like responses to trouble, an expensive option given a greater need for manpower, of course. Ominously, the "best and brightest" that Kennedy attracted to Washington in those promising days of the Great Frontier could not have agreed more.

The crew remaining overnight—RON—Irv decided to dine on base instead of going out "on the economy." The Open Mess had a rickety look and a packed earth floor. White linen-covered tables sat in a dimly lit dining room. Turkish waiters in white jackets, black trousers, bowties, and bare feet handed us pad and pencil on which we wrote down our orders, their English being limited. The lamb, pilaf, and wine tasted good. After dinner, we adjourned to the bar. Parting the wooden chain curtains, we walked through, still in our flight suits, as a bar on the far end stretching the length of the room beckoned. While having the *digestif*, we noticed that the low ceiling above the bar stools had a line of jagged holes in the plaster that we soon learned resulted from a fighter pilot ritual at Incirlik. Coming back from a mission where there was an encounter or close call of some sort, after duty the crews gathered at the O club, tossed off a few shots, and an initiate stood rigidly at attention with his arms clamped to his side, fists doubled and on the seams. A squadron buddy perpendicular on either side effected the ritual. Cradling their fellow pilot's clinched fists in their interlocked hands, they jammed him upward toward the low ceiling, the material of which was violently shattered by a crew-cut head. A good thrust, and there obviously were many of those, could blast the pilot's or nav's chin above the ceiling and out of sight. What were they thinking, you might ask? Who knows? But it was a local amusement invented in a rough land where crusaders 900 years ago, too, may have dreamed up crazy games of manhood and bravery.

Irv observed this evidence mildly amused. Our fighter pilot brethren, our comrades in arms, our countrymen, but we are not turned the same way, we transport airmen. Our airplanes are designed differently, and so are our temperaments, it seems. But neither MATS nor ADC aircrews are like their SAC counterparts, a serious group indeed.

The next morning, we were up early, cheerful as we were headed west where home was. At the base ops briefing the next morning, we drew up a flight plan to Torrejon Air Base east of Madrid, Spain. From there the next day, it was a five-hour, overwater flight to Lajes Air Base on Terceira Island in the beautiful Azores. With a light load of cargo, mail and packages from G.I.s stationed in Europe, we took on max fuel for a C-124 and flew directly from the Azores to Dover AFB with "go home power." Landing, the "Follow Me" truck met us at the apron, leading us to a parking spot. The Follow Me's presented a welcome sight any time at a military air base, signifying a safe ending to our flight. At the parking spot, an airman with a flashlight in each hand guided Irv, using throttles, brakes and nose wheel steering into exactly the yellow square upon which the nose wheel of the Globemaster would rest, aligned properly with other planes in a neat line, orderly. Another airman attached a ground power unit (GPU) to the airplane, and we shut down the engines. Like a bucket brigade, we off-loaded B4 bags and cases of Rose Mateus, (the old baggage drill effected at every stop-over since we were our own porters) and looked for the crew bus that would take us to the terminal. We donned ball caps and matching blue dickeys, and thus looking sharp, at least in our own eyes, strode through base operations to welcome hugs from dear wives awaiting us. We had covered 24,000 nautical miles in nine days and landed at nine different airports in six countries. We expended 66,000 gallons of aircraft-grade, high-octane gasoline, accumulated 90 hours of flying time, some of it highly pleasurable VFR, and delivered ten tons of cargo. We had helped defend the Free World. Crew members spoke about duty, honor, and country and generally thought they could probably do more along that line. Never characterizing themselves as *gung-ho,* they were yet willing to work hard and go far and wide, including into hot spots, and apply themselves to the occasion. Little did they know or care that their training and their aircraft were spearheading a burgeoning global U.S. military and civilian official presence which by 1962 numbered 850,000 people in 106 countries, perhaps the largest empire in history.[13]

2

"Rush by air"
Building an Aluminum Overcast

World War I, coming a little more than a decade after the Wright brothers' short flights at Kitty Hawk, had put the new air machine to military use. On battlefields in France and Belgium, soldiers in trenches watched dashing pilots sporting goggles and scarves in open cockpits flying just above them, tossing grenades and bombs overboard at the enemy. The war hastened development, and in the 1920s, General Billy Mitchell saw the coming value of military airplanes as an element of national power, a stance that brought him into conflict with the prevailing view of the Department of the Navy, which was indeed reluctant to give up the ship. Alfred E. Mahan's *The Influence of Sea Power Upon History, 1660–1783* (1890) had provided the basis for naval and military strategy thus far into the 20th century, as Admiral Mahan described steam-powered battle fleets as rulers of trade between nations. The fleet in turn would depend on a national commitment to building and maintaining capital ships with well-trained crews, modern armaments, and coaling stations, including strategically located islands under firm U.S. control. This basic belief created a reluctance among the admirals toward spending money on airplanes until the vision of the aircraft carrier began to take shape.[1]

On the other hand, the civilian sector was highly interested in speeding along aircraft designs and power plants. Lucrative U.S. government mail route contracts prompted engineers to design longer-range, heavier, all-weather airplanes and inspired entrepreneurs to bid for government mail contracts and envision new routes for passenger air service. Flying mail, cargo—and soon passengers—encouraged evolution of heavier, multi-engine airplanes.

MIT-trained aeronautical engineer Donald Willis Douglas, whose

Home to Dover, chocks in place, circa 1962 (courtesy Air Mobility Command Museum, Dover AFB, Delaware).

first job was as an aircraft designer for the Glenn Martin Company, started his own company in Riverside, California, in 1920 and thereon produced a single-engine airplane, the Cloudster, to compete for the distinction of being first to fly non-stop from coast to coast. While the Cloudster did not win this title, it did catch the attention of the U.S. Navy, which offered Douglas a contract to produce a pontoon-equipped biplane. The U.S. Army acquired four models of this plane from the Douglas factory and renamed it, secretly, the Douglas World Cruiser (DWC), which had as a mission the first round-the-world flight. In March 1924, the army dispatched a team of four DWCs to do just that. On September 28, seven months after departing Clover Field near the Douglas factory, one of the team completed this epic adventure and made its 36th landing of the trip in Seattle after 371 hours of actual flying time covering 27,000 miles. Though two of the four crashed en route, the mission was considered successful, and the Army ordered a cargo plane based on this design from Douglas Aircraft, designated the C-1.[2]

2. "Rush by air"

The C-1 had a single 433 horsepower Liberty engine that produced enough lift to carry seven passengers. Douglas built 27 C-1s, and in the robust decade of the 1920s furthered the connection between his company and the military, obtaining contracts for single and twin-engine airplanes. Busy with the military orders, Douglas left commercial airliner design and development to others like Ford and Fokker.

Fans of the action movie, *Raiders of the Lost Ark*, may recall scenes of the airliner that carried Indiana Jones to Nepal on one leg of his quest, the corrugated aluminum, three-engine Ford Tri-Motor. That machine, like the movie protagonist himself, spoke not of comfort, but of adventure with its quaintly romantic but rough-hewn look. Inside the Tri-Motor cabin, however, noise and vibration permeated, and by the 1930s, when the movie was set, something much better for passenger service had become available, an airliner built by Boeing Aircraft Company. In April 1933, citizens of Seattle watched with excitement as the Boeing 247 made its first public appearance and public test flight. Modern to the core, its two engines were embedded aerodynamically into the wings and offered ample power for the sleek aluminum airline, with its innovative retractable landing gear, to cart its ten-passenger load and reach its 150+ mph speeds over a range of 450 miles.[3]

Boeing, justifiably proud, promptly put the 247 into passenger service with its own United Air Lines. Since Boeing refused to accept orders from competing airline companies, Jack Frye of Trans World Airlines turned to Donald Douglas to build an airliner comparable to the 247. Douglas, despite little experience with commercial carriers, accepted the challenge. Less than a year later, the DC-1 was test flown and TWA, happy with its plush and noise-controlled passenger cabin, ordered 25 of the model, to be designated the Douglas Commercial (DC-2). So successful was its introduction that the Royal Dutch Airlines (KLM) ordered it for routes to the Dutch East Indies. President Franklin D. Roosevelt congratulated and personally presented Donald Douglas a trophy for developing the new overwater passenger plane. Development of air travel proceeded rapidly. Within two years, Douglas had lengthened, widened, and repowered the DC-2, creating what some have nominated as the greatest of all airliners, the DC-3 Skytrain. This plane satisfied the Pullman sleeping format suggested by Cyrus Rowlett, chairman of the nascent American Airlines. Good to his word, Rowlett ordered the first 20 DC-3s, which went into operation from American's central hub at Tulsa, Oklahoma, in 1935.[4]

The DC-3 could carry 14–28 passengers with a crew of five: two pilots, a navigator, a radio operator, and a crew chief for en route maintenance and cabin supervision. Two 1200 hp engines could lift 8,000 lbs. of cargo, fly at 10,000 feet altitude, and cruise at 192 mph with a range of almost 1,500 miles (Tulsa to New York, say). All the airlines, domestic and foreign, even United, clamored for DC-3s in their inventories. Perhaps the most important new customer for Douglas was Pan American, which with its fleet of 33 DC-3s expanded its pioneering of routes, landing fields, and passenger air service from South America to Europe to Asia. One industry historian estimated that by 1939, "ninety-three percent of the world's airline passengers were traveling in the ... DC-3."[5] In an increasingly dangerous world, the reliable and far-reaching Pan American Airlines in South America worked to keep countries it served loyal to the Allies, offsetting Nazi influences in the region as war loomed and as Latin American rulers considered which side to back. Pan Am, with its routes, offices, and services, its DC-3 fleet, its omnipresence, therefore could be and was an extension of American foreign policy.

The U.S. Army Air Corps in 1933 offered Douglas a contract for a military transport based on the DC-3 design, an airplane eventually designated as the C (Cargo)-47. The overwhelming success of the C-47 placed Douglas in a favorable position during World War II to develop larger transports such as the four engine C-54. Germany surrendered on May 8, 1945, a victory, according to Supreme Allied Commander Dwight Eisenhower, in part attributable to the C-47. Now instead of making war, the Allies used their armies to restore order and services to a devastated German nation, a duty that required even more air transport of cargo and personnel. Harry S. Truman had succeeded Franklin Delano Roosevelt, who died at Warm Springs, Georgia, on April 12, 1945, three months into his fourth term as president. Truman, a new player among the power brokers, arrived in Germany in June 1945 to help plan the occupation of Germany and indeed configure the post-war world. In July, at Potsdam (a Berlin suburb), with Joseph Stalin and Winston Churchill and their associates, Truman received a report entitled "The Test" from General Leslie Groves, overseer of the Manhattan Project. The test, of course, was of a nuclear weapon, and the report read by Truman deemed it ready. The atomic bomb had been *the* major priority of the Roosevelt administration even as the nation's huge industrial plants had turned out astounding numbers of planes, ships, arms, heavy machinery, trucks, jeeps, uniforms, ammunition, food, and countless other items of war. Having spent so much capital on building the world's first nuclear weapon, with Japan's leadership preparing for a stubborn defense of the homeland, and with the need to awe Stalin, it is difficult to see how Truman could have said anything other than use it. He approved the bombing order on July 25, 1945.[6] Perhaps Roosevelt with all his prestige and background could have declined the opportunity to obliterate an enemy city with one bomb, but not a new and unproven leader with so much at stake on the home front and in the post-war.

Relationships between the four powers (France was included at the insistence of Truman and received a slice of the American zone) that occupied, divided into sectors, and governed a defeated and devastated Germany, at first friendly, began to sour over ideological, strategic and personal issues. The United States had insisted on sharing Berlin, keeping the western part under their control even though it lay 120 miles inside the Russian zone of occupation. Berlin had been the capital of the Third Reich and was not only a mighty symbol, it had important geographical location on the continent. Some scholars have concluded that to understand European history, one must first understand Germany history, which itself necessitates understanding Berlin's history, a city with Slavic origins.[7]

In the sobering aftermath of the defeat of Nazi Germany, some American military leaders, notably George Patton and Curtis LeMay, voiced their deep suspicions about our powerful ally, the Soviet Union, a one-party, police state, Communist nation ruled absolutely by a paranoid dictator, Joseph Stalin.

That distrust turned out to be justified. One author wrote recently that "Four-power Berlin was always a bomb, the most dangerous place in the world."[8] Indeed, on June 17, 1947, the Russians shut down highways leading through their sector into Berlin. Canals were patrolled, and shipping stopped. Railroads were blocked. Stalin's wish was to force the West into abandoning Berlin with its 2.1 million people, most of whom were already trying to live on 900 calories a day and were slowly starving.[9] The rival powers floated two currencies in Berlin at the time, and the Soviets would honor ONLY *Eastmarks* for legal purchase of the necessities in East Berlin, where food and coal was available. If the West Berliners conceded the currency battle, it would insure that the West would lose Berlin, and, no doubt, would soon be out of Germany altogether. The world geopolitical picture would be considerably different, especially since 1947, when a Communist government under Mao Zedong began to rule the one-half billion people of China.

When 95 percent of the West Berliners refused the currency ploy, the Soviet Union played its trump card, and on June 25, 1948, the *Times of London* reported the severing of "western links with Berlin." In the story, the U.S. military commander in Germany, 50-year-old West Pointer General Lucious DuBignon Clay, stated that the emergency supply airlift, depending on the 48 C-47s and 30 British Dakotas on hand, was not a long-term solution. Yet the solution had to be airlift. To force through the land routes into Berlin might cause war, for which the Soviets had an overwhelming military superiority already in place.[10]

Clay was determined to stay in Berlin and keep the American presence there, including dependents, even while top military, cabinet, and congressional leaders advised President Harry S. Truman to evacuate the untenable city. Truman, however, agreed with Clay and announced, "We stay in Berlin. Period." That was a bold statement on the heels of which came an 11-month-long Berlin Airlift, bringing the Air Force to recognize its future and the need for transport and cargo airplanes.

In the first weeks, dauntless C-47s transported essential cargo, three to four tons per flight, into Berlin.[11] Coal for the upcoming winter, for example, was stuffed into duffel bags. With a great need to increase capacity and improve what began as a short-term, ad hoc solution to supplying the city, the Air Force called on its most knowledgeable hand, Major General William Tunner, deputy operations commander of the brand-new Military Air Transport Service—MATS—and a veteran of the "Flying the Hump" campaign to supply, by air over the Himalayas, Chiang Kai-Shek during World War II.

In West Germany, Tunner organized the airlift into near perfection as to schedules, routes, flying instructions, crews, maintenance, and *esprit de corps*. The airlift succeeded, Berlin was saved from Communist control, and the MATS budget increased. A dedication to building large-capacity transport airplanes resulted.

Tunner and his organizational skills and the Douglas airlifters had accomplished what had seemed impossible, that is totally supplying a city of millions by air. Through an investment of $200 million and 190,000 flights, the allies delivered 2,325,000 tons of supplies. The airlift cost 31 Air Force lives in 12 crashes. This gallant effort which saved the city brought on a new respect for giant transports. The Douglas-built, four-engine C-54, the Skymaster, cruised at 200 knots and had a payload of 26,000 pounds—13 tons, triple that of the C-47—and as the C-54 entered the airlift, its ability cut down the number of flights, hours, traffic, and costs during the airlift, demonstrating the efficiency of large cargo planes. A Douglas C-74 Globemaster I, tail number 65414, had flown into Gatow RAF base in the north of Berlin in August 1949, carrying 22 tons of flour, the runway barely capable of taking the considerably more weight involved in landing this new giant transport airplane of 172,000 pounds gross weight.[12] This plane could carry 25 tons of cargo or 200 passengers, and while it flew only 25 missions before it was reassigned in September, the rest of the fleet—four others—hauled Berlin-bound supplies across the Atlantic into Rhein-Mein, where it was transferred into the C-54s and so helped bring about the success of the airlift.[13]

General Tunner said, "the lessons we've learned from the airlift are tremendously important. We know, for instance that the future of military air transport ... is the big aircraft."

The figures kept meticulously by Tunner showed that 68 C-74s could transport the same cargo that in the airlift took 178 C-54s or 899 C-47s.[14]

The Berlin Airlift, even more than World War II, demonstrated that new American strategies must consider future probabilities of sending material and men to distant lands and duties, and that the overall strategic plan must include an inventory of quick response "big aircraft" that could deliver high-volume supplies and a high number of personnel to deal with military and civilian emergencies. Convinced, Secretary of Defense James V. Forrestal awarded a gigantic contract to Douglas Aircraft Company to build a gigantic airplane, with an open-ended number for delivery to the Air Force. The C-74 Globemaster had as a basic design the C-54 Skymaster, and the progression into a larger airplane did not end there. Douglas engineers were already re-designing the active duty prototype C-74 Globemaster I into a more commodious airplane with a better loading system and larger engines, which would be designated the C-124 Globemaster II.

Just before the Berlin Airlift, major changes effected by the Truman administration had come to the U.S. military establishment, and not just with Executive Order 9981 of 1948 that desegregated the Armed Forces. Truman sponsored the National Security Act, which combined the War and Navy Departments into the Department of Defense, and appointed Forrestal as its first secretary. The same act created the United States Air Force, separating this branch from the Army. The first Secretary of the Air Force, W. Stuart Symington, was sworn in on September 18, 1947, and a week later Gen. Carl Spaatz assumed the duties of U.S. Air Force Chief of Staff, marking the official separation of this branch from the U.S. Army. President Harry S. Truman signed the last transfer order two years later on July 22, 1949, completing the complicated separation process. The Air Force included the Military Air Transport Service. Other major divisions were the Air Defense Command, Tactical Air Command, and Strategic Air Command, "air commands," not merely an "air service," perhaps indicating a bias. After the advent of the C-141, which became operational in

1965, however, MATS was changed to Military Air Command, MAC. The jet transports were better and faster for pilots, evidently, and now could be included on a sort of a nomenclature par with their bomber and fighter airplane counterparts.

The C-124 and its immediate predecessors, the C-54, the C-97, and the C-74, defined for MATS even the location of its bases. The C-124 needed home bases with room for extra-sized ramps, huge maintenance hangers, and long, wide, concrete runways. The formula used then by the Air Force specified the ideal location for a base: 15 to 25 miles from a smaller city; infrastructure to support the base and its people; no polluting influences, human or otherwise; no ordinances against noise and round-the-clock operations. Better still, the town might donate the land for the base. MATS decided that its priority for location was along the Atlantic Coast, where five important air bases—Dover, McGuire, Charleston, Donaldson, and Palm Beach—would house 70 percent of the air transport resources of MATS. Travis in California and McChord south of Tacoma became Globemaster terminals on the Pacific Rim. The headquarters, though, was in the center of the country, 25 miles east of St. Louis, Scott AFB, Illinois, still today the headquarters of the Air Mobility Command.[15]

An experimental YC-124 first flew on November 27, 1949. Test flights at Edwards Air Force base continued with two Y models through 1950, even as manufacturing proceeded for the airlifter. In May 1950, the Air Force took its first delivery of a C-124. It had four Pratt and Whitney R4360 engines, each driving a three-bladed propeller with a rotating arc of 17 feet. Four hundred forty-six others produced from 1949 through 1953 followed, all built at a huge Douglas facility in Long Beach, California. None were pressurized, which limited the operational ceiling of the plane to less than 12,000 feet.

Douglas engineers working from C-74 Globemaster I blueprints substantially raised the cabin height, giving the Globemaster II fuselage a rather bloated look unlike any other American-designed airplane, a look rivaled by the Messerschmitt 323 *Gigant*, the largest land-based transport of World War II that carried panzers and artillery for the Wehrmacht, and by the British-built Blackburn B-101 *Beverly*.[16] Both planes had front-loading via ramps lowered on the ground by opening clamshell doors.

Front clamshell doors on the C-124, when opened, allowed two hydraulically operated steel ramps, each weighing 942 pounds, to extend to the airport runway so that rolling stock could drive right into the massive cabin. With cargo hold dimensions that measured 74 feet in length, 12 feet wide, and 12 feet ten inches in height, two army trucks could be fitted. Or a M-24 tank, or a helicopter with rotors folded on top, or 200 soldiers, or as it came to be in the early '60s, a Thor IRBM missile which was 65 feet long with a diameter of eight feet. Once the Globemaster delivered a Thor, its accessories, rocket fuel and a 2,200-pound nuclear warhead, typically carried separately in another Strategic Services Squadron or Air Material C-124, the weight of this atomic weapon reached 50 tons. At the height of the Cold War, these missiles were deployed in Great Britain and carried there by C-124s. Air Material Command used the Globemaster to carry outsized loads, such as the B-17 atomic bomb war head which weighed 42,000 lbs.[17]

The manufacture of the C-124 at Douglas Aircraft Company involved the facility, thousands of workers, high finance, government orders, and ship loads of materials. The basic material of the airplane industry and of the Globemaster was, of course, aluminum.

The Aluminum Company of America (Alcoa) developed the ore fields in central Arkansas and built a company town named, naturally, Bauxite. During World War II, as foreign sources became unreliable, the aircraft industry leaned heavily on the ore production from Bauxite, shipped by railroad from Arkansas to Alcoa mills in Pennsylvania. A *Fortune* magazine article in 1946 stated, "What won the war was air power, based on aluminum and Alcoa." The industrial colossus that the United States became during the war, potential energy converted to kinetic, realized the principle fear of far-sighted military leaders in Japan and Germany such as Yamamoto. Indeed, what other nation could produce 296,000 airplanes in six years, 1940–1945, for its army and navy? Except for wooden gliders and a few experiments, virtually all planes were built of aluminum turned out by Alcoa, Kaiser, and Reynolds, the major manufacturers.

In any sizable airplane, aluminum accounted for up to three-quarters of the total weight. Today's Globemaster III—the C-17—which has components of titanium, super alloys, and steel, still makes up 73 percent of its weight, in aluminum, which comes to 139,000 pounds of aluminum in each C-17.[18]

Douglas Aircraft used some 385,000,000 pounds of sheet aluminum in building the C-124 fleet. While the term "Aluminum Overcast" had been applied to the bombers of World War II, they were a fraction the size of the C-124 which, in fact, did cast a temporary shadow on ground over which it flew at low levels, making the phrase not quite as whimsical as before.

Seven manufacturing buildings stretched out along Lakewood Boulevard between Carson Street and Douglas Drive, used for construction of the Globemaster, totaling 1,200,000 square feet of floor space. Working in two shifts, 7,000 men and women workers assembled the giant plane from blueprints that would cover 100 football fields. The one-sixteenth to one-half-inch-thick aluminum sheets that made up the skin of the airplane were riveted to steel girders or ribs that had been fitted with tolerances to a hundredth of an inch. Douglas engineers designed the airframes in their offices in the same complex, and the combined annual salaries of C-124 production employees, half of whom lived in the city of Long Beach, amounted to $25,000,000 in 1950.[19] The manufacturing cost of each C-124 was calculated at $1,650,000 ($12,375,000 in today's dollars, and the Air Force accounting office in 1953 assigned each C-124 a value of $3,000,000).[20]

Something this size presented production problems that at times seemed insurmountable. More than 650 feet of aluminum milling machines turned out the spar caps, from six feet to 38 feet in length, required for the C-124 wing and tail surfaces. Unlike today's giant airplane manufacturing systems that depend on assembly of various sections—fuselage, tail, nose, made in separate operations in different countries—the C-124 was built from scratch in one location. One Douglas engineer recalled walking from the parking lot into his office, going through several factory buildings to get there, and hearing rivets being bucked and the smell of cutting oil in the huge work areas. The job of bundling electrical wires was usually the province of women workers who carefully and neatly incorporated and installed the miles of wiring harnesses needed in the Globemaster.[21]

The power for flight came from the largest gasoline engine ever mass-produced in the United States, the Pratt and Whitney 4360 radial engine. The company built 18,697 of these Wasp Majors between the engine's introduction in 1944 to power the B-50 and its eclipse by jet engines in 1955. With 28 cylinders and 56 spark plugs, each R-4360 weighed two tons, counting the 82 gallons of oil circulating through. The Aluminum Overcast therefore included eight tons of iron and steel in the engines.

The Douglas company had substantial Globemaster contracts—not only did they build the C-124A and C-124C models, the company contracted to convert the A fleet to C models. Although the product of a company famous for the DC appellation—Douglas Commercial—no Globemasters went to civilian use nor, for that matter, were any sold to foreign military, unlike the soon-to-follow C-130 which its manufacturer, Lockheed Martin, sold to Air Forces of 60 countries.

Douglas employees were excited about the Globemaster and shared

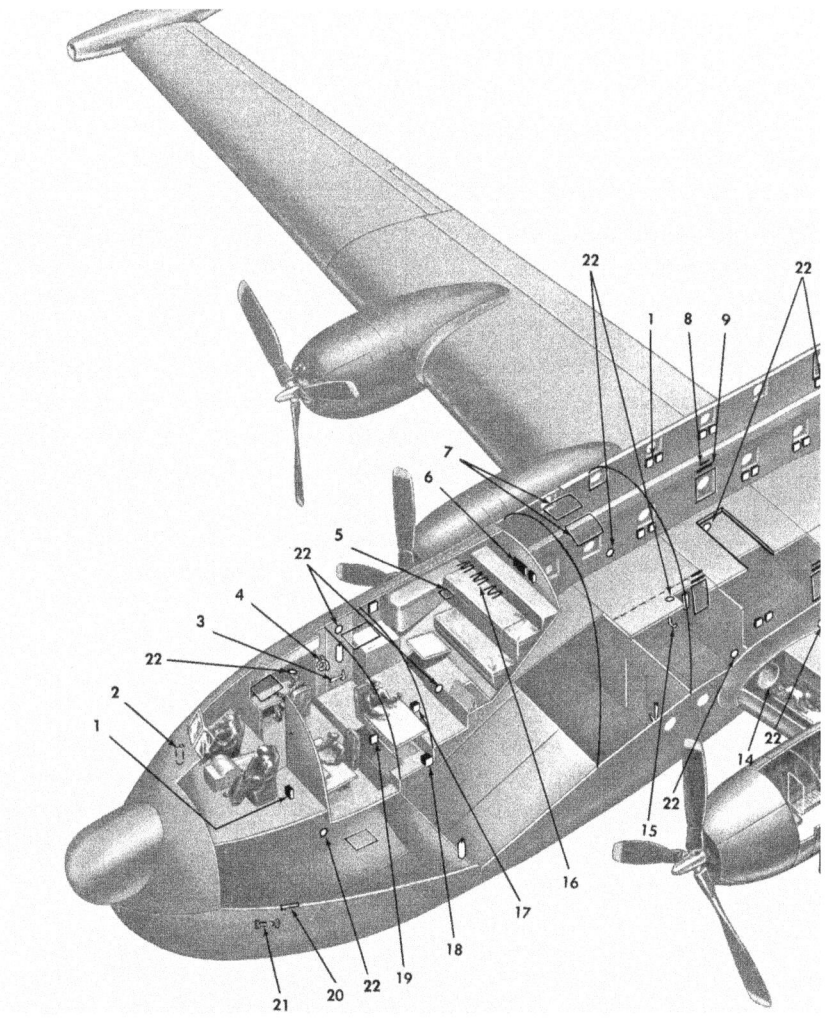

Image from C-124 Dash 1.

humor and incredulous anecdotes that highlighted the building experience, just as mechanics, maintenance men, and air crews had their war stories after the plane joined the Air Force. To many workers who had witnessed all the components merging together to create "an office building on wings," when the Globemaster II finally lumbered down the runway and took to the air, the completed airplane "seemed like a miracle." Each one of them, all 447.[22] Douglas employee Chuck Milner told a reporter that once, he crawled inside the fuel tanks and forgot the way out. He was rescued after he tapped out an SOS on the walls. The fuel tanks were huge, dark, and full of chemical vapors that could cause disorientation or even blackouts of anyone inside, and because of the hazards, a buddy system developed for those entering. Birds nested inside the flaps during the manufacturing process, and avionics installers swore that the cargo hull was so large, sometimes a rain storm would crop up.

One engineer said that the workers had hung 1,788 propellers, and if all started at once it would create a hurricane that could blow Long Beach off the map. Each C-124 had 156,000 feet of wiring (about 30 miles) that had to be carefully installed and verified. A full-page advertisement in the *Long Beach Press Telegram* on Tuesday, January 1, 1952, greeted New Year's Day readers as the production of the C-124 reached its peak in Long Beach and as U.S. troops in Korea were meeting the battlefield challenge of turning back some 900,000 troops of the Chinese People's Army. In the public service-type ad, a shipping tag at the top of the page read, "Rush by Air One Division of Doughfoots." The text specified the contribution to the nation's defense made by Long Beach and Douglas in producing "the world's largest air cargo carrier."

With "fleets of Globemaster IIs flying operationally all over the world for the U.S. Air Force," such marvels can occur as the dramatic example given in the advertisement of one C-124 that transported 35,000 hand grenades from Tokyo to a frontline air strip in Korea and flew back 160 wounded men from a forward hospital. The ad informed readers that a single C-124 Globemaster II could replace five C-54 Skymasters and land in the same air fields. This "enormous carrying capacity makes it possible for a fleet of C-124s to airlift an entire infantry division and all of its equipment."[23]

The Globemaster II was superlative, indeed. In November 1949, company test pilot William J. Morrisey made a 55-minute flight and returned to Long Beach Airport. The *United Press* news story was headlined "222-Passenger Transport makes its maiden flight." In April 1951, a C-124 made news when it flew 4,700 miles non-stop. Maxed out with fuel, a Globemaster took off from Hickam Field in Hawaii and, after a 22-hour flight, landed at Hunter Air Force Base at Savannah, Georgia. With headwinds throughout the route, the Globemaster averaged a 214-mph ground speed.[24]

The role of the Globemaster in 1950s national security was cited by President Harry S. Truman in October 1951 as he told 9,000 striking workers in Long Beach to end their six-week-long strike and settle their dispute with the Douglas Co. through the machinery of the Wage Stabilization

2. "Rush by air"

Poster circulated by Douglas Aircraft Company in the 1950s (author's collection).

Board. Truman wrote to Nat Feinsinger, chairman of the WSB, "The Douglas Co. is the sole producer of the C-124 transport and the Air Force has no other type which is capable of performing the mission of this aircraft ... continuance of the stoppage would impose a serious disadvantage for the Air Force."[25] Later in the week, the workers voted to return to work without a pay raise until the issue could be decided by the WSB. Donald

Douglas said of it that "every patriotic American concerned with our national defense will welcome the end of a work stoppage of such magnitude and duration."[26]

At the Long Beach manufacturing facility between November 1949 and May 1955, 447 factory-fresh C-124s were towed to the Long Beach airstrip for takeoff and delivery to the Air Force, a rate of seven flying behemoths per month or one every three workdays. When C model production ended in 1953, the A models begin their return to Long Beach, where 166 of them were refitted with wing tip heaters for de-icing and the nose thimble that housed the APS-42 weather radar scope which gave Old Shaky its caricature face. Long Beach was indeed a busy place because at the same time, the Douglas Company was in the process of manufacturing 289 jet engine-powered B-66s and was developing its line of magisterial jet age transports, most significantly the DC-8. As the last C-124 retrofit rolled off the line in May 1955, Douglas was re-tooling for the C-133, another giant transport plane, this one powered by turbo prop engines which gave it more speed, altitude, electronics, payload, and cost than the C-124. It did not, however, match the volume capability of the Globemaster, a fact that kept the venerable Old Shaky viable for another two decades, especially because of its importance to the material and equipment transfer halfway around the world from the U.S. to Vietnam. Neither did the C-133 improve on the safety record of the C-124, nor match the hours flown and multiple uses of the Globemaster. In the first six years of operation, C-124s logged one million flying hours, carrying air cargo a distance equivalent to a trip to the sun and back, or 8,000 times around the world. It flew in all weather conditions including, with modifications, an ability to withstand temperatures of minus 70 degrees Fahrenheit through 200 degrees above zero. Its capacity, range, and versatility were employed by five different branches of the Air Force: Military Air Transport Command which became Military Airlift Command in 1965, Tactical Air Command, Strategic Air Command, Air Material Command, and the Far Eastern Air Force.[27]

Douglas and its employees were a mainstay of the Long Beach, indeed the whole Southern California economy in those years. Michael Crowley, a just-graduated mechanical engineer from Arkansas, heard about Douglas from his aunt who lived in Orange County. Her neighbor in an across-the-fence conversation mentioned the jobs available. The young man came, interviewed, and was hired on the spot, launching his career in the aircraft manufacturing business. In 1965, Los Angeles replaced Chicago as the second-largest city in the U.S., and California became its most populous state. Douglas and its military contracts, including the C-124, played a big role in these demographic shifts because of jobs available in the industry. In 1962, Richard Nixon, son of a pious Quaker mother who had lived in Yorba Linda (where the Nixon presidential library is located) lost the California gubernatorial race to Democrat Pat Brown, and then in a piqué announced at a post-election news conference that the media wouldn't have Nixon to kick around anymore. He was wrong. Nixon defeated Hubert Humphrey in the 1968 presidential election at the height of the Vietnam War and the protests raging over its purpose and conduct. At the time, C-124s were delivering material and equipment to the war zone.

For all of Douglas' success in designing, manufacturing, and selling the big Globemaster transport—and other cargo and passenger planes of its day—the company faced severe industry competition. First, there was Boeing, based in Washington state and assisted by the low cost of electricity in the region created by the massive Grand Coulee Dam, the nation's largest hydropower facility. Unlike Douglas and other prime aircraft manufacturers in the United States during the World War II and Korean War era, Boeing made no fighter aircraft. Boeing's military contracts came with its success in the bomber field, the B-17 and the B-29.

Boeing's challenge to Douglas Aircraft for primacy in the airlift field became powerful with the Air Force contracts for the KC-135, the first of which was delivered in April 1957. The KC-135s would replace Boeing's KC-97, another airplane with a great following of users and former crew members. Boeing's commercial version, the 707, immediately appealed to the airlines. While Douglas won the contracts to build the massive C-133 Cargomaster, only 50 were built, and other companies entered the fray with more successful airlifter designs, notably Lockheed and its eminent turboprop C-130 Hercules (starting with A's that were delivered to the Air Force in December 1956, it is still being manufactured today as the H-model) and then its jet-powered C-141 StarLifter, which entered service in 1965. The StarLifter carried a navigator, but the planes were equipped with Inertial Navigation System—INS for short—a gyro-based acceleration sensor/computer tool that proved to be reliable and simple enough to operate without specialized nav training.[28]

To complete the Lockheed trifecta, its C-5 Galaxy was selected over designs of oversized transporters by both Douglas and Boeing. The first Lockheed C-5 entered USAF operations in 1968, in time for the last operational years of the C-124, so for a brief time they were peers. Supposedly agile enough to land on 4,000-foot runways, in practice the C-5 was limited in the number of airports it could fly into. While it carried a navigator, it was equipped with INS. In 1974, at Lajes Field as a Globemaster II crew was flight planning to a guard base in Tennessee, two C-5 navigators in the same room looked disappointed as their flight to Dover, their home base, was scrubbed because *one* of its two INS systems was inoperative. The C-124 nav had to suppress a "Oh, poor boy!" comment as his flight plan took him to Bermuda from the Azores right over the "Triangle" with the same navigation aids as Columbus had had. As a flight operations officer once said at Tan Son Nhut, "You've got to expect losses!" In fact, there were probably no C-124 flights cancelled because of an inoperative sextant or driftmeter.

Galaxies carried navigators, but the C-17 Globemaster III does not. And INS has been supplanted by the satellite age-derived Navstar Ground Positioning System. Beginning with the first launches in the late 1970s, the U.S. Air Force has ownership of and maintains a constellation of some 30 satellites equipped with atomic clocks that contain no gears or cogs and can provide accurate time and position for all users equipped with GPS—it's free—and has excellent coverage world-wide. Today, new cars and Boy Scouts alike can determine their position with this technology which spelled obsolescence for the celestial navigator.[29]

The C-17 was to replace the C-141 and be able to make rough field landings. It would eliminate the middle man in global airlift concepts, that is it could make the long trans-oceanic flights rapidly with high cargo or personnel capacity and then continue to forward areas without having to transfer the load from large plane to middle-size plane.

In other words, it was like its father, the Globemaster II, only much faster. Maybe as a verification, Douglas was selected to build it in Long Beach, as part of the newly merged McDonnell Douglas Corporation. This would be the last hurrah for Douglas at Long Beach. In 2013, Boeing, which acquired the McDonnell Douglas Corporation in 1997, announced that the last of the Globemaster IIIs would roll off the line in November of 2014. The Globemaster III manufacturing facility sat on the other side Long Beach Airport, where the 447 Globemaster IIs were built.

The buildings which once housed the assembly lines of the C-124 have been taken down. Where they once stood, a vast grassy acreage exists without apparent use and with an inconspicuous sign proclaiming it to be Douglas Park, although no children or dogs play there. Across the street a hanger stands where the C-124 was photographed in 1950 with a Thor, also built in Long Beach, under the *Fly Douglas* sign. The sign is still there, though it has been changed to read, *Fly DC Jets*. Small Boeing imprints are on the buildings now, but grass grows in the pavement joints. Fierce competitors have now been reduced to a single management and stockholder group. The Douglas archives, once housed in a separate building in Cypress, California, with vaults full of documents and records, have been moved inside of a Boeing plant building in Huntington Beach that makes secret military equipment. To access the archives, one must provide proof of identity and U.S. citizenship, and visits take no small amount of arranging. The archives are staffed by one person with volunteer help. Records showing the Douglas response to civil or USAF accident board reports regarding the C-124 may no longer exist, or if they do, they have not been made accessible by the company to all researchers.

So, what happened to Douglas, "undisputed industry leader and one of the nation's industrial giants?" The quotation is from Bill Yenne in his history of McDonnell Douglas, and he answers the question by outlining some mistakes made after Donald Douglas, a private man with a conservative orientation and driven by a perfectionist compulsion, turned the business over to his son, Donald Douglas, Jr., who although groomed for

Douglas building, now owned by Boeing, May 2014.

the position, nevertheless displayed few of his father's traits mentioned above. Costs, enormous costs, of developing the DC-8 and the DC-9, though they were successful designs, put company operations in debt. Officers of the Douglas Corporation began to look for a way to save the company. They found relief to the red ink dilemma in St. Louis with the deep pockets and proven management style of James Smith McDonnell. The two companies merged on April 28, 1967, under the leadership of McDonnell. Southern California continued to be the home to the Douglas Aircraft Company branch of the new corporation. Douglas, Sr., stayed on as an honorary chairman. Douglas, Jr., was replaced a year after the merger. Ironically, Donald Douglas, Sr., and James Smith McDonnell died within six months of each other, McDonnell on August 22, 1980, followed by Douglas on February 1, 1981.[30]

While continuing to be a major contributor to the nation's aerospace industry, McDonnell Douglas would be supplanted in the military airlift business by Lockheed Corporation of Marietta, Georgia, with its succession of great airlifters, the C-130, C-141, and C-5. All these airplanes were designed with a navigator station including a periscopic sextant vent in the pressurized C-130 Hercules, but soon the navigator was required only on missions of low level or paratroop drops, where training in low-level routes and release points for the air drop were needed. Often the nav adjusted these calculations while en route, updating targets according to changing conditions. It would take an advanced computer to reconcile all this new and variable information that an experienced navigator could do on the fly.

In the meantime, Boeing commanded the field of U.S. commercial passenger aircraft manufacturing with its succession of 707 through 777 models, emerging as the dominant company in the West. In the mid–90s, some Douglas engineers began to see the handwriting on the wall when CEO Harry Stonecipher tightened already severe cost cutting and reduced company spending to the point of not changing office light bulbs and having engineers empty their own waste baskets. The company disbanded its MD-12 superjumbo project, an airplane with more passenger capacity than the Boeing 747. This economy resulted in short term accumulation of larger cash reserves attractive to potential buyers, but looming as a long-term liability since cash inflow dropped drastically. The sale came in 1997 to archrival Boeing Company, which acquired McDonnell Douglas Corporation in a $13 billion stock swap. The merger honored contracts to complete the production of the C-17 Globemaster III and the fighter airplanes already on the assembly line in Southern California.

Vacant lots of "Douglas Park" in Long Beach (May 2014) where the C-124 Globemaster was once manufactured.

C-17s which went operational in 1991 need only two pilots and a loadmaster. Indeed, that advanced air drop computer had come along, which crunches data from a variety of sources such as parachute ballistics, wind factors, weather conditions, terrain, and the Coriolis effect to give the pilot a precise release point. The C-17 specifications of cargo capacity, passenger capacity, and short-field landing capability were almost exactly that of its predecessor, the C-124. A wide difference existed, however, in mph and altitude because of the jet engine factor, and crew numbers were cut in half because of the computers. Speed killed the need for a celestial navigator. Advanced avionics guaranteed that the nav would pass out of the crew compartment and into aviation history.

After the 1997 buy-out, for the first time since its biplane days, Boeing was building military cargo planes and fighters. Boeing Corporation ceased building planes in Southern California. The USAF took its 233rd and last delivery of a C-17 Globemaster III on September 11, 2013. Some 17 more were produced in 2014–2015 and sold to foreign customers.[31] With closing of the Long Beach facility, Southern California is without a major aviation assembly line and no military plane manufacturing (and without the 3,000 salaried non-union and 1,050 union worker jobs connected to the industry), ending an era that began when Donald Douglas arrived at L.A.'s Union Station in 1920 with plans in his head to make transport aircraft.[32] That cessation marks the end of the line for the family of Globemasters and of the shipment of huge amounts of aluminum to Long Beach, where they were made.

3

"The West Point of the Air"
Undergraduate Navigator Training

Prince Henry of Portugal established a navigation school in 1420 at Land's End near Sagres at the tip of the Iberian Peninsula. Henry, the youngest son of King John I "The Great," had no hope of elevation to the throne. That role would belong to his older brother, Edward, but Henry, when 21 years old was made governor of Ceuta after John I's conquest of this Moorish city across the strait from Gibraltar.

At Ceuta, Henry dreamt of further, even grandiose, conquests of the African Muslims. In so doing, Portugal would roll back the dominance of Moors and Arabs over Christianity on the south rim of the Mediterranean.

Islamic dominance of that portion of the Old World carried with it control of the lucrative spice and silk trade to the East Indies. Situated farther west, Portugal and Spain were at a distinct distance disadvantage compared to the Mediterranean city-state trading powers of Venice, Pisa, and Genoa, which had worked out diplomatic agreements with the sultans and emirs ruling over lands through which caravans carrying pepper cargo traveled the Silk Road from the East. Transferring silk and pepper cargo from the backs of camels into their galleys at ports such as Byblos, Venetian merchants brought the goods home to re-distribute them via rather sophisticated business channels throughout Western Europe. If that seems like a great deal of trouble just for some spices and clothing material, then it was. What is not as plain is just how much money could be made in these transactions, often resulting in fortunes, lifetime incomes, and even acquisition of land for those who were successful in the trade. Some of that wealth filtered down even to the lowest tars on the trading galleys.[1]

When by conquest in the ninth century, Arab true believers spread Islam from its provenances at Mecca and Medina across north Africa and

Lt. James R. Benson and fellow students in Undergraduate Navigator Training set up sextant for celestial class, 1961 (courtesy Nicki Benson Lepard).

along the fertile crescent into Persia and Turkmenistan, these robed conquerors created, in effect, a cordon cutting off Europeans from direct contact with trading founts in the East, a noose that Prince Henry, trained as a cavalry officer, intended to slash to pieces when he established a clearing house of nautical knowledge at Sagres. But his sword would be navigation.

Some key navigation tools were not developed by Europeans, such as the magnetic compass by Chinese mariners, and Arab sailors had improved the astrolab, used to fix position by observing the height of the sun at noon above the horizon. Europeans were, however, good map makers and rationalists, and with their maritime orientation and well-built ships, men of the sea. Sailing over the oceans provided know-how for European pilots. Even with a lodestone compass, getting it encased so that it could work while at sea and then accounting for variations and deviations, complicated piloting processes. Experience was the teacher.[2]

The printing press offered a seminal advancement in technology for spreading information, and Henry proved to be an able organizer and collector of geographical knowledge and navigation tools. Like any good geographer, he, or the scholars he attracted to the school, questioned travelers, especially those returning to Iberian ports from sailing south along the west coast of Africa, thus bringing scientific inquiry regarding navigation to the forefront.

These scholars of Sagres seemed convinced of a heretofore undiscovered river. In their imaginations, such a river ran across the African continent from west to east, equivalent to the south-north-running Nile. If this river could be discovered and navigated, then Portuguese ships could reach Abyssinia and the mythical Christian kingdom of Prester John, located, according to Iberian imagination, behind the Islamic regions. Such a link-up could reverse the cordon effect. The old military axiom of flank the enemy and then roll them up could be at hand.

Of course, none of this was reality, but many a Portuguese sailor, sallying forth in the new ship designs such as the caravel capable of long ocean voyages, attempted one or another of West Africa's rivers flowing into the Atlantic. They could sail inland in less than three days, but instead of a waterway to Asia, they found valuable commodities within Africa such as gold and ivory, along with captives who when taken back to Portugal and Spain were dispatched to those who found slave labor profitable.

In science, even negative results, if carefully recorded, are gainful, so over a number of years, the African coastal charts became more accurate and nav aids more reliable, emboldening Portuguese crews. The archive and learning enterprise at Sagres, much of which was in the hands of Jewish and Muslim astronomers and map makers, achieved some valuable firsts, including in 1435 sending a ship commanded by Gil Ennes beyond the dreaded Cape Bojador, which caused ships to sail far out into the ocean away from the sight of land and into the haunts, most believed, of gigantic sea serpents. Conquering this fear, visitation of the Azores and subsequent claim over those verdant and navigator-useful islands by Portugal followed, and discovery of the Cape Verde Islands came in 1456, the year of Henry the Navigator's death.[3]

Within the next 50 years, Portuguese pilot Vasco de Gama reached India even as Christopher Columbus, in the employ of the Spanish monarchs, sailed to the heretofore unknown Western Hemisphere and its new lands that in the excitement that his calculations were correct, Columbus called the Indies and the brown-skinned inhabitants, Indians. Both de Gama and Columbus supped from the table of knowledge prepared by Prince Henry. In his voyages, Columbus used dead reckoning as a primary nav aid and measured the speed of his vessels by paying out knotted rope lengths astern.[4] Thus, he logged progress across the ocean by how many knots are counted over a certain period. The term stuck around, and maritime and air navigation used the term knot as a measurement of speed.

In 1946, the U.S. Navy and the U.S. Army Air Force adopted the knot and the nautical mile as aeronautical units of speed and distance. A knot is defined as the distance of one nautical mile—6,000 feet or about 1.15 statute miles—covered in one hour. Six thousand feet is virtually the same as one minute of latitude on the global grid, thus a speed of 600 knots will be sufficient to travel ten degrees of latitude in one hour.[5]

In using a navigation instrument known as the Al-Kemal, the "guiding line," Admiral of the Ocean Sea (his official title) Columbus ascertained his circle of latitude from the deck of the *Santa Maria* by sighting Polaris through a notch cut into the top side of a piece of wood. A string attached to the center of the wood, with the end held against the tip of his nose, allowed a value to be read on a horizontal board that corresponded to the observer's position on the line of latitude. The marine sextant and the hand-held air navigation sextant used in C-124 overwater flights in the 20th century were nothing more than modern versions of the Al-Kemal. Development of the *Air Almanac* and sight reduction tables allowed the use of other heavenly bodies besides Polaris—the Pole Star—and instead of a single line of position, two or more can be used to ascertain position at the given time of observation, thus a "fix." A ship navigator on the ocean can be satisfied with one fix per day. When flying overwater, C-124 navigators sought a position fix each hour and 20 minutes.

Sailing west from the Canary Islands, Columbus happened onto a favorable line of latitude for crossing the Atlantic, or as he termed it, the Ocean Sea. His route, and the ease of its navigation, were among the most significant discoveries of his first voyage and opened the gates to the New World. The number of vessels from Europe crossing and crisscrossing the Atlantic exponentially increased after Columbus, bringing the two hemispheres into a contact unknown for millions of years, a separation that had resulted in the evolution of endemic fauna and flora species missing in the Old World: New World monkeys, turkeys, jaguars, tobacco, cacao, coca, tomatoes, and corn. Likewise, the inhabitants of the Western Hemisphere did not know of cattle, pigs, horses, sugar, or coffee. Nor did they have exposure to some biological viruses carried by European livestock—the poxes, that is—thus lacked immunities built up over generations in Europeans. Once exposed, the Native Americans died in droves.

The Portuguese accomplished what they intended to do and discovered a water route around Islam to the Indies. After de Gama's voyages to India, Lisbon rivaled Venice and Genoa as the merchant center of Western

Europe. While Columbus and the Spanish crown did not tap directly into this trading wealth from the east, their claims in the Western Hemisphere turned out extremely profitable. With so much wealth at stake, disputes over claims arose between the two Iberian nation states, and with no time for war, rulers called on Pope Alexander VI to settle matters using his Catholic jurisdiction over the two monarchs, both of whom employed the sobriquet Defender of the Faith. In Tordesillas, Spain, ministers from the Holy See and from the courts of John II and Ferdinand met and agreed on a line of demarcation. East of a line drawn 370 leagues from the Cape Verde Islands, all unclaimed and un–Christian lands would be within the domain of the Portuguese crown. All lands west, under the Spanish crown. It was to discover the boundary of this agreement in the Pacific, the other side of the world, that led to circumnavigation of the earth in 1519–1522 by the expedition of Ferdinand Magellan. Though Magellan, a Portuguese mariner sailing for the King of Spain, was killed in the Philippines because he unwisely (and oddly, as he was the oldest member of the expedition) took part in a tribal struggle for power there, one of his three ships, with 19 of the crew all close to starvation, sailed into Seville harbor in 1522, completing an epic and historic voyage. Ironically, Magellan died on Mactan Island, where the U.S. Air Force built a base large enough for C-124s during the Vietnam War. Will Durant, in his wondrous *History of Civilization*, wrote that "the discoveries begun by Henry the Navigator, advanced by Vasco de Gama, culminating in Columbus, and rounded out by Magellan effected the greatest commercial revolution in history before the coming of the airplane."[6]

Long-distance ocean navigation could not and did not remain a protected domain of Spain and Portugal. Quite soon boats of fishermen, adventurers, discoverers, settlers, and entrepreneurs based in England, Denmark, France, Holland, and other western European nations crisscrossed the North Atlantic. As Swedish historian Per Collinder theorizes, navigation art began when boatmen who plied the great grain-growing rivers encountered islands near the mouths of these rivers.

The Greeks applied the word archipelago to the Aegean Sea which separated Asia—the Orient or Morning Land where the sun rose—and Europe—the Occident or Evening Land where the sun set. Archipelago, as used today, means a sea with many islands. Indonesia and the Philippines, discovered for Europeans by Magellan and his crew, are fabulous archipelago nation-states. Ocean voyaging itself can be dated to 4,800 years ago. Navigating the vast seas that separated the hemispheres rested largely on experience, seamanship that is, being able to read the situation, currents, prevailing winds, and coming storms. Dead reckoning got many a mariner home safe then, as it would air navigators of the mid-20th century.[7]

Over a 200-year period, as exploring and colonization proceeded into every corner of the globe, England, creating an Empire "on which the sun never set," became the dominant sea power of Europe and the country at the vanguard of refining map- and chart-making and navigation equipment. While determining accurate latitude had long been possible using sun lines, the accurate calculation of longitude, a time-based measurement, remained an elusive target. Known was the time of earth's revolution—24 hours—and dividing that into 360° meant that every hour is equal to 15° longitude. The need was for a perfect clock at sea. John Harrison's longitudinal clock (chronometer H4) provided that, and Captain James Cook, in two lengthy round-the-world voyages, confirmed its durability and accuracy. The British admiralty breathed a sigh of relief for this great advance in navigation which would forestall coastal navigation errors that had led to some disastrous accidents, and it awarded Harrison a prize of 20,000 pounds sterling. Christopher Wren selected the site for the observatory at Greenwich near London on a site of higher elevation than surrounding villages that would house the most accurate clock in the world. Thus, Greenwich Mean Time (GMT) became the starting point for time zones and its signal the source of the C-124 navigator's time hack for overwater flight and the use of sight reduction tables for celestial navigation. Greenwich also became the start point of longitude, the Prime Meridian, or zero-degree longitude, replacing early points of origin including Alexandria, Cape Verde, Rome, Copenhagen, Jerusalem, St. Petersburg, Pisa, Paris, and Philadelphia.

Harrison died in 1776, four months before the American Declaration of Independence and just before James Watt patented a capable steam engine design, used to pump water out of coal mines at Newcastle, a city that became a metaphor for needless shipping and oversupply. The Iron Bridge was built, a well-known (and much visited) symbol of the Industrial Revolution, as the first construction of infrastructure using iron. But Greenwich became a more viable and lasting icon.[8]

In the 19th century, steam-powered steel ships reduced travel time and risks for ocean voyaging, using accurate maps based on a grid system, originally advanced by the Greek geographer/historian Ptolemy. Today grid lines are parallels and meridians that mark off latitude and longitude. Parallels are concentric circles starting at the earth's circumference, the Equator so called because it divides the earth into equal hemispheres.

3. "The West Point of the Air"

Meridian means long lines, and, on the map, we see them as vertical arcs stretching from pole to pole. Ship navigators used celestial sightings to mark their position on these grid maps.

In a sailing ship, top speed might mean 12 knots, so a day's travel might typically result in 300 nautical miles covered. A morning sun sighting might be used with noon and evening sightings to create three lines, the crossing of which revealed the position of the ship at noon, a reliable fix. Charting the path of the ship over a two-day period could reveal current factors and wind directions. This data could then be used for projecting the position of the ship and thereby an estimated time of arrival might be calculated, the ETA.

Navigators still used their experience to make estimates and correct a faulty sighting or instrument error. Eternal vigilance by the navigator, in the U.S. Navy the duty of the deck office and in the Merchant Marine the second mate, keeps a boat on course and on time.

In 1927, Charles A. Lindbergh crossed the Atlantic Ocean in his monoplane, the *Spirit of St. Louis*. The 33½-hour flight made "Lucky Lindy" an international hero. Lindbergh's 3,600 nautical mile route—New York to Nova Scotia to the Irish coast to Paris, France—was entirely forecasted using the compiled history of wind currents over the North Atlantic. Although the flight was not without its precarious moments with sometimes limited visibility, the wind speed and direction predictions proved accurate, and Lindbergh stayed on course, his weather data recorded on a sealed barograph inside the plane. Lindbergh followed a great circle route covering 139 fewer miles, a critical factor, than the straight (rhumb) line as depicted on this map:

Map from USAF, Air Navigation, Vol. 1.

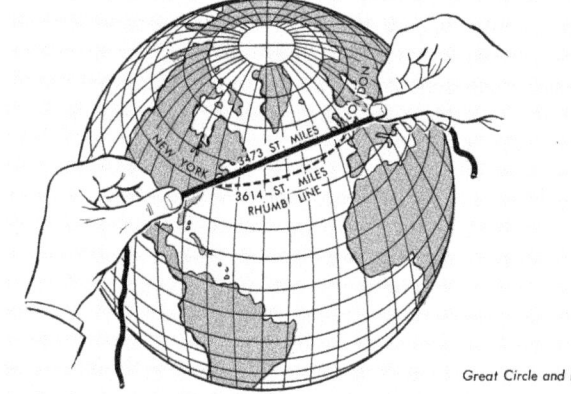

Great Circle and Rhumb Line

At an altitude of 900 feet above St. John's, Lindbergh could see "flat-roofed houses and stores, nestled at the edge of a deep harbor."[9] The *Spirit of St. Louis* flew on, the first airplane to overfly Newfoundland on the way to Europe. Beyond the thrill of departing the end of land in the New World, the vast Atlantic that now lay before him caused pangs of anxiety in Lindbergh, who wrote that the real navigation began there, what with the landmass of North America behind him and his destination far away. Lindbergh, a veteran of five years of flying experience totaling some 2,000 hours mostly overland, was to become a *bona fide* overwater navigator.

For this earth-shaking voyage, Lindbergh relied on charts the "same as you carry on ships." In response to a reporter's question, "Suppose you strike a wind change in the night and it drifts you far off course?" Lindbergh replied, "A navigating error wouldn't be too serious; this flight isn't like shooting for an island. I can't very well miss the entire European coast."[10] Mariners had long used this technique of landfall sailing.

But when Lindbergh, in the 23rd hour of the flight, arrived near enough to see the Irish coast, he was unsure exactly what he was seeing. The approaching landform seemed like a "desert mirage," he said. Just behind his pilot's seat, a navigation device called a drift indicator nestled neatly in a rack. To use it, Lindbergh placed the indicator in a bracket on the window and thereupon read the direction of the whitecaps on the sea. With the drift angle, the pilot could offset the compass to keep a true direction, but the system proved of limited value since to operate it, Lindbergh had to stop hand flying the plane and bend over to the sight, which effectively prevented flying straight during the time of the observation. Groggy from lack of sleep, Lindbergh refused to do that and wished that he had "traded the instrument's weight for another half-gallon of fuel."[11]

Lindbergh logged a description of his attempt to get directions from a fisherman off the Irish coast. He had talked to people on the ground before in his mail carrying days, so he glided down to 50 feet above a fishing boat and bellowed, "Which way is Ireland?"[12] In three passes, he never received an answer, so he opened the throttle and climbed away. A seldom used navigation aid to be sure, but a C-124 nav would have no trouble imagining the situation.

As had Columbus' monumental voyage, Lindbergh's monumental flight in 1927 opened the doors for many to follow in trans-Atlantic travel. His feat spurred on the development of bigger and faster, more powerful multi-engine airplanes. The U.S. government's profit incentives, airmail contracts for overseas routes, encouraged design and development of long-distance-capable airplanes. Juan Tripp's Pan American Airways pioneered

3. "The West Point of the Air"   51

routes across the Caribbean and into South America and built 93 radio and weather stations, an impressive privately-owned network to support overwater air traffic. By 1939, Pan Am was flying passengers between New York and France and between New York and England on Boeing airplanes known as flying boats because they landed on the water. The crew included two pilots, a navigator, and a radio operator trained in Morse code.

Nazi Germany placed emphasis on aeronautical engineering, and by 1938 the Focke-Wulf 200 could fly non-stop from Berlin to the United States and to Tokyo with one refueling stop. Navigation skill by pilots or a crew with a navigator was essential. Navigating the ocean currents of the Atlantic was an ancient art handed down in the pre–Gutenberg era from person to person. Charts and maps were of small scale and often inaccurate as late as the colonial period of America. Many seafarers and captains crossed the ocean, but with various approaches to navigational problems and with mixed results. Benjamin Franklin is credited with bringing scientific inquiry to Atlantic Ocean navigation, seeking as the King's Postmaster General to reduce the passage time of mail ships to the colonies even as he observed and noted the Gulf Stream (few contemporary scientists, if any, crossed the ocean eight times as did Franklin). With predominant westerly winds, reaching the New World from Europe had always been considered "going uphill." The return with favorable winds and currents seemed more like "going downhill." Once Franklin had identified and charted the Gulf Stream current, passages became more standardized and sea lanes developed.[13]

Air navigation used everything the mariners did to locate the vessel and chart the course, even to determining wave speed and cloud formation. In the early days of single-seat airplanes, pilots were their own navigators. Lieutenant Jimmy Doolittle of the Army Air Force tested Pan Am's "blind flying" procedures that heralded instrument flight rules.[14] Air navigation, dependent on knowledge of radio, map reading, DR, and celestial fixes, could help make flights and passengers safer. Air navigators were trained on the job, usually with Pan Am, which had its eye on Pacific routes and flying boat-style airplanes. Since no large plane could fly more than 1,500 miles without refueling, way stations were essential. Though a much larger body of water than the North Atlantic, the North Pacific offered some advantages to aerial crossing, in that it contained a bevy of islands providently placed for island hopping from California to Tokyo or Shanghai: Hawaii, Midway, Wake Island, Guam, and Okinawa.

Wake Island, 1,260 miles west of Midway, made up of three islets with no indigenous population, had gone mostly unnoticed, certainly unfrequented, by the United States since being acquired from Spain in 1898. Pan Am's request to the U.S. Navy in 1934 for a landing permit sparked efforts to find Wake on maps. In return for a five-year lease, Juan Tripp offered to pay $100 a year rent and to finance construction of aeronautical facilities. The request prompted President Franklin Roosevelt to place Wake and Johnson Island under the administration of the U.S. Navy, which chose Pan Am for the lease over an almost identical plan presented by South Seas Commercial Company, headed by Donald Douglas of Douglas Aircraft Company. To ease that pain of losing the valuable franchise, perhaps, Tripp invited Douglas onto the board of directors of Pan Am. Pan Am and the Navy kept a close working partnership. More than a few technicians and flying officers went to work with Pan Am after their Navy service. One left-out competitor for airline operations at Wake squawked: the arrangement rattled the generals and admirals in Japan, who felt threatened by this American breech of its marine defense line.[15]

Air navigation benefited from the engagement in the art and science by Fred Noonan, who, transferring his skills from the deck of a ship to the air, went to work as a navigation officer for Pan Am. He was aboard the China Clipper as it made its maiden run to Manila in 1935, landing at Wake Island en route. Noonan, renowned as Amelia Earhart's navigator on her lost circumnavigation enterprise, corresponded with P.V.H. Weems—author of *Air Navigation* (1931) and inventor of the Weems air computer—about methods and tools used to cross the Pacific in the flying boat. Weems, a former navigation instructor at the U.S. Naval Academy, responded:

Sketch by Francis Beaugureau of Captain P. V. H. Weems, USN, inventor of the Weems System of Navigation that appears in a Weems & Plath, Inc. brochure (author's collection).

> I used marine charts; a Longines second-setting watch set to G.C.T.; two sextants, Captain Field's improved type parallel rulers; and a Dalton Mark VII navigational computer ... actual navigation was comparable with such as would be practiced afloat—fixes were determined entirely by stellar observations at night.[16]

In 1940, the War Department contracted with Pan American Air-

3. "The West Point of the Air" 53

ways to train Army Air Corps navigators and at the same time opened its own navigation school at Barksdale Field near Shreveport, Louisiana.[17] The Pan Am school, located on the campus of the University of Miami, received its first cadets in August 1940 and five months later graduated 44 navigators in its first class, 40-A, among them Edgar D. Whitcomb, who would later author a book, *On Celestial Wings*.[18]

World War II began on September 1, 1939, with the invasion of Poland by the German *Wehrmacht*, ordered by der Führer, Adolf Hitler. The invasion followed a strategy of *Blitzkrieg*—lightning war—a new theory designed to maximally utilize existing national production capabilities and be over so quickly that no more war production facilities would be needed by *either* side. An important component of *Blitzkrieg* was the airplane, dive bombers and straffers such as the Stuka, not only for their firepower, but for the panic caused by their shrieking as they dove at military targets and civilian populaces indiscriminately.

The war, of course, was not over that quickly, and war production did become a deciding factor in its outcome. War production begins with machine tools and the ability to produce them, and the United States led the world in that key department, rivaled only by Germany.[19] The entry of the United States—the Third Reich, allied with Imperial Japan, declared war on the United States on December 9, 1941—meant among many other things that the aircraft industries growth would explode both quantitatively and qualitatively. So, too, would the need for and training of aviators. Randolph Air Base, a pilot training base, was dedicated in 1930 with the mayor of nearby San Antonio, Texas, calling it the "West Point of the Air."[20] During this period, all Air Corps pilots were trained at bases near San Antonio, Randolph primarily, but also at Kelly and Brooks Fields.

By 1942, with the progress of the war, the Army Air Force became a "subordinate but autonomous arm of the U.S. Army" and the number of training bases, including those for cadets, officer training, primary and advanced pilot training, navigation, bombardier (a graduate of which was Joseph Heller, author of *Catch-22*, one of the classic novels to come out of the war), and gunnery steadily increased to 438 at the beginning of 1944.[21] On July 7, 1943, the War Department set up the Army Air Force Training Command, with its headquarters at Fort Worth, Texas. World War II ended in 1945, and the AAF Training Command drastically reduced its training facilities to 34, divided into two training commands, Western Flying, headquartered still at Randolph, and Technical, headquartered at Scott Field, Illinois. Only at San Marcos Field did navigation training remain, a low priority in those days just before the onset of the Cold War, the Berlin Blockade and the subsequent airlift which placed a new premium on heavy transport airplanes.

Supporting efforts in Germany to supply a besieged city by air strained the Air Force's ability to train airmen in Texas. Reacting to the shortage caused by these efforts and by the steady and voracious needs of the Strategic Air Command, the Air Training Command sought funding for more pilot and navigator training. Ellington AFB near Houston became the basic and advanced navigator training facility, while bombardier school continued at Mather AFB near Sacramento.

The Cold War moved to another part of the world a year after the Airlift. North Korean army forces invaded South Korea across the 38th parallel on June 30, 1950. For the next three years, in the skies above the peninsula, fighters, including the romantic North American F-86 Sabre Jets and F-100 Super Sabres, battled their enemies flying Soviet-built MiG-13s and -15s in jet age dogfights, the planes engaging at higher speeds and climb rates than had occurred over the English Channel a decade earlier. To better deliver its nuclear weapons, SAC received the long-range jet engine B-47 manned by a three-man crew, pilot (aircraft commander), co-pilot, and navigator-bombardier (compared to the 11-man crew of the B-29 that was being replaced). No gunners were needed in the B-47 since it could out-fly fighter interceptors. All three B-47 crew members occupied ejection seats. The nav-bomb, who sat in the nose of the airplane, ejected downward, perfect except when the emergency occurred just after liftoff.

With a surplus of "observers," the category used in the previous era for navigators, radio operators, and bombardiers, the Air Force began to re-train this pool of flight officers for crew duties. For this purpose, it opened "flight observer" training bases at Harlingen, Texas, and James Connally AFB, Texas, joining Ellington and Mather, where non-pilot officer aviators were trained for flight assignments.[22] However, by 1956 this pool of experienced World War II aviators was depleted.

Two aircraft developments spurred an increase in nav training: the advent of the B-52 and the C-124. With high mass production of these multi-crew flying behemoths, demand grew for flight crew positions even as ROTC and other officer appointments trended down. In response, the Air Force sought a new source of young men and opened Officers Training School, OTS, to recruit and commission officers for flight training. OTS was a three-month school as compared to the six months of Officer Candidate School, the choice of servicemen without a college degree. OTS took only college graduates, most of whom were pre-set to stay in the Air Training Command pipeline for further training.

An entering group was termed a class, and OTS classes overlapped, so that upperclassmen "shaped up" the incoming group. A trainee assigned to latrine duty and new to the ways of the military asked an upperclassman (someone who had preceded him in the training by six weeks) what he was supposed to use for brushes. "The hand," he was told, "is the best instrument for cleaning!" College grads had entered a world of pain consisting of 5 a.m. wake-up calls, white glove inspections, beds made with "hospital fold" corners and tested with the bounce of a quarter, daily pull-ups and assorted physical training, KP duties, ass-chewings while standing at attention, and, worst of all, weekends restricted to base and something called CQ duty. OTC cadets shared miseries, but comradery, squadron competition, and the powers of discipline and gentlemanly behavior had habit, if not personality changing effects.

My first roommate at OTS, Paul E. Getchell from Portland, Maine, changed my college-boy habits. In March 1961, I arrived in San Antonio, Texas, at 3:30 a.m. on a Saturday morning, having flown in on a late flight from Little Rock, where I had been sworn in. I was met at the airport by an airman, driven to the OTS area in Lackland AFB, checked in by the CQ, and shown to my quarters. I was happy to hit the sack and ready for an uninterrupted "sleep in" until Monday morning. Instead, I was shaken awake Sunday at 6 a.m. by a broad-shouldered burr-cut who said in a commanding Maine accent, "Time to rise and shine! There's a parade for us to see." An hour later, I sat in a reviewing grandstand next to Paul, smoke billowing out of his big bowl pipe that could only be clenched by someone with a lantern jaw. We sat under the south Texas sun, waiting for the parade and the march of squadrons. It occurred to me that this was not a mandatory event. We were there out of our own volition, or more accurately out of Paul's volition. I marveled at this dedicated man who could roll me out of bed like that, thereby boosting me toward total commitment to the USAF and a new military life. We became trusted friends. He became a cadet colonel chaplain at OTS and a respected peer leader in the group.

OTS counted enough ex-college band musicians to muster a drum and bugle corps that accompanied drill. The military tenet, "Parades Build Morale," was chalked on the day room wall. Cadets were taught to march, properly stand at attention and salute (not too rigid and not too relaxed—just right), drill, and dress with precision that demanded tailored shirts and spit-polished shoes. We may not have articulated the feeling that came with close order drill or why one relishes it after a time. It was as historian William McNeil has interpreted, a "muscular bonding." Marching, McNeill wrote, made us "feel good about ourselves, satisfied to be moving together, and vaguely pleased with the world at large."[23] Daily calisthenics served the same purpose. We were fit and felt invincible.

With graduation came commissioning, albeit as reserve, not regular officers. After the ceremony, we, a fresh class of Air Force second lieutenants, looked for a favorite drill sergeant who in an ageless tradition saluted their former charge,to be given in return a silver dollar. These NCOs, one Sergeant Red Elk, had built into each OTC-trained Air Force officer a certain lasting pride in being just that, had taught them how to march sharply, keep the shoulders square and the gig line straight, and

OTS, 1961. Paul Getchell is front row center. Author is front row right (courtesy George E. Price, Jr.).

3. "The West Point of the Air"

bear the confidence not only of youth, but of a gentleman. We knew then and now that we owed them much more than a silver dollar for this conversion from college boys to U.S. military officers.

Newly commissioned OTS officers had training assignments awaiting, most to navigator schools, pilot school at the time being very selective. A few sought missile badges instead of wings. It was a rising occupation, and metaphorically, they were the mammals. Navigators, at their height in the early 1960s, would be the dinosaurs headed to extinction.[24]

Many of these training bases, as well as OTS, Air Training Command (ATC) headquarters, and the airman indoctrination center at Lackland AFB, were in the Lone Star state. Training Center superiors sometimes seized a newly graduated navigator who struck them as instructor talent, such as Ohio-born Lieutenant Robert Fox. Fox, like others selected because of their intellectual abilities, spent the duration of their active duty service not out there on the front lines battling their country's foes, but rather in the "Texas Air Force," as these instructors whimsically called their world.[25]

For acceptance into nav school, a favorable interview with a panel of rated Air Force officers got a prospective aviator recommended for further testing, which included a Standard Nine (Stanine) scored test that consisted of a series of drawings of airplane attitudes as viewed out the window of a cockpit, for which the tested person identified the plane as being in a turn, a roll, a climb, or other aerial maneuver.[26] A high score on the eye chart and a qualifying Stanine rating meant pilot school. Flawed vision could mean navigation school. Chuck Yeager had specified his superior eyesight as his great advantage in aerial combat. He could see enemy fighters before they saw him. Nevertheless, the award of nav wings meant that a student had mastered the art of air navigation, and a duty station and crew position loomed ahead. These young men fresh out of college, average age 22, seemed guided by the unspoken urge to "*Carpe diem*! Seize the day, boys. Make your lives extraordinary."[27] UNT took 11 months, and classes at James Connally AFB and Harlingen AFB, Texas, would have 20 students starting out. Undergraduate Navigator Training or UNT involved mostly second lieutenants—brown bars—throwing in the occasional pilot school washout who had been around long enough—18 months—to wear on his collar the silver bar of a first lieutenant.

So how did the young OTC and scattering of ROTC men take to learning the fine and historic art of navigation at these ATC training bases? First, it meant that aviation rating was attainable, which meant extra pay. Second, though it was not pilot wings, nav wings had a certain distinction, something indeed for a young officer to be proud of. Thus motivated, these college graduates settled down to life in the barracks, the great majority being single men, and returned to the classroom to sit under instructors of various talent and empathy but held in awe by the second lieutenants. If not in awe, then in fear of being washed out or struck in the head by a capacitor thrown by a radar instructor with a short fuse at students who were cutting up in the back of the room.

After a few weeks of classroom orientation, students donned newly issued flight suits and reported to the flight line for a day in the airborne classroom. Some nav trainees had never flown until they strapped on their chest parachutes and boarded a Convair-built two-engine T-29 "Flying Classroom" navigator trainer plane at James Connally or Harlingen.[28]

The non-pressurized T-29 had 14 student stations, each with radar, ADF radio, and loran. The upper fuselage had plexiglass bulges called astrodomes for hand-held sextants. Students were introduced to the driftmeter; the T-29 had five of them piercing the lower fuselage to allow these periscopes to observe drift by sighting ground references. Student navs had a map table, had plotted out the route, and at some point in the long flight, each had a turn as lead navigator, giving headings and ETAs for turning points by intercom to the pilots. An instructor graded our performance. The excitement was great, and only a few went queasy in the stomach.

James Connally in Waco, Texas, used four training routes, out-and-backs with turn-around points at Meridian, Mississippi, Walnut Ridge, Arkansas, Hutchinson,

Second Lt. Jim Adams tightening his parachute harness before a T-29 training mission, early 1960s.

Kansas, and Dalhart, Texas. The Dalhart route was favored by instructors because once past Dallas, little air traffic, blue skies and a vast flat landscape meant generally uneventful flights that even student navigators couldn't screw up. Below for much of the leg was the Llano Estacado, that once boasted a cattle ranch so large that its brand, XIT, meant Ten in Texas, covered ten counties that is. A group of Chicago businessmen obtained such a huge parcel of land in return for constructing the state capitol building down in Austin. The red sandstone building that resulted from this *quid pro quo* rises five feet taller than the U.S. Capitol dome. Maybe Texas deserved its own Air Force after all.

To a certain extent, T-29 pilots turned to headings given to them by the lead navigator, the other ten or so students at their tables in the cabin of the T-29 trainer flight-followed using Mercator and ONCs to plot the out-and-back course. ONC stood for Operational Navigation Chart, and each covered a specific area. If one collected all ONCs available and had a wall large enough to tape them together, a floor-to-ceiling world map could be constructed. Navs, like architects, were instructed to use well-sharpened pencils. To assist this dictum, each T-29 had a hand-cranked pencil sharpener. Scuttlebutt had the Air Force paying an exorbitant sum ($16 each) for the purchase and installation of these simple machines, but accuracy in plotting fixes was at stake, and over the ocean, dramatic as it sounds, then so was plane and mission! Erasers, especially for some navs, are important, this nav being dependent on one of the largest and best, the Red Ruby always handy on my table. Sun lines and DR nav legs came first in the training after ample classroom time in the basics of these techniques. What wash-outs that did occur typically came during the celestial or the grid navigation segments. Rigorous classroom instruction, hours in the planetarium and practicing with the sextant, and practice flights in the T-29 filled most duty time during the 50 weeks of UNT, but physical training, the occasional parade, and officer leadership courses in the curriculum honed military bearing.

Most weekends at nav school were held open on the class schedule. The Officer's Club hosted Happy Hours and Sunday morning brunch that included Bloody Mary's, the well-known (and overrated) hangover remedy. On Friday afternoons, the O Club, a going concern with young men on the base and their dates from the colleges, drew them in with live music and 50-cent beverages. Officer traditions and songs dating back to who knows when were learned. In retrospect, it appears now that it was these on-base happy hours that instilled tradition and pride of service in young officers. On weekday nights, nav students studied until late and then

Nav student table on T-29 navigator trainer, 1961.

maybe ventured outside the gate to a tavern like "The Casino" with pool table and juke box (Bruce Channel's "Hey, Baby" was a hit in 1962), operated by a jolly Lebanese named Mitch, or stayed in and roared with laughter listening to a Mel Brooks-Carl Reiner album or to the Vaughn Meador spoof of the First Family, all in good fun, of course. Kennedy could take a joke. What he couldn't take was embarrassment at the hands of the Communists. We were getting ready, us young navigators, to stop any chance of that happening.

Volkswagen dealers in Texas found a market with nav students. Bugs—Beetles—were economically good news (showroom price of a 1961 VW: $1,861) especially in Texas, where service station gas wars sometimes drove the price of a gallon of regular down to 12 cents. VWs were exotic since there were so few of them on the road, had no gas gauge, and no factory-installed seat belts. The James Connally commanding officer ordered that all vehicles would be retrofitted at the motor pool with this emerging safety measure, at a cost of five dollars for driver and passenger sides. Installing them was mandatory. Using them was optional. Seat belt laws, air bags, and children's car seats were far in the future. For that matter so were satellite GPS, digital cameras, and iPhones.

3. "The West Point of the Air"

After almost a year of such activities, training, learning, and comradery, graduation date came along, and wings were pinned to the proud chests of those who had completed Undergraduate Navigation Training.

Next in what the Air Force called a pipeline, most graduates from 1955 through 1970 went from UNT to Mather AFB, California, for advanced school and to obtain a bombardier rating. Out of Mather, most assignments were to SAC bases. Who were we, being readied for Curtis LeMay, who personalized dropping atomic weapons on the enemy? We came from colleges like Bucknell, Canisius, Marshall, Tennessee Tech, Merchant Marine Academy, Kansas State. We were all male. Our class had one African American and none with a Hispanic surname.

Training in California had a whole different feel to it, as though one was on the verge of something meaningful about to happen. Not many nav students washed out at Mather, due to concentration and the thrill of an operational assignment which was within reach. Inspections were rare at Mather, and weekends were free to sightsee and party down, after studying, of course. More of the student nav-bombs were married; the single men, though still in the majority, found themselves invited to cozy, neatly kept apartments and duplexes of their newly wedded classmates for home-cooked meals and a game of bridge. A certain refinement thus settled over the nav trainees, though most still thought, with pride, of their becoming SAC-trained "killers." With bars in California open until 4 a.m., there was enough time for the nightcap after the gentle evening. At Mather, navs typically got their first visit from a life insurance salesman from a firm specializing in high-risk occupations like aviation. At the age of 24, one, of course, could never die, and life insurance seemed a remote consideration even though the salesman could talk the talk since he was invariably a retired Air Force officer supplementing his pension.

Nav-bomb students sought mastery of the MA/6A system, a radar tracking system used by the B-47 Stratojet bomber and early versions of the B-52. Installed in the Mather T-29s were advanced electronic tools designed to develop navigator-bombardiers. In flight, students utilized a ten-inch radar scope to pinpoint targets with a control handle called a joystick by keeping crosshairs on a target, flying the airplane over the run-in right to the bomb release point. Once the bomb was on its way to mass destruction—in most cases it would be a nuclear weapon—the pilot regained the flight controls and began the acceleration needed to out-run the shock wave and climb to escape anti-aircraft fire or interceptors.

The hooded ten-inch scope reflected the landforms, physical features, and buildings quite distinctly, and for any student paying attention to his studies and equipped with good vision and a logical mind, there was no mistaking the San Joaquin Valley from the bowels of the T-29 trainer (meant to simulate the bombardier crew station in the B-52, which sat in the center of the plane, slightly lowered and far from any windows, the better to see the scope and relentlessly concentrate on target precision). In later years, I casually wondered why Bakersfield and Taft, working class cities, were chosen for targets, not, for instance, Monterey and Santa Barbara.

With bombardier school came the clearance needed to associate with nuclear weapons that we were to shepherd to their targets in the Soviet Union. Getting into that category of trust meant that in our home towns, FBI agents went about questioning friends and local leaders about our character and loyalty. If they passed this scrutiny, navigators could be cleared for Top Secret. Only the fictional "Eyes Only" stood higher in the public eye. At Mather, we navs became familiar with the most horrendous weapon yet produced by mankind. We were treated to films about atomic bomb testing on Pacific islands and in Nevada and scenes showing the awful aftermath of the explosions in 1945 at Hiroshima and Nagasaki. Thomas Wilson Ferebee, the nav-bombardier on Paul Tibbets' B-29 *Enola Gay*, used a T-shaped bridge over the Ota River in the central part of the city of Hiroshima as his target. Releasing the bomb from an altitude of just above 31,000 feet using a Nordin bombsight, an accurate and top secret optical device, the bomb when released dived straight at the target through cirrus and scattered cumulus clouds, exploding as planned, 600 meters above the bridge, an air burst. The 16-kiloton fission bomb gave off the light and heat of the sun, vaporizing anybody who happened to be at ground zero, leaving only x-ray images burned into chards deposited in a giant rubble pile created in two seconds after the explosion. The devastation was hard for us bombardier students to imagine, even looking at the photographs, until the instructor at Mather gave us a tidbit within our experience range. He said that it wasn't the heat or radiation that got most people, rather it was "the goddamn brick in the back of their head," what with a blizzard of debris zooming about.

Theodore "Dutch" Van Kirk, the nav on the *Enola Gay*, began his aviation career in a Sikeston, Missouri, pilot training base, washed out and was sent then to navigator school, wrote a book, *My True Course*, in which he stated that many bad things happen in a war, such as the firebombing of Dresden, the Rape of Nanking, the bombing of Coventry, England, and the Bataan Death March. In the second atomic attack on Japan three days later, the B-29 *Bockscar* had to divert from its primary target because of haze, dust, and smoke in the air from a massive air strike on the Japanese city of Kokura by 224 B-29s the day before, choosing to unload on an alternate target, Nagasaki.[29]

At Mather, navs trained for bomb readiness if the Cold War ever became a Hot War, which in 1962 seemed a very real possibility. In his book, Van Kirk said that any country should have the courage to do what it must to win a war of national survival. This philosophy was without a doubt the guiding morality of the navigator-bombardiers in training at Mather 17 years after the bombs dropped on Japan. Ironically, the 1964 black comedy *Dr. Strangelove* depicted the Air Force leadership in the "War Room" not in the least concerned with a moral question but rather the problem of how to recall Slim Pickens' B-52 before it got through to bomb Russia, an explosion that would trigger the Soviet Union's "Doomsday Machine." Although Air Force aviators laughed out loud during the movie, that was exactly what each, if they were in that situation on the B-52, would have considered to be the problem as well. Most of the navs and nav-bombardiers I knew were graduates of some liberal arts college and so presumably had had an ethics course somewhere in their curriculum. Yet no one ever spoke about the humanity of nuclear warfare other than over the sixth beer, sometimes when reflection time set in and the purpose of our training was pursued, saying something like, "those poor devils."

As the school neared completion in December, students looked eagerly toward their regular duty assignments and anxiously at the class standings which would determine their command, their station, their airplane, and their immediate future. A few assignments sent navigator-bombardiers to MATS to become transport qualified, or to ADC and TAC to take their place behind pilots in the tandem seat interceptors. Typically, the list of assignments "coming down" was leaked, as were the rankings. This led to conjectures about what assignments the top guys in the class would prefer. News came that out of 22 completers in my class, 14 would go to B-52s, five to MATS C-124s in Dover, and three to Donaldson AFB C-124s in Greenville, South Carolina. We had just heard that SAC policy, in accordance with the Kennedy administration's desire to reduce the number of SAC bases and the massive maintenance costs, had increased alert time to 50 percent of the squadron, up from 33 percent. That meant, of course, more time in the alert shacks for B-52 crews. Unfazed and as predicted, the top two graduates in the class chose SAC bombers. They wanted to save the world. My three roommates and I—we had driven out in a convoy of our four cars from Arkansas to Sacramento the previous

May and upon arrival rented ourselves an off-base, two-bedroom apartment in Rancho Cordova, the better to save money—all chose the transports. We wanted to see the world. Two dedicated nav-bombs near the end of the class standing list flipped a coin to see who would go to the SAC base at Minot and who would take Altus.

In this way the United States Air Force equipped itself with aerial navigators for duty in the huge and national security-essential air planes of the immediate post–World War II era. Size and power of that generation of air planes had increased dramatically in a few short years of development. For example, the 1950 C-124 could carry 15 times as much cargo as the 1938 C-47, the 1950 B-47 15 times the bomb load of a 1941 B-24, and the 1956 F-105 flew four times as fast as the 1942 P-47.[30]

Whether we went to SAC or MATS, all of us nav-bomb graduates— now first lieutenants—had one more school to go before reporting to the operational side of the Air Force. And it was a big hurdle: The Air Force Combat Survival Training at Stead AFB, Nevada. Reporting date for our class was January 6, 1963.

Stead is just outside of Reno, Nevada. Like Lackland, it has no squadron of airplanes. What it has is a cadre of airmen who provide ample learning opportunities for escape, evasion and survival training. This is in case an aircrew is downed behind enemy lines. In early 1963, we were about a decade removed from the Korean War, and the military was highly aware of the Chinese and Korean interrogation techniques and treatment directed at captive Americans in that conflict. Starting with classroom instruction on the Code of Conduct, we trainees passed on to workshops and instruction designed to increase our chances behind enemy lines. We had parachute lessons, judo lessons in the gym, boarded a 20-man life raft in the pool, field dressed small mammals for the spit, and whittled out wooden spoons with our combat knives. We took a course entitled "fishline sextant" that taught how to use items in the survival kit, including cigarette packages, candy, flags, prophylactics, and, of course, U.S. dollars. The curriculum included instruction in COIN or counter-insurgency.

After a week of intense classroom work, study halls, and testing, we received the "final briefing" for the "resistance lab." One evening, dressed in flight suit and flight jacket, we were taken to an obstacle course where we crawled through barbed wire under live fire for about a hundred yards. At the end of it, we were "captured." Our captors searched each individual and confiscated items like cigarettes or chocolate. We were taken to a long, four-foot-high Quonset hut where softball-size rocks and small boulders had been dumped on the dirt floor. All you could do was sit or lie on the rocks; standing or kneeling was impossible. We didn't talk much, being a bit dazed. It was very cold and very uncomfortable. In the morning we were placed in solitary cells, and periodically someone would be put into a narrow box. We were not fed. After about 36 hours, we were "interrogated" and threatened with more in-the-box time. We didn't spill our guts, though, recently having been refreshed on our prisoner rights under the Geneva Convention. Other than that, how could we have? We didn't know anything to tell.

The next morning, we were "released" from our Resistance Lab Training and mustered into a supply building. Feeling normal again, we now had a couple of classroom days on subjects such as "land navigation" and "air recovery." Supply issued each of us two down-filled sleeping bags and, for every six of us, a parachute. We were about to embark on the evasion and survival part of the program. It would take five days. When we got off the buses in the Desolation Wilderness Area of the Tahoe National Forest with our survival kit, our rolled-up sleeping bags, and a topo map, a freezing rain hampered our knot-tying ability as we strung up parachute tipis over the long poles at the site. Is the tipi waterproof? No, not exactly. And how do six men fit in a tipi? Every man's head is to the center with the feet extending out like the spokes in a wheel. Of course, the foot of the sleeping bag extends outside the parachute and is soon icy.[31] The next day we spent building a small cook fire and over it drying out the down-filled bags. Someone had smuggled in a bag of instant mashed potatoes. I had no doubt that is what my life depended on. That and the three packs of smuggled multi-flavored Lifesaver candy mints. I vowed to never, ever be without a package of Lifesavers. Of course, I have gone back on that vow, but they still have a place in my heart.

The next day, each group of six set off at staggered times to keep separation. Over the next three days, we land-navigated toward rendezvous points where "friendly partisans" met us with hot soup and gave us the next coordinates. Crossing streams and with steep inclines to traverse, the group did not stay together. It came down to the two- or three-man buddy system. If caught, the "enemy" punched a training card we "evaders" carried. Anyone getting three or more punches had to repeat the course with the next class, truly a credible threat that kept us moving and staying low.

Most of us going through this demanding physical test in the middle of the winter in mountainous terrain were in our 20s and had the advantage of coming straight there from Air Force schools, where physical training each week was part of the curriculum. A few in the group were older, transferred to a unit that required this survival school, extremely difficult for a 40-year-old individual who was a bit out of shape. Once it stopped snowing and with clearing skies and getting a handle on the environment, it became not such a bad outdoor trekking experience. We could, on some nights from some high point clearing about the pine trees, see the bright lights of Reno. A few days later, we would be amidst those lights, trying to regain some weight with a steak at Harrah's.

In our "Big Picture" lectures at Stead, an officer had told us of the new concept in the nation's defense strategies. President Kennedy understood the meaning behind world-wide conflicts and had moved the military toward a counter-insurgency stance. A total reliance on "massive retaliation" by SAC was giving way to manning and equipping a larger, mobile army which would need global airlift. Airlift would be taking part of SAC's budget. Airlift crews would have to be survival trained, such as we just went through, because their new duties would be taking them right to the gates of the enemy.

My Mather roommate, George Price, from Nashville, Tennessee, slender of build to begin with, lost 15 pounds in the Stead survival training and trek, about average, but on him it looked dramatic. He had temporarily lost hearing when one of the survival instructors, impersonating an enemy soldier who had infiltrated our bivouac, found us asleep, so fired his blank pistol just above George's right ear. This gunshot wake-up call was supposed to embed a concept of "Eternal Vigilance." We were relieved at the end of the Combat Survival Training and happy with our certificates. After a T-bone and taking in the sights of the biggest little city in the West, we clambered into our cars and, gobbling peanuts, candy, and raisins drove east, George to Greenville, me to Dover. My three years as an active duty transport navigator aboard a Globemaster II were about to begin.

4

"Ike's Bluff"
Cold War and Civil Wars

The second-smallest state in the Union, Delaware has three counties—two at high tide, say the residents. The middle of those three counties, Kent, is home to a large United States Air Force base. During the Kennedy administration, Dover AFB received and embraced the 1607th Wing of MATS. Dover was almost the counterpart to the giant of WESTAF, Travis AFB in California. Almost, because headquarters of EASTAF was not actually at Dover, but 70 miles up the road at McGuire AFB, New Jersey. The 1607th Wing, however, had 53 C-124s, and to fly them, three squadrons of aircrew numbering 330 pilots, 170 navigators, 240 flight engineers, and 139 loadmasters.[1] Two squadrons with 27 C-133s and crewmembers were based at Dover, too, along with "tenant" units of SAC equipped with KC-97s and ADC equipped with F-101s and F-106s.

Coming to an operational unit after two years of Air Training Command presented a new life for crew members, where real work meant real opportunities to serve the country and see the world. Here, neophyte transport navigators checking into their squadron got, among other orientations, a guided tour of their operational airplane. The flight line buzzed and roared with airplane activity. At Dover, with its diverse mission, C-124s parked in rows near the terminal were impressive with their stately size and perfect alignment. Barely visible at the end of the field, the SAC tenant unit arrayed its KC-97s on a separate ramp that veered directly onto the runway in case of a scramble. At the supply store, navs picked up brown leather nav kits and flight suits on which they would sew MATS and squadron patches. Med techs plunged into an arm three syringes at a time to inoculate us against Yellow Fever, Cholera, and Plague.

C-124 rises above a parked C-133 at Dover, circa 1962 (courtesy Air Mobility Command Museum, Dover AFB, Delaware).

Airmen posed for pictures and obtained passports necessary for the global mission of C-124 crews.

Bachelor officers moved into a row of BOQ's. Base housing granted married officers an allowance with which to rent off-base. The largest apartment complex in Dover was named after Caesar Rodney, a Founding Father of the Revolution. As presented by teachers in local elementary schools, Rodney rode the 70 miles from Dover to Philadelphia in a driving rainstorm, arriving on July 1, 1776, to break the tie in Delaware's three-man representation at the Continental Congress, using the phrase, "I vote for Independence." Rodney did his part in the American Revolution and stayed active afterwards. He died in 1784, though, before the Constitutional Convention. His legacy to the new United States lived on, and Delaware became the first state to ratify the new Constitution as it emerged from the Convention in 1787, earning its right to the nickname, "The First State," which still appears as a motto on automobile license tags. Just a few miles from the Caesar Rodney Apartments is the capitol of Delaware, a colonial brick building fronted by the Dover Green, where in the 1960s, on the corner of the grounds, a whipping post stood to which a repeated misdemeanor offender was sentenced to receive a flogging of 20 lashes, a decision upheld by the Delaware Supreme Court. He was never tied to the post for administration, however, as the court of public opinion halted what most people thought of as over-the-top punishment.[2]

Dover had prominent town-life features such as a weekly market for the conservative Mennonite farmers who came to town in their enclosed one-horse buggies. Delaware rural roads have a lane for horse traffic, and the city designated a parking area for the conveyances. Bearded men with wide-brimmed hats, plain clothes, and females wearing no makeup, hair in buns covered by a white cap and floor-length dresses, talked earnestly with each other, dealing with issues in a world much different from that going on at the air base a few miles to the south.

Rehoboth Beach, 30 miles down the coast from Dover, boasted fresh-caught seafood and the Bottle & Cork ("World's Greatest Rock 'n' Roll Bar"), where college kids, young officers from Dover, staffers from inside the Beltway, and Philadelphia secretaries mingled in the summer to converse, dance, do the limbo, and maybe watch a sunrise from the beach.

Near Dover AFB, a village, Kitts Hummock, fronts Delaware Bay, which is protected from crashing ocean waves by a peninsula of land occupied by the state of New Jersey, 80 miles across the bay toward the rising sun. That bit of shelter creates a special habitat occupied, by among other sea creatures, something called a horseshoe crab, because it looks like the underside of a horse's hoof. It consists mainly of a large, soft shell and a six-inch spike of a tail that it can point straight up, which it will do as it scrunches down to cover its body in the beach sand. This crab has no edible meat, and if a beachcomber or swimmer happens to step on the spike, well, it feels like stepping on a 20-penny nail. Yet it is a unique form of life requiring this unique habitat. Edible crabs, along with clams, abound in Delmarva. As a newbie to this fare and being from the Ozarks, I asked my East Coast friend what baked clams tasted like? "Well," he said, "sort of like chicken." "Really," I replied. "And what does lobster taste like?" "Sort of like chicken, too," Thornton answered. I mused on this new information.

Bars and taverns strung out along the beach highway have frequent clambakes to go along with their shuffleboard tournaments. Pucks are called quakes in Delaware, further distinguishing the small state which in 2008 saw its favorite son, Joe Biden, elected to the vice-presidency of the United States, on the ticket with Barack Obama, the first African American to be elected to that high, precious office, and Commander-in-Chief of the U.S. military.

C-124 crew members arriving at Dover for the first time from Air

Training Command stints, where they had lived and worked in the spacious states of Texas and California, are immediately struck by the nearness of everything around Dover. Washington, D.C., lies just two hours away, New York City four. Philadelphia, Baltimore, and Atlantic City are in easy driving distances. Although nice to think about, such getaways for Air Force officers were rare, as flying schedules, training, and duty assignments made for long work weeks and short weekends. Pilots seemed to spend every waking hour studying, simulating, staying current, or checking out some skill in the plane. Navigators had some of these duties, too, but for the most part, time each month was spent away from home station on a flying mission. Rated officers were capped at 330 flying hours for a quarter, and typically that meant about 100 hours per month, which translated to about 15–16 days out of 30 on a trip. Most of those C-124 trips from Dover were directed to Europe.

A priority purpose of the 1607th mission was to keep NATO allies supplied with material. In 1960, the U.S. Army had more than a half-million soldiers and airmen in Europe.[3] Although these American soldiers were not supplied all or even mostly by air, the crisis of the blockade and subsequent Berlin Airlift brought recognition of a need for heavy transport airplanes in case ground-based supply systems failed. To keep the air supply channels open and lubricated, many missions were flown seemingly for that purpose. A perhaps apocryphal story circulated about one C-124 delivering a single I-beam to a NATO base and a second C-124 loading it for the trip back home.

In 1954, the newly created 1607th at Dover AFB received its first C-124s, then fresh and unfatigued. In the same year, Globemaster IIs from another base, the 62nd Troop Carrier Wing at McChord AFB, carried French troops from their home stations in Europe to Dien Bien Phu, where the great battle for French Indochina—Vietnam—was occurring. Perhaps the reinforcements were too little, too late, but a major lesson learned was the reliability and power of the C-124s in that all 13 of them assigned made the 22,000 nautical mile circumnavigation of the globe successfully in an average flying time of 119 hours—actualizing a new day for troop transport where a full division could be deployed from thousands of miles away in a very short span of time.[4] The Globemaster, with its dogged reliability and its voluminous cargo bay, won over air strategists. Consequently, numerous airlift and Atlantic crossings were in store for these huge airplanes of MATS, especially those of the 1607th, extending by the mid–'60s to all airlift wings when C-124s were landing daily in South Vietnam. Thus, the heyday of the C-124 was dawning.

4. "Ike's Bluff"   71

Dover's first C-124 arrived on May 1, 1954 (courtesy Air Mobility Command Museum, Dover AFB, Delaware).

Dover C-124s, as much as any transport airplane, represented Air Force responses to the realities of 1961–1963, that is the commitments of the Kennedy administration to a military designed for counter-insurgency actions rather than relying on nuclear warfare. This in turn led to the U.S. Army's commitment to Air Cavalry units dependent on helicopter transport to fire zones. Increasing aggression of North Vietnam toward South Vietnam, an emerging hot-spot 10,000 miles from the United States, gave opportunity for trial.[5] With military jet airlifters still on the drawing board and but a few C-130A Hercules turbo-prop ready to carry out missions, the Globemaster II size, operational numbers, trained crews and maintenance proved able to meet demands of the American Century.

While not diminishing the airlift missions needed by NATO, NORAD, and humanitarian causes, the 1607th, through gigantic exercises, trained its C-124 crews for the meet-them-on-the-ground national strategy of containing Communism. Formation flying, paratroop drops, short field landings, and engine-running off-loads signaled a day when airlifting counter-insurgency forces to faraway places, like Vietnam, and landing them in forward positions would be the norm.[6]

Dover AFB was perfectly situated to combine the NATO and the Air

C-124 three-ship formation flies over Dover AFB during 1963 air show.

Cav support missions. With an elevation of less than 30 feet above sea level, 10,000-foot runways, and proximity to sea ports and cities of the Eastern seaboard, Dover had advantages for sustainable airlift operations.

Local people looked up to see three- to nine-ship C-124 formations, as they plied the skies above, but never did the odd-looking Globemaster develop a romanticism that attached itself to the awesome bombers or the sleek fighter airplanes sharing those same skies. Unfair maybe since Dover C-124s carried nuclear weapons, too, albeit just for transporting and always safety armed, but nevertheless real atomic bombs. One ill-fated occasion on July 28, 1957, concerned a C-124 that lifted off from Dover with three nuclear weapons and one nuclear capsule aboard. The fissionable core was not installed in the bombs, which was indeed a fortunate safeguard on this mission. Shortly into the flight, the Globemaster lost #1 and #2 engines on the port wing of the airplane. To maintain altitude for a return to an emergency field, the aircraft commander ordered the jettison of cargo through the freight elevator well. The first weapon left the plane at 4,500 feet altitude, and the second was jettisoned at 2,500 feet. No detonation occurred even as the bombs hit the surface of the water. The nukes sank to the bottom. Search efforts could recover neither

4. "Ike's Bluff"

weapon nor associated debris from the ocean. The C-124 landed safely at the Atlantic City airport.⁷

Even with some highly exotic and newsworthy uses of Dover C-124s—such as the world-wide tour by a Globemaster exhibiting the Mercury capsule that had been piloted by astronaut John Glenn, making newspaper headlines—the airplane seemed irrelevant. But rising events in sub-Saharan Africa demonstrated otherwise.

In 1962 a Globemaster II carried John Glenn's space capsule Friendship VII on a four-month, round-the-world tour (courtesy Air Mobility Command Museum, Dover AFB, Delaware).

In the summer of 1960, a United Nations peace-keeping force arrived in the Congo, much of it transported by Dover Globemasters. The *Delaware State News* headlined, "Dover Planes Leave on New Congo Mission" detailing movement of 19 C-124's charged with transporting 2,000 Irish troops to Katanga province along with 147,000 pounds of cargo, each Globemaster to cover 12,000 miles in a round trip from Dublin to Kamina Air Base in the Congo.⁸ This unfolding civil war signaled a departure from John Foster Dulles, Secretary of State in the Eisenhower administration, and the limited response inherent in Dulles' "Massive Retaliation" strategy to deter aggression. Emerging threats could not be properly met with a single foreign policy that relied upon SAC to destroy the enemy if they dared attack us or one of our allies or clients. "Ike's Bluff," as it has been termed, was to stare down any unruly behavior anywhere and especially if complicated by our chief adversary, the USSR.

The Greek Civil War in 1948 had prompted the Truman Doctrine, in which the president had specified that U.S. power would be used to stop the spread of Communism. The Marshall Plan, a corollary, had sought to use money as the instrument to prevent that spreading, thus originating U.S. foreign aid programs. Harry Truman ran for re-election in 1948 and won a surprising uphill battle against the Republican challenger, New York Governor Thomas Dewey. Dixiecrats, wildcatting Southern Democrats irate over the military integration Executive Order 9981 issued by the president, fielded a segregationist candidate, Strom Thurmond, taking many of the South's Democrat electoral votes away from Truman.[9] Dewey was formidable in his own right and was widely predicted to win the election over the divided Democrats. Truman, whose prospects for victory looked dim, campaigned hard and won the election.

The American people decided, perhaps, that Truman's experience was the best bet at this crucial time when the U.S.–U.S.S.R. alliance that had defeated the Nazis was coming apart. A Communist coup in Czechoslovakia deposed popular president Edvard Beneš, who died in September 1948 after he resigned in the face of Soviet troop intervention. The Berlin Airlift that started on June 26, 1948, continued until September 1949. These threats led to meetings to prepare for mutual defense by Western European countries in 1948, a forerunner to the inclusion of the United States and Canada in forming the North Atlantic Treaty Organization (NATO), the treaty signed in April 1949.[10] With bipartisan Congressional agreement, NATO would insure globalization of United States aims and responses.

While that provided comfort for our European allies, their nerves were still frayed by the monumental Red Army facing them across the "Iron Curtain." If attacked, NATO forces, small in comparison, would be overwhelmed by the Red Army, which would, of course, bring on the spread of Communism. U.S. troops in Europe formed not a stout line of defense, but only a "trip wire" which if triggered would result in "the launch." With Western Europe at stake, a launch would occur. That strategy preoccupied the Eisenhower administration that followed Truman's, and massive retaliation developed as a national strategy. But that strategy could not account for confrontations that were starting to occur in the developing world.

In the late 1950s and 1960s, independence movements in former colonies broke out around the world. In African countries, violent conflict between leaders and groups vying for political power often accompanied wars of liberation, even after independence had been won from the imperialistic European powers who with the Berlin Conference of 1889 had systematically divided up the "Dark Continent" between them. King Leopold of Belgium staked a claim to the interior of sub–Saharan Africa as his private possession. It was called the Belgian Congo.

Bisected by the Equator, the Congo, a vast land in the middle of the great continental plateau of Africa, is one of the hottest and rainiest places on earth. Its river, the Congo, carries an immense volume to the sea, and 90 percent of the population lives along the river, which acts as a great inland artery. Beyond the river settlements stretched enormous, unbroken rain forests. But unlike the Amazon, the Congo does not provide ocean vessel access from its mouth in the Atlantic into the interior. Two-hundred-foot escarpments that appear at the edge of the plateau 100 miles inland from the coast prevent further passage. Ship-borne cargo from the sea cannot enter the Congo basin, the physical geography of the continent thus isolating central Africa and its people. Imports from outside reach inland markets in the country via bearers or by air transport.

As Belgium slowly granted measures of independence, the Congo, colonized for 80 years and further held back by imperialism, saw no unified indigenous government emerge. In June 1960, Congo became independent but with no consensus. With rivals for power gearing up for armed conflict in pursuit of their aims, the U.S. and the U.S.S.R. saw a need for getting a foot in the door. In the Congo civil war, both sides settled on the use of surrogates rather than nuclear threats to advance their interests. This case tested Khrushchev's theory that the Soviet Union could compete with the United States and win—*my vas pakhoronim*—in emerging African states such as Egypt, and now the Congo, without setting off massive retaliation.[11] Congo, like many other former European colonies, was not under the defense umbrella of NATO which, with U.S. insistence, adopted at its founding charter a clause excluding territories below the Tropic of Cancer.

With Belgium administrators and military officers staying put in the former colony, much was about to go wrong. Patrick Lumumba, the elected Prime Minister and a charismatic socialist, asked for United Nations assistance as he faced a serious threat of secession in Katanga province from his rival, Moise Tshombe. Tshombe, a Methodist and former businessman—what's not to like? Western diplomats might have thought—had hired white mercenaries, led by former Belgian officers, to battle Lumumba's Congolese government troops. Noting that chaos was about to descend in central Africa, UN Secretary General Dag Hammarskjold responded to Lumumba's request by sending a substantial international military force to the Congo to intervene in the crisis. The United States and the Soviet Union agreed to provide the airlift.

In January 1961, the 19 C-124s, aided by four C-130 Hercules, provided help for beleaguered Congolese. The mission included evacuation of Europeans, mostly Belgians but some 400 Americans who worked or served in the Congo as well. Dover AFB C-124s took on a lion's share of the airlifting, flying 9,000 troops from nine countries and 4,500,000 pounds of cargo picked up from nine airfields stretching from Ireland to

UN troops loading on a Dover AFB C-124 at Elizabethville, Congo, 1961 (National Archives).

Pakistan in an operation initially dubbed Operation Safari, a designation soon changed to Operation New Tape. Globemasters carried troops in and out of the Congo, including a contingent of 500 United Arab Republic soldiers to Equator province.[12]

Katanga had one jet fighter, piloted by a Belgian, that ruled the skies, "playing a key role in the fighting" until Swedish fighters arrived and gave protection to ground forces of Lumumba.[13] Showing a high level of international cooperation achieved by Hammarskjold, India sent fighter planes to do air battle and give air support for United Nations troops as well. Katanga was worth fighting for since within it lay uranium and vast copper deposits, making it resource rich. Copper had been mined and exported from there since the first millennium. The 1960s were the beginning of affluent years in the United States, and the housing boom needed copper imports, driving the market upward. Over the next 20 years, world copper production doubled.[14] Oil was still cheap on the world markets, but copper was not.

The warring factions trumped Hammarskjold's indecisive efforts to use the multi-national force in any meaningful way to stabilize the elected government, which caused a desperate Lumumba to request support from the Soviet Union. This appeared to reduce Congo independence into a minor league version of the Cold War, where battles occurred between Maoist factions and those who were not Marxists, each supported but not controlled by one of the super powers. "Not controlled" was a key to the rise of a dictatorial regime uncommitted to either side, but brutal and exploitive in its own way.

The airlift to the Congo logged 40,000 flight hours, most of that in the first year and a half when C-124s from the 1607th were virtually the only MATS aircraft used in New Tape.[15] From European bases such as Chateauroux, France, isolated airways to Leopoldville (now Kinshasa) took Globemasters 22 flight hours. Many missions bound for the Congo stopped over at Wheelus AB, the American-operated field near Tripoli, Libya. Navigators flight planned in base ops there, using incomplete charts of the African continent, much of which in the pre-satellite era remained as uncharted as in Henry Stanley's day. ONCs depicted most of the massive Sahara Desert in white, meaning scant navigational knowledge of an area comparable in size to the lower 48 states. Sandstorms that reached flight levels impeded use of celestial in flights over the Sahara. Radio beacons as well as airport towers operated only during daylight hours, if then."[16] A usual preflight briefing for the intrepid 1607th crews that carried troops and material to this war zone in the Third World came down to: fly south for ten hours and pick up the Leopoldville RDF.[17]

Dover crews flew across the continent mostly VFR, which offered wonderful views of the most spectacular landscapes and wildlife in the world, and landed with troops or material at stop-overs like Addis Ababa, Ethiopia (airport elevation 7,625 feet), Entebbe, Uganda, Khartoum, Sudan, and Leopoldville in the Congo. Pakistani troops carrying field packs and wearing their unit berets boarded at Karachi, carrying carbines and automatic weapons. Crews bunked in the airplane, in a vacated dormitory at Lovanium University in Leopoldville, and at the Lake Victoria Hotel, and once a Belgium family departed their villa so suddenly that they left their dinner on the table. Aircrew members wore civvies and were sustained over the course of a typical 20-day TDY by a flyers' nutritional standards: a can of Beanie Weenie, dessert of Oreos, and topped off with a Winston or Marlboro cigarette.[18]

As one C-124 pilot told it, "A crucial navigation beacon, Lake Awasu, between Stanleyville and Addis, was never on the air.... Finally, we located the village and spotted the antenna and the shack which housed the generator. We buzzed the village and even dropped a note, but no joy. It finally came on the air the day we left for home and we later learned that to turn it on, a soldier was dispatched riding a donkey from Addis on a nine-day trek."[19]

At Leopoldville, Congolese troops boarded a C-124 and marched the crew off the airplane at gunpoint. Some were jailed and three were struck repeatedly with rifle butts. Eventually released, the crew received the Air Force Commendation Medal, and the three who had taken the physical beatings were awarded the Purple Heart, perhaps the first time that had occurred in Sub-Saharan Africa. Anti-aircraft incidents occurred as well. In December 1961, a Globemaster II was hit by enemy ground fire on landing approach to Elisabethville, the capital of Katanga province. The C-124 landed safely even though the gunfire put one engine out of commission.[20]

Lumumba was murdered in 1961, after being captured, held, and beaten unmercifully by Congolese soldiers in the cargo compartment of a C-130 flown by an Australian crew. By 1965 pro–Western Moise Tshombe had been exiled. Ironically, Daj Hammarskjold was also a casualty of the Congo crisis, killed in a crash of a U.N. Douglas DC-6 airliner in September 1961 over the Congo-Zambian border while en route to negotiate a cease-fire between UN non-combatants and Katanga troops of Tshombe.[21]

Army general Mobuto Sese Seko, whom the United States backed as a capable politician, consolidated power and exercised it to create a dictatorship that lasted 32 years, from 1965 until he was weakened by prostate cancer and deposed in 1997. In 1971, Mobuto, who channeled billions of dollars reaped from copper resources into his private Swiss bank accounts, renamed the country Zaire in what he termed the Africanization movement. To publicize his world image, Mobuto promoted a spectacular heavyweight championship fight in 1974 between Muhammad Ali and George Foreman. An award-winning documentary entitled "When We Were Kings" revealed the political tensions of that bout and indeed the whole era. C-124s are not mentioned, though of course Ali and entourage and Foreman, whose baggage included his German Shepherd, arrived by airplane. Foreman may not have known that this breed of dog was an unpleasant reminder of colonial repression.

Isolation for people of central Africa continues into the 21st century and makes the Democratic Republic of the Congo—the name was changed back after Mobutu's fall—one of the more unpredictable countries in the world. The experience did show that through uncertain surroundings and hardships in operating the Globemaster on its mission to the Congo, it was a reliable, large-scale airlifter. Remarkably, not a single C-124 was lost in fulfilling this UN mission. The C-124 showed that it could take a punch. Could it be that this record dispelled any doubt in the Pentagon of the capability and the reliability of the Globemaster in dispensing U.S. military power to the far corners? The Congo offered a proving ground for a vigilant, ongoing, global U.S presence to meet the exigencies of the Cold War, and the C-124 crews and planes proved equal to the task. The U.S. would and could compete with the Kremlin in the emerging countries. The Globemaster would and could provide the airlift for global gamesmanship.

Not that the end results of the Congo game and U.S. and U.N. intervention was all that positive where making the world safe for democracy was concerned. Indeed, if analysts had been on their toes, they might have gleaned a better understanding about the after-effects of outside military assistance without much cultural awareness. The African airlift and American participation in it did not offer a promising model for continuing the U.S. export of its interests into places unable to change centuries of nondemocratic rule. Capable though the airlift might be, the experience proved that favorable outcomes were difficult to achieve.

Even as the Congo crisis subsided, C-124s continued a full schedule of strategic airlift support to Thule, to NATO forces in Europe, to the Caribbean, and to the Far East. Even with the MATS full commitment to overwater airlift duties, an obvious shift in mission readiness and aircraft and crew duties had occurred. Joint service exercises began to dominate the scene. Proof by experiment was needed for limited war options. Training operations dubbed Swift Strike, Desert Strike, and Gold Fire burnt an extraordinary amount of Air Force time, energy, and resources in the early '60s. And to where did it lead? To Vietnam, of course. The Kennedy administration sent the first helicopters there in 1961.

In two years of joint exercises, MATS proved that it could respond to changing Pentagon priorities. Military planners sought to place in operation Commander-in-Chief John Kennedy's reasoning that counter-insurgency forces would be a more effective method of stymieing Communist advances in the Third World during this world-wide Cold War period. On July 21, 1963, in the southeastern United States, 75,000 men launched a one-month-long inter-service war game termed Operation Swift Strike, the largest peacetime maneuver in U.S. history. An integrated Air Force-Army combat force, firing blanks but noisy enough to awaken imaginations of the American Civil War in this Southern area, demonstrated its ability to "meet a military emergency *anywhere in the world.*" (italics added)[22] MATS succeeded in transporting 34,000 troops and

27,000 tons of material into an area while training for assault of enemy troops and re-supply of forward positions. Operation Gold Fire followed the next year, moving the combat zone to the foothills of the Ozarks, perhaps better to simulate the terrain of the central highlands. C-124s, along with the sturdy C-130s, hit the ground hard, practicing short field landing techniques in limited runway and facility airfields like Walnut Ridge, Arkansas. These maneuvers claimed much time and budget resources of Dover and other MATS bases as crews practiced lifting and dropping troops into battle zones. Congo had demonstrated the long-range and extended time capabilities of C-124s. The stateside exercises conditioned aircrews no less than the troops for even more direct involvement in world trouble spot crises. The Globemaster II played an essential role in the preparatory exercises and in the early years of combat in Vietnam but received little recognition for performance of that role. An example of that is in an *Air University Review* article entitled, "USAF Airlift and the Airmobility Idea in Vietnam," which barely mentions the C-124 while concentrating on the contributions, laudable to be sure, of the C-123s and C-130s deployed in early stages of the war.[23]

C-124 formation dropping troops from the 101st airborne over the Kentucky countryside, early 1960s.

Not only training, but fighting equipment seemed to be designed especially for Southeast Asia and counter-insurgency strategies to be implemented there. The M16 plastic stock rifle, for example, issued to U.S. soldiers in 1963 was thought by its designers to be as effective as the Soviet bloc AK-47 Kalashnikovs for *jungle warfare*. It replaced the wood stock M14 for U.S. Army troops in Vietnam. Bell developed an improved UH-1, the D model, that joined the U.S. Army inventory in 1963 and could carry 12 soldiers with heavy armament on a 290-mile round trip.

In Asia, insurgencies with Marxist leanings in Malaysia, Indonesia, and the Philippines worried American military and civilian administrators. But in Vietnam, worries advanced into preventive military measures with the sending of U.S. Army advisors into the field to mentor South Vietnam soldiers. The Congo Airlift and the joint military-airlift exercises that followed it were, in retrospect, natural forerunners to full U.S. commitment to contain Communism by battling insurgency on the ground anywhere in the world. Korea had been a little different, a far-off war on the Asian land mass, a predicament that West Pointers since Douglas MacArthur had sworn to avoid. The Korean War had been forced on the United States because the government of South Korea was in danger of being extinguished, and Japan, nearly defenseless, could be in peril if the U.S. folded in Korea.

Vietnam, however, presented more options, not a cut-and-dried-fight-them-here situation. The domino theory certainly decried the fall of friendly Southeast Asian governments to Communist arms, but even so, bad as that would be, it was not catastrophic to most Americans, not like losing China had been or Japan would have been.

At the same time, rapid increase in aircraft technology meant that the C-124 was nearing the end of its prominence as a MATS airlifter. The C-130 Hercules could fly across oceans with cargo and troops and land in forward areas. Charleston AFB received the first C-141 in December 1964. Many more were in production. The Boeing 707 rolling off the lines in plants in Washington and Kansas would become as successful as the Douglas C-47 had been in its day, able to carry cargo and a lot of soldiers at much faster speeds. Both airlifters were available in 1965. In 1965, the *Airlifter* reported replacement of C-124s by brand-new C-141 Starlifters, a jet transport developed by Lockheed and built at Marietta, Georgia, and at Oklahoma City's Tinker Field. In statistics given by the article's author, A2C Walt Rykiel, the Globemasters of Dover had logged 870,000 hours in the air and covered some 174,000,000 miles into most corners of the Earth.[24] During its 11 years of duty with the 1607th, 32 crew members were lost in the five deadly crashes that occurred. Ironically, the 1607th's other strategic heavy lifter, the turbo prop C-133 Cargomaster, also built by Douglas, had five crashes in the same period in which 33 crew members died, a total of 65 airmen between the two giant Douglas airlifters lost by the 1607th ATW from 1957 to 1965.[25]

In 1965, however, the 285 Globemasters that remained in the MATS inventory gave strategic military planners a huge resource in airlift and in planning. Enough perhaps to tip the balance toward favoring U.S. military deployment with active combat troops and equipment to Vietnam. In 1965, the stateside large-scale maneuvers ended. The training was over, and the real war about to begin. Globemaster navigators would be called on to use their skill to guide planes over the vast Pacific to a war zone 14,000 miles away.

5

"Hairy conditions"
Over the Oceans

Juan Trippe's Pan American Airways and Howard Hughes' Trans World Airway, pioneers in long-range air transportation, set standards for "highways in the sky," including late-afternoon and evening departure times for eastbound planes crossing the Atlantic. A MATS crew from Dover AFB could depend on a 2000 hours departure (8:00 p.m.) when scheduled for a mission to Mildenhall AB, England, Rhine Main AB, Germany, or Chateauroux AB, France. That put the sun and wind at their back en route to these typical destinations in the Cold War years and a night sky for celestial navigation. The commitment to the North Atlantic Treaty Organization meant a constant stream of men and material flying out of the United States toward Europe. Every day, C-124s departed Continental United States or CONUS, as the military jargon had it, routed over the North Atlantic using dead reckoning (DR) and weather forecasts to plot efficient routes and landings.

The basic C-124 crew had a pilot (the aircraft commander), a co-pilot, a navigator, two enlisted flight engineers, and a loadmaster. On duty, MATS airmen wore sage green flight suits, lightweight and durable, made of a synthetic material, Nomex, which had strong, heat-resistant fibers. These were known to the quartermaster as CW-27/P and were used with color variation in the film *Ghostbusters*. Flight suits had simple rank insignia, name plate with wings, and a squadron or MATS patch. Crew members wore or packed the nylon MA-1 summer flight jacket with blaze orange silk lining.

The jackets were convenient, light, warm, and managed to look none the worse for wear even with months between dry cleaning. Some guys brought along a spare flight suit. Others sent theirs out to be washed on stopovers that boasted a Visiting Officers Quarters (VOQ), usually staffed with local civilians who had a side business of overnight laundry service. If that service was not available after days of flying from station to station, the crew member simply stood his flight suit in the corner until donned the next morning. Black, lace-up combat boots called, incorrectly, brogans and a squadron ball cap completed the uniform for MATS crews. Some units eschewed the ball cap in favor of the garrison (overseas) cap that could be stuffed in a pocket when not in use. No one wore a "fifty mission crush" wheel hat as World War II bomber pilots did.[1] In the 1960s, on trips where diversions extended the planned length, MATS crew members might run short of cash, and hardly anyone had a VISA or Discover card. A few might carry American Express Travelers Cheques, which were readily accepted and exchanged for local currency (this is no longer as true), conjuring a favorite jibe: You can tell a MATS crew member because they're standing around in a flight suit scratching their ass trying to cash a check! One zippered pocket of the flight suit kept flight orders that listed each crew member's name, rank, serial number, crew position, and security clearance (Secret or Top Secret) and gave authority to proceed on an airlift mission of from two weeks to a month in duration. The orders included a table marking monthly flying time for each crewmember so that no one unknowingly exceeded monthly or quarterly limits. The flight orders directed the crew to use government quarters and meals when available.

A mid–1960s USAF flight suit with MATS insignia.

Airmen wore a chain with dog tags and a P-38 can opener.[2] Regs prohibited wearing rings which could cost a finger with an unfortunate snag.

Short haircuts and dark aviator sun glasses completed the picture. One in a hundred guys had a tattoo. We carried no arms and wore no parachutes in flight on standard missions. On drops, sometimes the second nav in the back by the exit donned a parachute. When in combat zones, all wore holsters with a .357 Smith & Wesson Magnum and trained to use them in periodic visits to the firing range.

On a normal mission, loaded with 21 tons of cargo and with 36,000 pounds of 115/145 octane fuel, the range of the C-124 was 1,840 nautical miles.[3] The air distance to Chateauroux from Dover was 3,513 nautical miles, so a Globemaster with cargo could not reach the European continent without refueling. Depending on the time of year, weather conditions, and initial destination, the routing went through Labrador, Newfoundland, or the Azores and sometimes both. In many cases, the Globemaster flew from Dover to St. John's, Newfoundland, or Harmon Field, proceeded southeasterly to Lajes Field in the Azores, and then, the next day, on to Torrejon Air Base near Madrid or to an airfield in France, in effect making a zigzag path across the North Atlantic. Airmen overnighting at Chateauroux AB looked forward to the local French onion soup and the escargots, culinary delights, the latter especially if heavy with garlic butter. Chateauroux became associated with the United States Air Force in 1951 and during the Cold War was considered a front-line base, home to about 8,000 Americans. The village people near the base befriended Americans and tried to communicate even though few airmen spoke French.

Chateauroux AB sits 232 kilometers south of Paris in mid–France and 98 kilometers east of Tours, the site of an 8th-century battle (732 AD) in which French knights under the leadership of Charles Martel ("the Hammer") defeated a Moorish army which, beaten, turned south and recrossed the Pyrenees to establish an Islamic presence on the Iberian Peninsula that lasted until a truly momentous year in Spanish history, 1492. Flexing his muscle in the light of this victory over the Moors which some claim as the salvation of Christianity in western Europe, Martel built a ruling dynasty that a century later produced Charles the Great, Charlemagne, "The Father of Europe."

In 1958, the French people elected another hammer, Charles de Gaulle, to head the Fifth Republic. It was a time of need, with the Moors or, in modern parlance, the Algerians, who were battling the French Foreign Legion, not at the gates of Paris, but in North Africa. The solution to de Gaulle was Algerian independence, granted in 1962. In 1966, de Gaulle decreed that France's military would go it alone and withdrew French forces from the military arm of NATO. De Gaulle's government informed the USAF that it must leave Chateauroux and 12 other air bases with flight operations in France. The cessation after April 1, 1967, left the American Century proceeding without an Aerial Port Squadron in France and indeed without much help at all from France, ironically our vital ally during the American War for Independence.

Stimulated by the needs of World War II, the United States had developed airfields to ferry prop planes and support air cargo planes crossing the Atlantic to the European Theater of Operations. Airfields built at Harmon and Goose Bay in Newfoundland, Kindley AFB, Bermuda, and the most alluring of all, Lajes Field in the Portuguese Azores Islands, were heavily used during the Cold War, being standard stopovers for MATS crews. With so much familiarity, protocols or at least routines were established and passed on by word of mouth to a succession of airmen from Dover. The class six store—the military designation for the branch of the Base Exchange (BX) that carried alcoholic beverages—at Lajes, for example, had shelves of a Portuguese sparkling wine, Mateus Rosé. The quaintly shaped bottle and the bubbly and tasty contents were a favorite for taking back home, not to mention cartons of cigarettes priced as low as 90 cents, or nine cents a pack. Portuguese settled the Acores, anglicized to Azores, after their discovery and mapping by navigators sailing for Prince Henry in the 15th century. Columbus' first port of call returning from his epic voyage to the New World in 1492 was Sao Miguel, now the capital of the islands. Nine volcanic-origin islands are situated in the archipelago, seven with settlement. The third island, Terceira, was picked as an airfield site because of its relatively good weather and the satisfactory amount of open and level land on the Lajes plains. In 1933, Juan Trippe and his Pan American network, which included British airlines, negotiated with the Portuguese government for coveted landing rights in the Azores. Portugal's Mussolini-styled leader, Antonio de Oliveiro Salazar, had just come into power, and Salazar wanted the protection of Britannia for his vulnerable Atlantic Ocean province.[4]

So Pan Am again was in the right place at the right time for Lajes AB. During World War II, Pan Am passed control of this "airstrip in the middle of the Atlantic" to the Air Corps. Officers at this remote but essential base sought to build their own amenities such as an O Club and, in 1953, a golf course. Some of this wonderful American spirit of can do and making the best of a military situation by civilians-turned-soldiers is captured in classic postwar movies such as *Teahouse of the August Moon* and *Don't Go Near the Water*. Lajes AB and golf course in the Azores could have been a candidate for the kind of pranks and shenanigans at the core of such movies.

5. "Hairy conditions" 87

The friendly, peasant stock people encountered on Terceira live by fishing and farming. Volcanic rock walls enclose small lots used to pasture dairy cattle. Farmers chain one leg of the cow to a stake and during the day advance the stake further into the field so that the animals graze the grass in an orderly fashion and do not trample fresh grass or "shit it up."

MATS regulations limited crew duty time, from reporting for the preflight through last landing, to 18 hours for the basic crew. Adding a man at each position augmented the crew and extended the duty to 24 hours. The C-124 flight deck had three bunks, each designated for a specific crew position, where a pilot or engineer could doze for a couple hours at a time.

Once refueled at St. John's, Newfoundland, the crew had about nine duty hours left so promptly taxied to the runway and lifted off, bound for Lajes AB, located on Tericera. This 1,471-NM leg over the Atlantic required careful navigation since weather, especially winds, could be unpredictable. The unpressurized C-124, by rules of flight, was assigned to altitudes of 7,000 or 9,000 feet ASL when headed east 001–180 degrees, meaning that most of the time the airplane was in the thickest of the weather, which even if without thunder cells often obscured the stars and planets needed for a celestial reading.

Halfway on this leg, the navigator who wants a definite fix turns to his sextant, his most accurate aid. The navigational sextant gets its name from the "one-sixth" of a circle that forms its arc of observation and calibration and was considered, at the time of its creation by Sir Isaac Newton in 1699, an improvement over the octant, an earlier device used to shoot the stars as relative to the horizon of the observer. Above the nav station, C-124A models had a plexidome bubble within which navs shot the stars with hand-held sextants, carried over from the same system as on the C-47s. On C-124Cs, in the crew compartment a periscopic sextant extended beyond the skin of the aircraft, and the nav stood on a stool, using the eyepiece to sight and identify three stars to calculate lines to be plotted on the ONC.

When the first star was placed in the middle of the viewing mirror, a process known as calibrating began. The nav turned a knob to keep the star centered in the sextant bubble for a period of one minute. He then— there were no female navigators in USAF in the 1960s[5]—swung the sextant to locate the second star, and when it was identified positively, did the same calibrating. And then the third body—stars were more difficult to identify but at the same time provided better lines of position (LOPs) than the planets. Taking the readings afterward, promptly—not a second to waste because unlike a ship at sea, the airplane, even if a C-124, did not stay in one place very long—to a table which had its own gooseneck lamp, the nav plotted the three LOPS using the calibrations and a sight reduction table. The result, if all went properly, that is if the nav had the correct stars, the pilot maintained a steady course, the sextant had not been jarred into an error, passing clouds did not interrupt the calibration, and the math was correctly calculated, then the star lines on the map when drawn converged in a point, the precise location of the airplane at the mid-point of the observation. The LOPs, when constituting such a "pinwheel," made the fix reliable, and the navigator was satisfied about the position. The lines sometimes created a small triangle, not too bad, and the fix was pretty certain in his mind. The nav placed a dot in the middle of the triangle, measured the angle to go, and notified the pilot of the new compass heading and ETA. A few times, however, the LOPs resulted in a huge triangle, or no triangle at all. In those cases, DR became the standby, and an element of educated guesswork injected itself into the navigational headings. This caused a bit of uneasiness and, among the more conscientious navs, a compulsion to plunge immediately into calculating a fresh reading of stars.

If things were going well, the nav might even retire to his bunk behind a swing-up door that covered the stairs leading down to the cabin, for a 15- or 20-minute refresher nap in the middle of the night and in the middle of the Atlantic crossing. The on-duty engineer would switch on the exhaust fan right above the nav pillow to wake his nav in time for preparing paperwork for the next hourly position fix. Engineers rarely slept in their bunks, preferring it seemed to climb down the spindly 23-step ladder from the crew compartment to the cabin, where he might stretch out on a bunk bed in the aft compartment where the loadmaster hung out. Pilots, though, getting rested for the upcoming landing often alternated in their bunk, usually sleeping for a couple of hours at a time. That left one pilot seat open, and navs took advantage of that opportunity to sit in front, sometimes even flipping the autopilot to off to hand fly the huge plane for stretches of otherwise boring time.

Samuel Eliot Morison, biographer and admirer of Christopher Columbus (Cristobal Colon) wrote that "Columbus was a dead-reckoning navigator [but] made colossal mistakes every time he tried to determine latitude from a star."[6] Columbus, of course, made vital contributions to ocean navigation but never accepted that his initial calculations were incorrect, and in his fourth voyage (1502–1504) he thought himself to be in the East Indies and just around the next bend would be the path to

5. "Hairy conditions"   89

Cipango (Japan). On the other hand, there was Francis Drake, who in 1577–1580 circled the globe, always knowing where he was. Drake returned to England sailing across the Pacific with his ship, the *Golden Hind*, loaded to its beams with treasure worth 950,000 pesos d'oro removed from Spanish America, his crew healthy and soon to be wealthy. He presented Queen Elizabeth with a crown made of silver and emeralds liberated from the *dons*. Elizabeth's relative, King Phillip of Spain, demanded that she return the treasure and hang Drake as a pirate. Instead on April 4, 1581, Elizabeth, the Protestant queen, knighted him. Sir Francis Drake's secrets? English gamesmanship (keep calm and carry on) and an unsurpassed ability in celestial navigation.[7]

Four hundred and fifty years later during America's century, celestial navigators used 36 first- or second-magnitude stars selected for astronavigation, although 57, not all visible from the northern hemisphere, are listed in the *Air Almanac*.[8] Celestial observations from an airplane differ, of course, from the mariner platform where panoramas can stretch to the horizon and the *day's* travel might be 185 nautical miles. The Plexiglas dome did present a workable view of the sky from the flight deck of the C-124, and motion of the airplane, unless it was up and down, did little to disturb the view. While even partial clouding gave the sensation of here one minute, gone the next, clear nights over the Atlantic did occur. To find the right star, pre-calculations from the sight reduction tables gave the quadrant and altitude of the stars to be used in the fix. Positioning the viewfinder of the periscopic sextant with these values allowed a smaller field to scan through the lens. When it went as planned, the star, even if a low magnitude like Polaris, the North Star, was clear within the scope of the sextant lens. The nav then swung around to find the other two, which were ideally 120 degrees apart for perfect triangulation.

Such navigation, when all went right, was a power, a sort of learning that brought self-satisfaction. When it did not go right, the nav used every LOP in his quiver to determine the aircraft position. The electronic aids were Loran and Consol. Sometimes a line of position could be obtained from a low-frequency radio wave. With the weather briefing before the flight, the nav would become acquainted with en route low- and high-pressure systems that determine velocity and direction of winds. Since at least the 18th century, sailing ship navigators had logged data about weather systems. Over time, this empirical evidence took on truisms that were passed down all the way to the aerial navigators flying C-124s. Such as, with the wind at your back, the low pressure is to the left. In the Northern hemisphere, winds in a low-pressure center circulate in a counter-

D-1 periscopic sextant used in a Globemaster.

clockwise direction. Conversely, the high-pressure winds move clockwise around the center. In the Southern hemisphere, those directions are reversed as is the Coriolis effect, which is why water exiting a bathtub drain or a toilet bowl in Australia swirls in a clockwise direction and why a visitor from the USA will feel something is different down under, beyond that those cobbers drive on the wrong side of the road.

Empirical observations by ship navigators were grouped for general principles by meteorologists and published by a Dutchman, C.H.D. Buys Ballot, so the law of wind at the back, low to the left is named for him. Nathaniel Bowditch published his book *The American Practical Navigator* in 1802, and updated editions included the Buys Ballot law. Bowditch sought to assist ship navigators in dead reckoning across the oceans, the same task confronting C-124 navs.

An aid in finding wind direction and velocity for dead reckoning was a low-tech method, but one that proved critical at times. The B-6 drift meter, a gyro-stabilized optical device the barrel of which projected from the bottom of the aircraft, allowed a straight-down view of the waves to 10,000 feet below the airplane. The nav (no other crew member would even come close to the drift meter) could view the sea below the plane.

5. "Hairy conditions"

Using the reticle, which was a ground glass plate with a grid etched on it, to align white-capping waves and then timing the swells with a stopwatch, a nav could determine ground speed and wind direction, and make a reasonable estimate of wind velocity. The nav compared this data to the preflight winds to make corrections for a dead reckoning fix. The driftmeter could also be angled upward to scan the bottom of the wings or the fuselage in case the pilot or engineer suspected a problem there.

The Loran 9 system received signals from stations along the coast lines of the NATO countries. The operator superimposed two signals displayed on a cathode ray screen and then did a lot of interpreting and counting. Some accuracy could be had if the nav's experience level was high enough to differentiate one-hop sky waves from ground waves, all of which were subjected to various types of interference, some of it deliberate since there was a Cold War going on and both sides had their kit of dirty tricks. To pick up the signals, Loran 9 utilized a trailing wire antenna to which was affixed a heavy, lead torpedo-shaped weight and played out from a reel in the aft of the C-124 fuselage. The nav, by trial and error method and with use of the toggle switch that reeled the bulb in and out, tried to match the antenna length with that of the radio wave. Imagine the Globemaster in the middle of the Atlantic flying less than 200 knots at an altitude of 9,000 feet between solid cloud layers with a cargo of squealing pigs (true), towing an eight-pound lead torpedo at the end of a 150-foot wire. And then imagine the butterflies in the stomach of the navigator as he fine-tunes the Loran 9 to get a reading from the yellow lines on a green background so that he can plot a reasonable position and make a course correction, which only he knows

Driftmeter in its alcove on the starboard side in a C-124 cabin, 1965.

Panel at the C-124 nav station showing the trailing wire antenna switch, radar, and other controls.

is both imperative and impossible. If Lajes was found and the Globemaster entered the landing pattern, more misery could be had if the trailing wire "in" toggle switch was somehow overlooked on the nav's landing check list before touchdown, leaving the lead weight free to bounce along the runway, which resulted in its separating from the wire or being dragged to the parking spot, fraying the nerves of many an A-model navigator.

It was, therefore, of considerable relief to navs when Loran 70 systems, an improved design that could be more precise in locating the aircraft and with built-in antennas, replaced Loran 9s on most C-124s.

As the flight path neared the European coast, the navigator might of necessity figure an LOP using Consol, a British system of dot and dash signals sent out in a fan-like pattern. The broadcast originated from any one of the five low-frequency operating stations built in Europe during the latter days of World War II. For a Consol fix, the nav tuned in the radio station and pressed the headset against his ear, counting the number of dots or dashes he heard in one minute. He plotted the results on a Consol chart which yielded an LOP. The American version, Consolan, broadcast its pattern of dots and dashes from two stations, one on Nantucket Island, the other located at Atlantic City, New Jersey. Consolan broadcast range extended to about 1,500 sea miles at night. The stations, thought by budget planners to be primarily for aviation but little used by modern jet aircraft, went off the air in 1972 as an unnecessary expense. Too bad it fell to the axe, as it was a popular nav aid for off-shore boaters along the Atlantic coast.

The C-124 navigator had these tools available for the Atlantic flights along with more esoteric aids like "pressure lines of position" (PLOPs), radio compass direction signals, air plotting, and radar. One favorite was the Ocean Station Vessel (OSV), operated by the U.S. Coast Guard, ships fixed to a certain point in the ocean, literally cruising around in a circle. Flight navigators contacted the radio operator below on an assigned frequency and received in return a radar identification and a definite position from the sailor friends below. In daylight, navs scanned the surface for a visual sighting of a 378-foot cutter below. That contact was generally a good feeling for both sides, and a few personal words might be exchanged such as "What's for dinner down there?" or "What's showing tonight in the movie lounge?" While Atlantic airways were not as lonely as in Lindbergh's day, traffic remained light with plenty of open space, and it seemed radio operators on the ships rather enjoyed the contact which broke up long stretches of radio silence and were, after all, the duty to which they were assigned.[9]

In the Pacific, there were only two OSVs, one manned by the Coast Guard and one by the Canadian nav. Instead, atolls provided reference for overwater navigators, specks of land, some of which were long enough for airplanes to land there on World War II-constructed strips, Johnson Island and Canton, for example.

North of Hawaii sits Midway, which gave its name to one of World War II's most famous sea battles. Today, the once-crucial base has been virtually abandoned by the U.S. military, not much being there now save a bird preserve that includes an estimated one million creatures known to science as *Phoebastria nigripes*, to birdwatchers and civilians as the black-footed albatross, and to three generations of military flyers as the gooney bird. Ninety-eight percent of the world's population of these birds hang out around Midway.

Gooney birds, due to their clumsy behavior and preference for hanging out at air strips, were both amusing and nuisances to air crews. As such, stories abounded about these birds, and G.I.s being G.I.s added their fun. One U.S. Navy EC-121 Constellation pilot noticed four gooney birds

Johnson Island viewed from an overflying C-124 in 1965.

hovering in the wake of engine #3 on a C-124 getting ready to taxi nearby. As a practical joke and obviously with little else to do, the Connie pilot radioed the Globemaster crew and asked them to push forward the throttles, because he wanted to see those birds fly. And fly they did, the engines' powerful backwash gusting the surprised and summersaulting birds along the tarmac. Once a gooney bird on the wing of a C-124 positioned himself at the fuselage and with comical flapping made his takeoff run toward the wing tip, only to abort just before the No Go decision. Making a second attempt, the gooney used every bit of the 74'-long aluminum runway to get himself airborne.[10] Getting liftoff speed was difficult for these large-bodied birds and precipitated an energetic use of their long wings, the only times in their flight when that was necessary, so adept were they at finding and using air columns and updrafts. Albatrosses become consummate gliders when aloft, able to fly great distances with minimal effort.

The durable Douglas C-47 had a company name of DC-3 Skytrain, while the British called their version Dakota, a wry acronym standing for Douglas Aircraft Company Transport Airplane.[11] G.I.s bestowed endearments on their beloved C-47 as it helped them win the war. But the best-known nickname, "Gooney Bird," had to be brought on because of its ungainly appearance but flying safe reputation. One veteran summed it up this way: "Aerodynamically speaking, the albatross should not be able to get off the ground, but since it is so goofy, it does not realize this and flies anyway." Like the C-47 and other airplanes including the C-124, the gooney bird's awkwardness of appearance on the ground and on the takeoff morphed into a certain stately gracefulness when airborne at cruising level.

Douglas designed the Globemaster to deploy troops and military material. It was used by SAC to carry nuclear weapons and Thor IRBMs, deadly stuff. But other tasks came to it of humanitarian or rescue nature. When the C-124 landed and taxied to the parking ramp in some foreign place like Ethiopia, the Congo, or Honduras, it presented what had to be a friendly sight with its plump look, clown's nose, and grandpa's chin line. It squeaked and squalled while rolling, vibrated the rivets while flying, and took forever to go anywhere, it seemed, whether in the air or on the ground. But it had that helpful, non-threatening appearance. Only among some, it was rumored, was there a forbidding shudder when the giant clamshell doors opened, and the twin ramps slowly unfolded, looking to a primitive person steeped in superstition too much like the serpent's forked tongue.

Carrying loads, whether into Berlin, Vietnam, or any other place of American interest, was the purpose of transport airplanes, their crews, and their command. The loads might vary and did, from pigs to breeding beef bulls to Thor missiles to Hueys for the 1st Air Cav. A C-124 left Kelley AFB loaded with nine bulls, each encased in a crate, all prize-winning and selected by agriculture officials from the Alliance for Progress and headed to Argentina. Weather at the first stop over Howard AFB in Panama was so hot and humid, the bulls were off-loaded and placed in the shade with periodic hosing down, so they might better withstand a typical day in the tropics. The crew reappeared from quarters the next morning, and the crates with the bulls bellowing in top voice were once again wheeled up the ramps into the cargo bay of the Globemaster. Another day in flight and a landing in Argentina accomplished the mission.[12] In similar fashion, breeding stock from blue ribbon farmers in the United States were sent overseas via C-124s to destinations in other countries seeking to improve their livestock courtesy of the United States in the 1960s and 1970s, the good neighbors. In the same tradition, a 1996 Bill Murray movie, *Larger Than Life*, winds up with surplus elephants from the San Diego zoo being loaded into a Globemaster III for transport from California back to India.

For years, until C-141s begin to roll off the production lines in Oklahoma and Georgia and go operational in 1965, the Globemaster carried out missions of great political importance to the United States, often setting distance or cargo records and its flights being reported with datelines such as:

> Karachi, Pakistan, May 6, 1954—United States Air Force C-124 planes carrying French paratroopers to Indo-China have been refueling at Mauripur military airfield here today and flying on via Ceylon.[13]
>
> Dover, Delaware, January 9. 1961—Dover planes leave on new Congo Mission. C-124's will deliver 2,050 Irish troops and 147,000 pounds of cargo between Dublin and Katanga Province.

During the Cold War, SAC clamored for a base within striking distance of major cities in the USSR over a polar route, an itch satisfied by improving a World War II outpost in northwestern Greenland a mere 807 nautical miles below the North Pole.[14] This airfield site, at the end of a long fjord, was suggested by Danish explorer Knud Rasmussen and confirmed by USAF Colonel Brent Balchen, the name Thule being taken from medieval atlases which designated remote or forbidding locations with the Latin term, *Ultima Thule*, literally at the end of the world.[15]

Thule is ten degrees of latitude above the Arctic Circle, where on a summer solstice, the sun travels 360 degrees around any fixed observation spot, never dipping below the horizon, Land of the Midnight Sun! Conversely at the winter solstice, when the apparent location of the sun is on the Tropic of Capricorn, S23° 2', the sun does not appear above the horizon in the arctic, resulting in 24 hours of darkness, except that is for full moons, bright star light, or illumination from the Aurora Borealis.

After Thule's construction in 1951, Dover supplied the base and Sondrestrom AB, a little further down the west coast of Greenland. In addition, the U.S. constructed a chain of radar stations in northern Greenland known as the Distant Early Warning (DEW) Line, maintenance and operation of which required an aerial supply line from the states to be provided by Globemasters.

En route to the Arctic, Dover crews landed at Goose Bay, Labrador, to refuel and to rest the crew. Goose Bay, although seeing 75 inches of snow annually, was not as cold as Thule, where MATS C-124s have landed when temps were minus 76 degrees Fahrenheit. A 1955 press release from Douglas Aircraft Company about the capabilities of the airplane pointed out that C-124s had been modified to "withstand temperatures as low as 70 degrees below zero and 200 degrees above [Fahrenheit]." C-54s on the northern run had chronic failure of cabin heaters. One C-54 pilot asked passengers, after cabin heat failed again, if they wanted to continue, which would mean eight and a half hours at 30 degrees below zero. The 25 passengers voted to continue and burrowed into arctic sleeping bags provided by the loadmaster, who checked the shivering human cargo periodically for frost bite. All survived "the most uncomfortable flight ever."[16] No wonder departing Thule passengers preferred to board Old Shaky, which had reliable heaters.

Strategic Air Command sent B-52 crews to Thule on three-week rotations and supported them with their C-124s. Dover Globemasters did the rest of the supply, carrying among many items for the remote base mail, parts, medical supplies, clothing, and cases of Tuborg. Danish observers and administrators stationed there preferred their own national beer. These Danes followed a custom from their culture of finding just the right depth in the tundra to bury their beer so that it achieved the exact temperature deemed best for drinking. Denmark, a member of NATO, gave permission for its ally, the U.S., to operate Thule as an enclave in Greenland and provide Cold War protection for Greenland, the world's largest island and subject to Danish claims and control since the age of Norse exploration. Some people of Greenland, now an autonomous region of Denmark, have campaigned for full independence by 2021.

Activities in Greenland and Alaska proved that the C-124 could operate satisfactorily in arctic weather settings. Navigation in polar regions, where lines of longitude sharply converge and magnetic compass variation is severe, requires the use of grid navigation techniques. While there is no alchemy associated with grid, far from it indeed, pilots are not generally schooled in this navigation technique and so view this means of direction finding with great anxiety. It means un-slaving the N-1 compass from its magnetic source and depending on the gyro to keep a steady heading reference. It means setting that N-1 to an arbitrary value, namely a heading derived from measurements on a grid field superimposed on the air navigation chart. It means putting complete trust in the navigator. Navigators with a deep understanding of mathematics love the system. Positions on the grid chart are verified by celestial lines, and headings are given in the grid, not magnetic, direction to the airport. Grid navigation makes going to Greenland or Antarctica worthwhile to navs.

Submarines cruise below the surface in the Arctic Ocean, which measures 14,150 feet in depth under the North Pole. Thick ice covers most of the ocean above the Arctic Circle, which is latitude of 66° 33' North, so explorers have reached the NP location in dog sleds. Icebreaker ships in the summer months can get near the pole. One dream of Thomas Jefferson and many others, including America's first millionaire, John Jacob Astor, was to find a northwest passage that connected the Atlantic and

Pacific. Now with global warming, in the summer ships can sail through the Arctic Ocean into the Pacific.

Antarctica, on the other end of the earth, the antipode as it was once known as, is a continent. No subs can travel below the South Pole, it being a land area. At Little America, temps of minus 70 degrees Fahrenheit are typical in the winter months (June, July, August), with ferocious storms mixed in. Antarctica subjects an airplane in its transit to high wind velocities and blizzards that can obscure vision and put air strips suddenly invisible to the eye. The nav, the pilots, and the airplane are under more demands than flying anywhere else. Thus it was appropriate, perhaps, that the first airlifter to enter this zone in support of research stations there was a C-124 piloted by no less than a major general, Chester McCarty, commander of the Eighteenth Air Force, a reserve branch that specialized in airlifts. McCarty's C-124 air-dropped a rocket-shaped transmitter over the South Pole, and the flight marked the first time that a USAF plane had navigated to the "bottom of the world." The "bomb bay," actually the wench-driven loading platform of the plane, had been used to parachute nine oil drums over the pole, followed by the "Grasshopper," which was described by a *New York Times* reporter aboard the C-124 as something that "comes to life as compressed air 'legs' shoot out in such a manner that it gets to its 'feet' and a radio antenna thrusts upward. It then begins transmitting weather reports from the isolated areas into which it had been dropped."[17] And this before NASA and the sophisticated moon walkers and probes of its day. Colonel William G. Forwood, commander of the Sixty-first Troop Carrier Group, TAC, piloted the first landing at the McMurdo ice strip a year later.

Named for Alexander McMurdo, a British Navy commander and explorer of Antarctica and located along the Ross Ice Shelf some 850 miles from the South Pole, the site became the main landing area and supply depot for polar science in the International Geophysical Year (IGY) which began on July 1, 1957. Globemasters were selected to air drop and airlift

Icing

Image from C-124C Dash 1.

5. "Hairy conditions"

equipment and suppliers for Operation Deep Freeze, a U.S. Navy project developed to support the IGY.[18]

The IGY engaged world scientists to comprehensively study the earth and its environment. As part of this 18-month study, the U.S. Navy undertook material support for seven scientific research stations on the Antarctica continent in what was dubbed Operation Deep Freeze. To supply those stations, the Navy called on MATS, with its C-124 "behemoths as the backbone of these expeditions." In October and November, Globemasters flew personnel and cargo to McMurdo Sound from a staging base at Christchurch, New Zealand. The first of these missions airlifted 33 men and 8,650 pounds of cargo over 2,200 miles to McMurdo, a one-way trip of 12 hours. The Globemaster weight could be handled on an "ice strip" still sound enough at the beginning of the Southern hemisphere summer. While the ice strip was reported as an excellent surface, all did not go well 100 percent of the time. In late October 1956, a C-124, tail number 52-982, skidded after landing and struck a snow berm at the end of the runway, collapsing the nose wheel and damaging the clamshell doors. Such a disabled C-124 curtailed valuable space at the strip and presented evacuation concerns. To solve the problems, a decision was made to repair the C-124 into flyable shape. A month later, two Globemasters were dispatched carrying supplies for the base and men and equipment to fix the disabled Globemaster. One from Norton AFB, California, had aboard 22 civilian technicians who volunteered for extended duty at the bottom of the world to effect the repairs. The first of these two rescue planes, tail number 52-983, approached the strip on November 28, 1956, and eerily, experienced the same sort of landing accident, skidding into an ice floe, collapsing the nose gear. So on the ice strip were now two disabled behemoths. Despite objections by U.S. Navy brass that the repair project was "hopeless," the Norton C-124 flew in the next day.

Alas, it skidded and collapsed its nose gear, a trifecta. The USAF and Globemasters were now zero for three in the Antarctic summer of 1956. Fortunately, no crew members or passengers were injured with these mishaps, and there is a happy ending to this remarkable series of events. Working in high winds and below zero temperatures, and with a threat that ocean currents might break the ice airfield away from the mainland, the repair team succeeded in only 12 days in getting 52-982 airworthy enough to fly to New Zealand. The workers turned to 52-983, and on December 19 it too was flown out to New Zealand. Thereafter, with a nose gear braced and welded into a non-retractable position, this Globemaster, christened "State of Washington," made it back to Norton on January 21, 1957.[19]

This C-124 slid off the runway after landing at McMurdo Sound (1956).

The last of the three C-124s, the "State of Oregon," was unrepairable and was salvaged at McMurdo, where the cabin served as a storage shed. The two that were repaired, which ironically had been side by side on the Douglas production line, went back into MATS service until mothballed in 1970 and 1971.

A year later, pilot James Thomas, who was making a round trip to resupply Byrd Station, 800 miles from the home base at McMurdo, found the ice strip at McMurdo completely socked in. Descending to 7,000 feet, ice on the wings forced him to climb and seek an alternate landing site 400 miles away at Hallett Station. There, the landing was aborted in conditions of 30 mile an hour crosswind and a blizzard that reduced visibility to 200 feet. The plane flew back toward McMurdo, where the storm had somewhat abated. Thomas put the giant C-124 down on his third approach with three hours of fuel remaining in the tanks. The Globemaster had been in the air 13 hours, manifesting another heroic event of the Old Shaky period.[20]

In December 1957, glaciological equipment and accessory drilling parts were parachuted from Globemasters to enable deep drilling in Antarctica, the first such experiments conducted there using a rotary well-drilling rig powered by compressed air to reach depths of 300 meters.[21] Dr. Paul Allman Siple inspected the station. It was the 49-year-old scien-

5. "Hairy conditions"

tist's second time at the South Pole, the first as a Boy Scout accompanying Admiral Richard E. Byrd's expedition there in 1928. On this 1957 occasion, Siple flew out on a C-124 from McMurdo to Christchurch, New Zealand, 2,220 miles, most of which was covered with the Globemaster operating on three engines.[22]

The involvement of MATS and TAC C-124s with Antarctica exploration continued after the IGY, and so did the risks. When in February 1958, the ice strip began to crack, a C-124 which had just landed the day before, hurriedly took off for New Zealand to complete its round trip. Usually in the beginning of winter, February in the antipodes, the ice is solid enough to accommodate the 190,000-lb. airplane, but in this case the sounds and lines of ice fissures caused the hasty retreat. Perhaps that haste had something to do with the endangerment of the plane on the return, when an oil leak caused a fire in one engine. This, in addition to one engine already lost, meant a hazardous landing, which the pilot accomplished in Christ Church, whereupon the 60 people aboard clambered out safely. The fire was extinguished by the plane's own system.[23]

A U.S. Navy Seabee stationed at NAF McMurdo Sound from September 1960 to August 1961 remembered that the sound froze solid to a depth of eight feet, thick enough to hold a C-124, but he witnessed many a "hairy landing on the 10,000-runway carved into the ice."[24]

Far from the "hairy conditions" persistent in polar regions, the central Pacific is nevertheless an area of isolation. One of the intermediate stops for C-124s and other prop planes crossing the Pacific was Wake Island, actually three small atolls. Named for a British captain, William Wake, who reported it to the admiralty in 1840, the island was surveyed by Charles Wilkes of the United States Navy, who had with him the naturalist and artist, Titian Peale.[25] Pan American landed their Pacific Clippers there in 1935 after constructing a small station, the first human inhabitants of the island, and from that time thought of the island as PanAm domain. It had that kind of location and that kind of romance. Tiny, but perfectly situated for this purpose, Wake was blessed by what navigators called a perpetual high-pressure system right over it. That meant unfailing good weather for taking off and landing airplanes, which was a gift because not only was Wake tiny in size—barely big enough for the runway lengths needed—but it sat truly without peer, or alternate landing field, in the vast North Pacific. The Air Force did not staff the airport, the flight services, or maintenance at Wake Island. It was and is civilian control, and as such had a different atmosphere, good, but different, with piped-in Barbara Streisand crooning "Happy Days."

The flight time from Hickam to Wake, 2,001 nautical miles, about ten hours average flying time with tailwind, needed some 30,000 pounds of fuel. On top of that, regulations required 4,500 pounds of fuel for one hour and 45 minutes holding time, since there was no landing alternative. Rain showers occurred at Wake Island several times each month—it gets 40 inches of rainfall a year, just enough with conservation to be water self-sufficient. Nevertheless, rarely did a transport plane go into a holding pattern at Wake because of low ceilings or a socked-in airport. With about 34,500 pounds of fuel, a peacetime gross takeoff weight limit of 185,000 pounds, and an aircraft of 101,000 pounds, that meant the maximum cargo was 49,500 pounds or 25 tons, same weight as a D-7 bulldozer. One Globemaster, one crew, one bulldozer. Delivery time to Tan Son Nhut from Peoria, Illinois, was six days, about the same amount of shipping time for a book order from Amazon in 2014.

The advantage of good weather! If every place had constant good weather, then flying would be so much more fun and safer. That must be what a general had in mind during the "flying the Hump" days from India to China during World War II. Tired of being faced with scrubbed missions in getting the precious cargo over the highest mountains in the world because of the forecasts, one day, he ordered, "From now on, there will be no weather."[26] Generals then and now, when promoted to that first star, attend a special school that instructs them how to act as though they are God, and their wives attend a similar school. Their service hats have darts, thunder clouds, and lightning bolts on the visor, a mural sometimes referred to as "scrambled eggs." When such a hat was spotted, junior officers invariably went the other way, seeking to keep the lowest profile possible.

Since high pressure tends to create predictable winds, navigation to Wake usually conformed to the preflight route as to headings and ETAs. A good nav, of course, kept up with the celestial shot plotting and made corrections to headings if need be. Blue skies with the occasional cumulus clouds over a blue-green expanse of water and usually in daylight hours made for an enjoyable time. Navs noted the weather on their logs for each fix, and the jargon of the day, "clear as a bell," was par for the course. Naturally, a military spicing of the jargon occurred, and widely spread on those logs was the notation, CAFB, meaning "Clear as a f*ing bell," verily, revealing a jaunty feeling in a trouble-free flight.

The Wake airport TACAN reached out about 180 miles, which meant that only in the case of a monumental navigation error and/or monumental neglect by the pilots could the C-124 miss the island. Nevertheless, it

5. "Hairy conditions"

Wake Island in 1965.

was a satisfaction for navs when the needle pointed dead ahead when the TACAN locked on.

Most approaches were straight into Wake AB runway 28 in clear weather, so pilots had ease of mind. The R-4360 engines seemed to like all the pleasantries about the leg, their hum relaxing the flight engineer, too. Since cargo was rarely unloaded at Wake, the loadmasters were in for a light duty day as well. Thus, when the crew bus arrived, the mood was usually jovial, especially after checking to see results of nose wheel roulette. Each crewmember marked his name on one of the spokes before takeoff at Hickam, and if your spoke pointed to the runway, you bought the drinks. Not that it was too hard a hit, as beverages at Drifter's Reef, the only bar on the island, were modestly priced, and at happy hour practically given away.

A dining hall staffed by Filipino waiters provided a plate lunch any time of day. Filipinos had a special dispensation spelled out by a National Defense document to work for private contractors at Wake Island. In the aftermath of World War II, with subsistence agriculture in the Philippines on the wan as a means of making a living and as Fernando Marcos became chummy with the U.S. government, the two countries signed a treaty allowing migration of Filipino workers to American defense installations

MATS airman at Drifter's Reef, Wake Island, June 1965.

5. "Hairy conditions"

in Pacific commands. That agreement continues to this day. The private contractor for management of Wake Island was Brown and Root, a Texas corporation.[27]

Crew members who showered had to remember the procedure: step into the shower; turn on the water for 15 seconds; turn off the water and lather up; turn on the water again for 15 seconds to rinse. That is a Wake Island shower, and a good conservation practice anywhere, not that anyone in the Air Force at that time was anywhere near being environmentally green. Far from it.

Filipino workers on Wake had dorms, their own mess hall, and a day room with table tennis set up, the main indoor recreation on the island. Filipino aces were all return and finesse with their game, playing close to the net, using a lot of spin and drop shots even while playing with the old sandpaper or thin rubber-dimpled paddles. In the mid–1960s, a C-124 nav found the workers' hangout, waited his turn to get a game, and went into offensive mode with his forehand smashes and hard serves. On each time through, he made it a point to visit his acquaintances and play a game or two. He felt welcomed. On a trip coming through Wake from Tachikawa, the nav brought high-tech paddles with the dimples turned inward and glued atop a sponge filling, an equipment innovation that had helped elevate the Japanese game into one of the best in the world. Landing at night, the nav went straight to the dorm, found the sleeping room of a special Filipino friend with whom he had often played the game, and presented him with the paddles. Both nav and worker were so excited, even though it was midnight, they went straight to the day room and played for a couple of hours, perfecting new spins and kills with this state-of-the-art equipment.[28] Hands across the table tennis net and across the sea, and the evolution of a game!

Usually C-124 aircrews had 15 hours on the islands, until the beginning of the Vietnam War stage system of "delivery without delay," which made the length of the stay quite unpredictable. If a guy had time to kill, walking the beach or swimming in the lagoon sort of allowed the feeling of being in a tropical paradise. Except, of course, there were no bathing beauties or surf boards, just artifacts—concrete bunkers, hulls of sunken ships, and unexploded ordinance—of the great battle for Wake Island in 1942 as the Japanese Imperial Navy dislodged the small U.S. Marine detachment which defended with great vigor and heroism. Pan Am employees and contractors and Marine survivors of the battle were taken captive and sent to China for the duration of the war. Hollywood made a movie entitled *Wake Island*, released in 1942, starring William Bendix,

Brian Donlevy, and Robert Preston, all killed in the movie version. No women were cast in the film, which was one of the biggest hits of the year with five Academy Award nominations.

During the build-up to the war in Southeast Asia, Wake became a major stop in the C-124 stage system of airlifting materials. In the 1964 election, anecdotal evidence suggested that Republican candidate Barry Goldwater, Jr., Arizona Senator and National Guard fighter pilot, had garnered wide and deep support among U.S. Air Force officers. He did not, however, have wide support among U.S. voters, as he carried but three states and lost 2–1 in the popular vote. Goldwater wrote a book entitled *Conscious of a Conservative*, and backers coined a phrase to identify their candidate: "In your heart, you know he's right." Influenced perhaps by General Curt LeMay, Goldwater was not about to back off on the reliance on nuclear power as a means of national defense, a policy developed when President Dwight D. Eisenhower *knew* there was *no* chance of a nuclear exchange because the USSR simply didn't have the means of delivery. Eisenhower reluctantly approved U-2 spy flights, not to prove that the Soviets had missiles and bombers aimed at us, but to prove to Dulles and the military, that they *did not*.[29] That there was such a vast U.S. superiority impelled Eisenhower to warn the nation in his

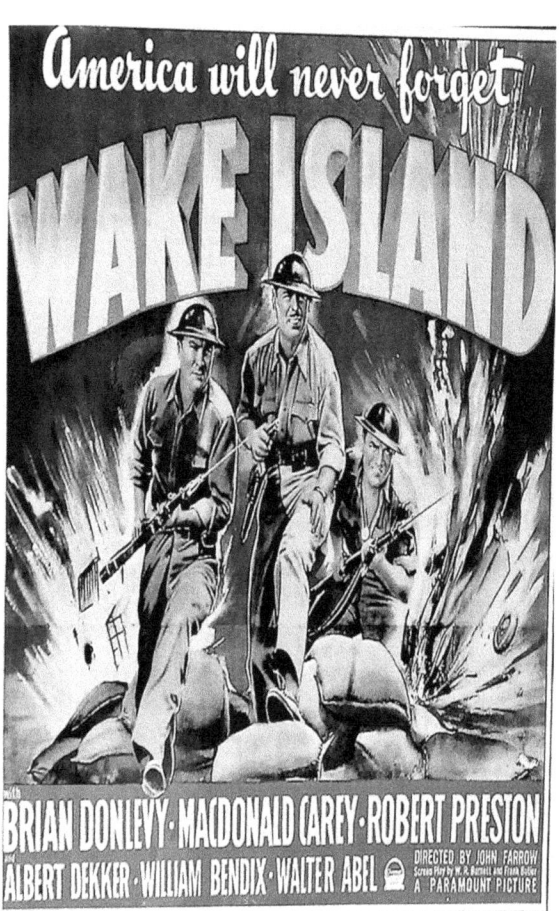

Poster advertising Hollywood's 1942 release of the movie *Wake Island*, featuring a star cast (author's collection).

5. *"Hairy conditions"*   107

farewell address, delivered on January 16, 1961, of the dangers of the military-industrial complex, which of course found a big USSR threat to our way of life a godsend for increases in the national defense budget, much of which would go their way.

This balance had changed a bit with the development of huge Russian rocket boosters by the time of Goldwater's candidacy. Not that the senator from Arizona was all gloom and seriousness. He had revealed a rich sense of humor in recorded ripostes with President John F. Kennedy, but that was tested during the 1964 campaign when the Democratic Party purchased national TV ads that turned the Republican Party's tagline into, "In your heart, you know he *might!*" with a mushroom cloud in the background.

Many Air Force officers privately supported the war about to begin in South Vietnam, but paradoxically disliked the Commander-in-Chief who was calling for it. Lyndon Baines Johnson did not exude toward the military the charisma for which he was known in the Senate cloakroom. Moreover, LBJ was a career politician, an occupation suspected by the military (and vice versa) since the American Revolution. LBJ's wife, Lady Bird, was an astute businesswoman whose investment in an Austin, Texas, television station had provided financial stability, even a degree of wealth, for the family. Scuttlebutt cast Lady Bird as a silent investor in a corporation that had secured the government contract to maintain Wake Island. Brown and Root had assisted LBJ's campaigns in Texas since his races during the Great Depression, and various legislation backed by Johnson in the Senate favored the Texas Corporation. In 1965, Brown and Root joined three other giant corporations to form RMK-BRJ, "one of the largest civilian-based military construction conglomerates in history," and received $2 billion in contract work in Vietnam and other Pacific sites such as Wake and Guam.[30] In this American Century, Brown and Root were absorbed into Haliburton Corporation, which still receives these contractor awards from the Pentagon. As mentioned, the Filipino workers at Wake Island during the Vietnam War period were imported by and under the supervision of this contractor.

From Wake Island, C-124s typically flew on to Guam, Clark, or Tachikawa. The practical and dependable aerial supply line across the Pacific enabled the Vietnam War in its early stages, and in this period, the Globemaster lived up to its name.

6

"Birthplace of Winds"
From Attu to Zaire

Pan American clippers set up routes, airports, and customer service across the Atlantic and the Pacific, and when the same happened to the Caribbean, pilots in competing companies said wryly, "All oceans belong to Pan American, irrevocably, absolutely, by order of God and the President of the United States."[1] Much of the early Pan Am Caribbean traffic focused on the "Pearl of the Antilles," Cuba, so-named by the Spanish colonizers, the adelantados and the empersarios, because of profits that could be realized from a grant in Cuba by the Spanish crown. These for-profit grants to Spanish nobles included not only *huge* tracts of land but the minerals in it and the people on it, a built-in labor supply for gold-mining or tobacco-growing enterprises. The descendants of Cristobol Colon today receive ten percent of all profits derived from the New World by the Spanish government.[2]

Halfway around the world, the Spaniards, because of the voyages and claims by Ferdinand Magellan, established the "Pearl of the Orient," Manila. Both "Pearls" were loosed from the Spanish Colonial System because of the 1898 Spanish-American War. In the Philippines and Cuba, America replaced Spain as the "bearers of the 'White Man's' burden," meaning, in those days of unvarnished racist lingo and images, that the U.S. now had a self-imposed duty to prepare these adopted non–Anglican states for a democratic future based on our morals and institutions, particularly our common law.

Having experienced 405 years of rule by Spain, this American impertinence could not stand, and Cubans demanded full independence. Because of this, or in spite of it, democracy did not take root in Cuba, and dictatorships were the typical governmental forms until the mid-20th cen-

6. "Birthplace of Winds"

tury. So far as Pan Am, American tourists, the Baccardi brothers, and eventually the Mafia were concerned, dictatorships had an upside. The downside, however, included a huge gap between haves and have-nots and the highest infant mortality rate in the hemisphere on the largest and most fertile island in the Caribbean.

Pacific skies from the cockpit of a C-124, in 1964.

The inevitable revolución came in the 1950s. Former right-handed pitcher and University of Havana law student Fidel Castro and his followers overthrew Fulgencio Batista's autocratic government in January 1959. When the Castro regime nationalized American and Cuban big businesses, the Eisenhower administration imposed sanctions on the key export and economic mainstay of Cuba, sugar, beginning a half-century of hostilities between the United States and its neighbor 90 miles away.

That conflict had implications for the U.S. Air Force, including MATS. Other autocratically-ruled states in Latin America had to be accounted for so that the Marxism did not spread to susceptible small countries right under our noses. For the record, the Castro-led government trained doctors and lowered the infant death rate to the lowest in Latin America, evened the onerous burden of bringing in the sugar by requiring everyone to share in the labor of the cane harvest, expelled Mafioso-run night clubs, and kept the quality of cigars to an acknowledged best in the world. But Marxism is a heavy price to pay for these successes, and the U.S., egged on by furious Cuban exiles, stood on alert.

Castro found a new big customer, the U.S.S.R., for the U.S.-boycotted sugar exports. The Soviet Union in return sent military hardware to the Cubans, including nuclear-weapon-tipped missiles and state-of-the-art fighter planes. The less-than-deft handling of the Cuban situation by the Eisenhower and Kennedy administrations no doubt amused the Politburo, which gave the Russians an opportunity to install missiles which could easily reach, say, Houston. The missiles got the attention they deserved, the U.S. went on war footing during the 1962 Crisis, and fighter squadron leaders dusted off their "MiG Alley" posters from the Korean War. One

OTS training officer, a blond-haired, muscular ex–fighter pilot nicknamed "The Hawk," had a wall picture of an F-100 on the tail of a Soviet fighter. The message was clear, and our training officer loomed heroic among us trainees who only mildly wondered why he was in this rather undemanding desk job. This was, after all, what we were about, even if we were bound for Nav School. We were officers in the world's best Air Force, about to go to war with the other superpower!! We were 20-something, could not die, unless we ourselves jumped on the hand grenade, which we would do willingly, unless a quicker someone beat us to it.

After the Crisis subsided—Secretary of State Dean Rusk said, "We're eyeball to eyeball, and I think the other guy blinked"—a lingering result for low-flying airlift crews was avoidance of Cuban air space in flight plans to reach Jamaica or Haiti, or even Puerto Rico. Puerto Rico is, as Columbus described it, a beautiful island, and came under American authority during that same 1898 war with Spain, a war caused by and won by the U.S. Navy, and well before there were any airplanes, much less an Air Force. Hence, Puerto Rico was a U.S. Navy domain, which still uses one of its small satellite islands as a target for their cannon and missile practice despite the occasional protest demonstration by Puerto Rican activists. Air Force airlift crews, when landing at Roosevelt Roads Naval Air Station, universally called the motor pool CQ with a request from a "Lieutenant so and so for a car to be brought round for our aircraft commander, Captain so and so." If the CQ was a greenhorn and had only been through basic training in the Navy, then it just might work. Not that we needed a car that bad, just wanted the tweaks the prank provided with our service rival, who out of a rich tradition call their O-6s captains, a rank equivalent of an Air Force bird colonel.

Periodically, people of Puerto Rico—who migrate freely between the mainland and the island and who serve in the United States military as American citizens—face a referendum in which they have three choices: become fully independent; continue as a "commonwealth" of the United States; apply for statehood.[3] The track record is a vote of about 33 percent for each of the choices. If the latter was ever the people's choice, and if the United States Senate sent an enabling act to the president who signed it, Connecticut would drop to number four on the list of smallest-area states.

Beautiful and small as it is, Puerto Rico held a major Air Force installation, Ramey Air Force Base, home to SAC's 72nd Bombardment Wing until closed in 1972. Ramey's 3,000 acres, perched on the northwest tip of the island, served as a staging point for operations against a suspected

6. "Birthplace of Winds"

Communist military coup in the Dominican Republic in April 1965. The Johnson administration was in no mood to wait and see the political stripping of striking rebels, mostly working class and farmers, who sought to overthrow a rightist military government that had succeeded the autocrat Rafael Trujillo. Even though the buildup was proceeding in Vietnam, MATS diverted C-124s from five bases to carry paratroopers from Fort Bragg, North Carolina, to Puerto Rico and then on to the Dominican Republic to insure that the rebels under the leadership of Colonel Francisco Caamano would fail in their attempt to, in their words, restore democracy and constitutional government.[4] Some 42,000 U.S. soldiers shouldered arms in this fracas, occupying the Dominican Republic as part of a Pan American force that included soldiers from Brazil, Paraguay, Honduras, Nicaragua, and El Salvador, none of which were at the time exactly democracies.

The Air Force set up a landing strip in a combat zone near the capital city of Trujillo City (now Santo Domingo). At this strip, Globemasters and crews from as far away as McChord AFB, loaded with paratroopers from Fort Bragg, made assault landings to discharge these troops from the 82nd Airborne. C-124s came under fire while landing and typically off-loaded with engines running, keeping ground time to a minimum. Crew members holstered the same Smith & Wesson .357s as in Vietnam. It felt like war, and, though short, war it was until the "Constitutionalistas" were overwhelmed and defeated. Then, the "Yankees Get Out" signs were taken down, new elections were held, and order restored under the rule of Joaquin Balaguer, worse than Trujillo, critics said, which would have taken considerable doing if true. But here would be no backdoor entry for Communists in the Caribbean, as had happened in Cuba. Vigilance focused on Nicaragua in the late 1970s as the U.S. financed the Contras, opponents of the democratically elected Sandinista government. In 1983, President Reagan ordered an invasion of Grenada to prevent a leftist government from taking power.[5]

In 1965, the Air Force inventory listed 380 troop and cargo carrying C-124s (less SSS planes and losses) while the C-130 fleet numbered about 340 planes.[6] With these navigator-equipped, propeller-driven, non–GPS C-124s and C-130s, MATS and the Air Force had proved that the U.S. could fight two wars half a globe apart at the same time. If, that is, the wars did not last long.

Vigilance on Caribbean revolutions continued into the Reagan years, focused on Nicaragua in the late 1970s as the U.S. financed the Contras, opponents of the democratically elected Sandinista government. In 1983,

President Reagan ordered an invasion of Grenada to prevent a leftist government from taking power.[7]

On January 3, 1959, Alaska became our first non-contiguous state and 49th overall. Hawaii, with a larger population but with far less area and natural resources and further from the mainland, would follow in August, reconfiguring the stars on the American flag for the second time that year. Admittance of these two states came not easily because of still-active Southern resistance to the 1954 *Brown* decision and to the Civil Rights movement in general. Congressmen representing the ex-Confederate states worried that expansion of the Union would dilute their considerable influence in the legislative branch of the federal government.

Alaska's state flag features the *Ursa Major* constellation, the Big Dipper and the North Star of *Ursa Minor*. Obtained from Tsarist Russia in 1867 and defended from Japanese military operations in 1942, this giant, northernmost state received much attention from the U.S. military during the Cold War, it being so near to the Soviet Union. Of course, that attention meant air transport, which meant Globemasters. Support for the installations and exercises in the north country came mostly from the 7th and 8th Air Transport Squadrons, assigned to McChord Air Force Base as part of the 62nd Air Transport Wing.[8]

McChord, located between Fort Lewis and Tacoma, Washington, is 1,263 NM miles on a rhomb line heading of 322° to Elmendorf AFB, near Alaska's largest city of Anchorage. En route to Elmendorf on an overland route paralleling the islands of the Alaskan Archipelago, C-124s sometimes encountered phenomena known as a mountain wave. Terrain features in that area can disturb normal wind flow, much like a rocky bed in a fast-moving stream. Strong winds can have their velocities doubled or even tripled in some cases. Because the airplane is in an air mass which is picking up speed, the ground speed of the airplane might increase, in the case of a C-124 above 300 knots, even as the pilot throttles back and cuts true airspeed (TAS) to just over 100 knots. That charging air mass makes for a shortened flight time and gives a smooth, quiet ride as well, but alarms a crew when the C-124 airframe is moving at such a speed, which seems to exceed performance limitations. The uneven terrain in the archipelago landscape can lead to air turbulence and make altimeters give false readings, a situation made more dangerous by the frequent foggy conditions at C-124 flight levels.[9] And "fate is the hunter!"

Eielson AFB, the northernmost Air Force base in the United States, is 214 NM north on a heading of 17° (NNE) from Elmendorf. Eielson is a half-hour flight from the Arctic Circle (72 degrees 20 minutes North latitude). At Eielson, a daylight landing in summer could occur at ten p.m. local time. Sundown on the Summer Solstice, June 22, comes at about midnight, with sunrise at two a.m. That means a *bona fide* barfly in Fairbanks that time of year might never see the short nighttime. Conversely, six months later, he might not see daylight.

Flying directly from Fairbanks to Tinker AFB, Oklahoma, took the Globemaster over the Klondike region and across the 141st meridian that separates Alaska from Canada's Northwest Territories. The route is via airways, meaning no need for celestial aids, so the nav only monitored the flight path on radar and radio. But it is a lonely terrain over which to pass. Operators of the VOR/TACAN stations seem as islands of humanity in the taiga, their remoteness multiplied by endless snow. Looking down from 10,000 feet and seeing a thin blue curl of smoke from an isolated cabin interspersed within this vast pine forest led to a sort of an empathy with the hardy station operators. Together we seemed to be at an existential moment, the only people on earth. The excitement generated by an approaching airplane must have been akin to that of a lighthouse keeper along some rocky coast in spotting a vessel bobbing in distant swells.

Early in 1965, C-124s from McChord departed nearby Fort Lewis, airlifting troops and equipment for a two-week-long Alaskan exercise, navigating up the archipelago by radio beacons and map reading. The APS-42 radar gave a clear picture of the islands, and a navigator who stayed on top of the route had no trouble picking out landforms and confirming headings and ETAs even with an undercast, a typical situation in that region. The planes landed at Big Delta, Alaska, on the Yukon River some 50 miles southeast of Fairbanks, inland where it gets very cold. The 50 soldiers aboard had been quiet on the six-hour trip, perhaps dreading what they were about to encounter. This cold weather exercise had them outfitted in arctic

TACAN station drawing (in *Air Navigation*, Vol. 1, 6–46).

wear, which included triple-insulated rubber boots, orange in color. Soldiers clopped down the ramps in these huge brogans into whirling winds, snow, and 60-below-zero temperatures. The men seemed not anxious to leave the relative warmth of the cargo bay into this environment, but the loadmaster and their own NCOs hustled them up so off they went to their bivouac site and to, no doubt, some miserable nights. The crew kept engines running, and as soon as the last troop cleared, drew in the ramps, closed the clamshell doors, and taxied to the makeshift runway for takeoff to less drafty quarters, the Air Force way! In this exercise, Operation Shoehorn, the aging, three-story-high C-124s from the 62nd TCW at McChord used tiny, snow-covered, sloping landing strips. The Distant Early Warning Line often required outsized, dangerous cargo, and the C-124 was the *only* way of getting it there.[10]

Arctic night exercises in drastic below-zero temps had occurred before as the U.S. Army maintained its readiness. In 1956, a formation of three C-124s dropped a battalion of 82nd Airborne paratroopers from Fort Bragg near Thule, Greenland. After landing on the icecap, the troopers assisted each other and constructed snow shelters and ice block igloos for quarters during the operation, which lasted from February 13 to March 14. They, like the Big Delta troops, waddled like penguins in their triple-insulated boots and arctic parkas.[11] The global mission included polar regions, and these troops were being dropped as an exercise to practice defending the Distant Early Warning Line ("dewline") from enemy ground attacks. The line of radar stations stretched along the Arctic Circle from the Alaskan tundra, across northern Canada into Greenland, and commanded a big budget. To satisfy the public opinion and Congress about its worth, in the spring of 1956, the Air Force remodeled a C-124 building in special accommodations for a press tour of the 3,000-mile-long early warning system. Thirty writers from U.S. and Canadian organizations, including the *New York Times* and *Maclean's* magazine, slept in arctic bags on special stretchers arranged three-high and dined on French

Image from C-124C Dash 1.

6. "Birthplace of Winds"

pastries, king crab legs, and hot biscuits. The C-124, nicknamed "Dewliner" by its pilot, Capt. Thomas O. Aultman of the 14th TCS from Greenville AFB, South Carolina, made nine landings at construction sites and supply strips from Yellowknife to Cambridge Bay on Victoria Island. The coldest temperature encountered was 32 below zero at a site by the Gulf of Boothia Bay, Canada. The trip was arduous but enlightening, and in appreciation of the airplane, crew, and amenities, one newsman reported in his story that "there was never another press tour like this one" in, he said, the "Flying Flophouse."[12]

Alaska, our largest state, of course has many ins and outs and what have yous, including the continent's highest peak at 20,310 feet above sea level, Mount McKinley, or Denali in the Native American tradition. While no Globemaster could fly directly over it, we did pass by its eastern flank en route from Eielson to Elmendorf. At 9,000 feet altitude, on a clear day crew and passengers could see the mountain on the starboard side, from the air at that juncture a stunning sight. It was named for William McKinley, Jr., of Niles, Ohio, who happened to be campaigning for president of the United States in 1896 when a gold rush to Alaska occurred and a prospector named the peak after his choice of candidates. The gold seeker must have been connected in the past directly or by blood line to the GAR and to American expansion. McKinley was a Republican, a former Union Army officer (the last of six consecutive GAR veterans who became president in an era dubbed by Mark Twain "The Gilded Age"), declarer of war on Spain, annexer of Hawaii, and the third president to be assassinated.[13]

Dick Maher, a soldier stationed at Elmendorf in the 1950s, remembered his service basketball team flying as passengers on a C-124 to Fairbanks to play in an inter-service tournament. His photographs of

A soldier's snapshot of a C-124 at an air show in Alaska in the 1950s (courtesy Dick Maher).

paratroop drops in Alaska with snowy mountains in the background reveal a major mission of the Globemaster at the time. Another mission was static display during Armed Forces Day and other goodwill gestures to the public. The Alaska airbase picture of civilians lined up to board the C-124 via the loading ramps is an example of how the Air Force warmed the public up to its giant airplanes. The caption could have read, "Come on in, there is plenty of room!"

A part of the United States lies beyond the 180th meridian, which situates it in the Eastern Hemisphere. The Aleutian archipelago, 279 islands strong, became a U.S. possession with the rest of the Alaskan peninsula in 1867 via a treaty with Tsarist Russia arranged by Secretary of State William E. Seward, a holdover from Lincoln's cabinet. The Aleutian Islands are characterized by weather just as Hawaii and the Azores are, only in the other direction. Constant winds suddenly appear, so violent that they have been dubbed with a name, williwaws. Add perpetual mist, fog layers, horizontal rains, chilling ice and snow, the occasional earthquake, and sudden shifts in the weather, and the picture is not pretty. It gets worse moving westward toward the end of the chain, all the way to Attu, say. Attu and its smaller neighbor, Shemya, had names given to them by the native Aleuts, "Cradle of Storms" and "Birthplace of Winds." Mountains rise in the interior of Attu, a 42-by-17-mile island. Left over from World War II are some berm quarters dug into hillsides with grass growing on the roofs and dirt floors, sub-terrain-constructed because buildings and wind socks can stand only so much.

At neighboring Sheyma, a reinforced structure, though, arose during the Cold War to challenge these powerful weather elements: a large hanger, the doors of which were almost always shut. The hanger with the doors closed housed a Lockheed SR-71 Blackbird. Few Americans have or had ever seen one of these fantastic spy planes, let alone see it take off. With missions that took it into Soviet air space at altitudes of up to 80,000 feet, cruising at world-record speeds of 2,100 mph, it was a state-of-the-art successor to the U-2s of the Eisenhower administration. This impressive airplane was so secret in the mid–1960s that not even top-secret clearance airmen such as C-124 crews were allowed an up-close look or to intermingle with Blackbird crews. To talk with a SR-71 navigator (recon systems operator in that plane) would have been a perfect way to pass crew rest hours on amenity-less Sheyma Air Base, but no such luck. Ironically, the technology of air navigation advanced significantly with the accelerated development of the inertial guidance system deemed essential for the Blackbird's mission and came soon after to the new airlifters on

6. "Birthplace of Winds" 117

drawing boards such as the C-141 and the C-5. Technological advancements spurred on by the Cold War doomed the overwater celestial navigator, who had risen to a career peak with the C-124s, C-130s, and C-133s.

Most McChord crews who flew into Sheyma just wanted to get out on schedule, sometimes hard to do. One tactic was to flight plan, take up positions in the plane, start engines, taxi to the runway, and ... wait. Wait until the preposterously stubborn fog, clouds, and mist would lift just enough for the tower to declare the field above minimums and clear for takeoff. At which time the crew lost no time in squaring up and pouncing on the throttles to get airborne before the ceiling fell, which assuredly it was just about to do.

Attu has location as one redeeming factor and a second positive in its appeal to birds, which are attracted to the island despite hardly a green tree there. Birds fly in from two continents with their finest plumage on display for the opposite sex and for birders. Attu, at a longitude of E173°–30', is closer to Tokyo than to Seattle, which is the reason that McChord airlifters were making marginal landings at an outpost that would be on anyone's (except for birders) short list of "Godforsaken places in the world."[14]

Seven months after Pearl Harbor, in June 1942, the Japanese Imperial Army seized Attu, which had at the time a population of some 40 Aleuts and two schoolteachers. The Japanese had occupied American territory, which would have been a psychological victory if anyone other than the military in the United States had known. The public didn't hear about it though, because the military and the government kept it mum. Deprived of a public relations coup, the Imperial Army promptly forgot about the regiment it had left there on American territory, and in 1943, the U.S. Army got around to taking the Aleutians back. But they first had to withstand Banzei suicide attacks from the 2,500 Japanese soldiers who preferred death to surrender or maybe to another year on Attu.[15]

The Japanese toehold on Alaskan land spurred U.S. construction of the Alcan highway, with Canada's full approval, to build an airport on Attu, and to fortify Dutch Harbor, further east on the chain, with nationalized Arkansas guardsmen.

Just like the other great empires in world history, the American version did not give up its territory gladly, regardless of how inconsequential that land might appear. Outposts such as Attu and Sheyma were part of the perimeter defense of the United States and were used aggressively during the Cold War. Essential to their construction and to their maintenance was airlift, and an airlifter with the volume and willingness of the

Globemaster, which certainly lived up to its name by flying into these stations.

Dutch Harbor, a port and commercial trading facility since the 1880s located on the island of Unalaska about midway along the Aleutian chain, is a vestige of Russian control of Alaska, the Aleut, or Unangan, people, and the incredible fur-bearing animals that were the bonanza driving investment in these remote, foreboding islands. After their successful assault on the outer islands, the Japanese continued the threat by bombing Dutch Harbor, which is far more settled that Attu and Shemya, a regular suburbia in comparison. They did not attempt to land troops, but the scare was there and so increased American commitment in the Aleutians.

The airport at Dutch Harbor sits on a small plain with high peaks nearby. Fog is a constant here, too, and the harsh weather conditions even today cause about 20 percent cancellation of commercial flights in and out of the airport, which has a 4,100-foot runway. On one trip in, the co-pilot, a lieutenant colonel on a check ride at his new station, effected a directional radio approach for his instrument landing. This is an all-else-failing landing procedure rarely used and never when conditions are close to minimums, since Radio Direction Finders (RDF) are notoriously slow to react and thus can be unreliable. But this was practice and a bit of pilot swagger, so the co-pilot tuned to the radio beacon at the airport. He lined up to fly directly over it, at which time the needle on the compass card is supposed to swing 180 degrees to show passage. Using a stopwatch and after a pre-determined lapse of time, the pilot then pitches into the downwind leg and finishes the landing pattern. On the Globemaster, the navigator monitors the approach on the APS-42 radar. On this one occasion, after a long flight and at twilight with fog making it IFR conditions, the co-pilot followed the procedure while the pilot kept time. When the time expired as to expected needle swing, it had not yet done so. It could have been a strong head wind, an incorrect time calculation, or some other unforeseen problem—maybe a balky needle. Discounting the third of these possibilities, the pilot continued, flying without visual reference—in the blind—seconds passed and as they did, the navigator's radar screen (the pilot has a backup that shows the same imagery, but with a little less detail) clearly showed an obstacle ahead that was rapidly filling the screen. Interpreting the return to indicate a mountain, one that was looming at or above our flight level, the navigator requested a sharp climbing turn. Without argument, the pilot honored the request. The co-pilot's check ride ended at that point, the pilot asserted command, and the mountain was

6. "Birthplace of Winds"

avoided. After the missed approach, normalcy returned and a GCA landing was made.

The incident above is not something that navigators practiced. To be sure, they were competent in and checked out on ARA—airborne radar approaches—but only in rare cases were the conditions realistic. Even less realistic for navs was the willingness of pilots to trust this approach alternative. GCR—ground-controlled radar—was a typical instrument approach used by MATS pilots, but navs lacked the intensive training and the daily experience of air traffic controllers, and of course there was a vast difference in the capabilities of the radar equipment. Navigators could have been further trained, but that seemed a redundancy in depth. The APS-42 was precise enough for the approach tasks and in fact was standard equipment on the C-124C, causing the Bozo the Clown look with the radome at the forward point of the airplane. C-124A models, which did not originally have the airborne radar, were all retrofitted. The ten-inch scope of MA 6a/7a radar that navs trained on while at Mather in bombardier school preparing for SAC seemed so much more sophisticated that the APS-42, that not many navs had ultimate confidence in it either. That may have been the product of low-maintenance priority for it rather than any design defects. Out on the circuit, not many, maybe no aircraft commanders would delay flights until the APS-42 was in perfect adjustment, and in truth, away from a squadron's home base, not many electronic people could be found in the system experienced enough to take the radar set on a C-124 to the top of its game. Navs were left, then, most often with scopes that presented fuzzy images or were uncalibrated and therefore unreliable as to distances. Almost every one of the C-124 transport navigators at one time or another in their business felt the butterfly-in-the-stomach syndrome while peering at a radar scope reflection of intense cumulonimbus thunder cells at their flight level or at some bright, bright reflections from landform obstacles dead ahead.

GM's Delco Battery division made a commercial for television in 1958 depicting a Globemaster in the arctic and in an icy fog, dependent totally on ground control radar for the approach and landing. The GCA equipment was in turn backed up by totally dependable Delco dry charge batteries. A harrowing moment in the three-minute film comes as the primary electricity fails and the airman rushes to a cabinet to activate the battery-driven backup system. It works, and the C-124 lands safely. Realistic enough, certainly, but the navigator no doubt in such conditions was monitoring the situation with ARA as a backup, although that goes unmentioned in the film, which does have some good footage of a flying C-124.[16]

The statistics are rather chilling, too. Among the 39 airborne crashes of Globemasters, seven flew into mountains or high terrain near the destination airport. Three of the seven happened in Alaska. In addition, five more fatal accidents in the Globemaster occurred on final approach. The Cooperton, Oklahoma, C-124 crash occurred in a thunderstorm, and navs were aware of how to avoid such cells with use of the APS-42. Only in one mishap was navigation error cited in the accident report as the chief cause, but in all of them, a navigator was flight following at his duty station and surely was recognizing the danger he, the crew, and the plane were in.[17]

Pilots were far more accepting of nav advice while flying through or around a line of thunderstorms using the APS-42. Trying to pick openings was tricky, and while a path could look feasible for a few minutes, once in the line, the opening could quickly close as thunderheads built rapidly. The up and down drafts of a giant thunderstorm could put incredible stress on the airframe, equivalent, some instructors told us, of flying directly into the side of a granite mountain. At the C-124 typical flight level of 9,000 feet AGL, some anvil-topped cumulonimbus clouds could tower 30,000 feet above the plane. A procedure coming into the Philippines was to fly around a line of these tropical monsters, but sometimes the line kept extending, it seemed like, for hundreds of miles. One nav remarked to his pilot that if we kept skirting, we were likely to wind up in Red China. A bit of an overstatement, perhaps, but with a grain of truth so that the pilot took the plunge and the right-angle approach to penetration, a hazard-facing that turned out well that time and, fortunately, in the great majority of times. Plenty of these experiences, however, are shared by veterans of the C-124s.

7

"The Right Stuff"
Crewing Old Shaky

The first-built MATS Old Shakies were only 15 years old at the time of the Gulf of Tonkin Resolution in August 1964. Yet the Globemaster was an elder statesman in the fast-developing world of aviation. Its crews, however, were young. Aircraft commanders and flight engineers often were middle-aged, but co-pilots and navs were usually in their 20s, and loadmasters, mostly Airmen First Class, could be even younger. The routines and burdens of long-range transport flying, therefore, rested on the shoulders of the strong, those who could exist, even thrive on flight lunches, live in close quarters, go unwashed for long periods, urinate once or twice a day, put up with other people's cigarette smoke and cold coffee, take unexpected detours, operate even with a hangover, take ribbing, insults, and coaching, and keep smiling with brimming, maybe unwarranted confidence in the future, both near and far. Crew composition, in retrospect, gave evidence that the U.S. Air Force and MATS knew what it was doing, even though intuition spoke to one otherwise.

Early Air Transport Command pilot Ernest K. Gann wrote that pretenders among aircrew members were easily and quickly spotted. In his book, *Fate is the Hunter*, Gann defined the difference between fear (long-term, incapacitating, detested by any aviator worth his salt) and fright (short-term, adrenalin-producing, and known by all aviators). Cool, responsible, decisive, and honorable were the qualities Gann wrote about as shaping the best crew members, and as the "enterprise of flying the oceans" became abundant, good crews were treasured.[1]

Chuck Yeager had a lot to do with the way aircrew members, especially pilots, spoke, thought of themselves, and acted. Yeager was from West Virginia and spoke English with a regional drawl. It had not the

Image from C-124C Dash 1, 1965.

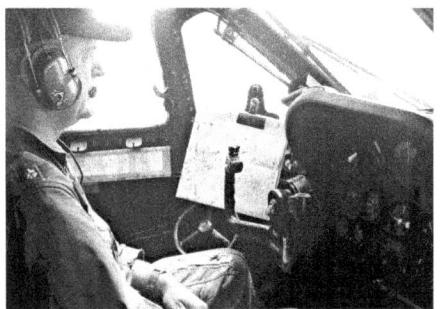 

Left: Major Frank Muscal piloting the C-124. *Right:* Major John J. Bibo in co-pilot seat.

clipped resonance of the North, nor did it linger like a deep South accent, say like those from Georgia. Only through the Civil War and secession did the loyal West Virginia, the mountainous third of the Old Dominion, escape political domination by the Tidewater elite of Virginia, and with it the distinct marling of vowels that cause "about" to be pronounced "a-boot." So with elements of the Appalachian claim to "Elizabethan English," with a panhandle that extended north of Pittsburgh, with coal fields, and with mostly rural lifestyles, the West Virginia speech developed its own brand.

7. "The Right Stuff" 123

Yeager typified that purely American speech and the toughness of West "By God" Virginia. He was an air ace in World War II. Among his 11 kills was a Luftwaffe ME 262, which was the world's first jet fighter and could reach a speed 150mph above Yeager's P-51 Mustang. In 1946, assigned to Wright Field in Dayton, Ohio, he put on many air shows with the F-80 Shooting Star, the Air Force's first jet fighter plane. From a list of highly qualified test pilots, some with engineering degrees, Yeager, who never attended college and who was assigned as a maintenance officer, was selected by Major General Albert Boyd to pilot the rocket-powered Bell X-1 to be the first person to break the sound barrier, a seemingly impossible feat because experts foresaw a mighty and never experienced shock wave that would tear apart any airplane. Indeed, that had already happened to a British experimental plane attempting supersonic flight in a dive earlier that year. The metaphor was of hitting a brick wall.

Yet progress required that it be tried. Bell Aircraft Company built the plane, the Air Force became the operator, Muroc Air Base, later renamed Edwards AFB in the Mojave Desert, became the Flight Test Center, and on October 14, 1947, on his ninth flight in the X-1 which he said flew so well, Yeager became the first human to fly faster than the speed of sound.[2] He not only survived, he became a pilot's pilot, a role model. Timing could not have been better. President Truman, on July 17, 1947, aboard a Douglas DC-4, had signed the last of a series of bills separating the Air Force from the Army. Thus, the United States Air Force came into being in the same year that one of its pilots became a marvelous hero to the flying community for his accomplishment.[3]

Thereafter, thousands of USAF pilots and air traffic controllers conformed to Yeager's efficiency of speech and his matter of fact descriptions of conditions even in the direst moments, as per country-cool Chuck Yeager would have said it. Evidently pilot DNA makes them extra-normal in the face of impending disaster. Often, it seems, that calmness and the complete confidence that it implied alone carried them, and their charges, through situations that could go either way. In fact, that is exactly the way Chuck Yeager put it. He said that he didn't know about the "right stuff," but that "my nature was to stay cool in tight spots."[4] If you are Chuck Yeager, you don't brag or promote yourself. Why on earth would you do that? Having flown 50 different airplanes, most of them fighters or experimental, he was selected to test fly a MiG-15 that the U.S. had acquired through a defection. Arriving at Okinawa, Yeager put it through its maximum performances as to speed, dive, altitude, turning radius, and weaknesses. His commanding officer Boyd, himself a renowned fighter pilot, looking at the

Yeager's analysis of the test flight, said, "and now we know more about its capabilities than the Russians do."

While with Air Logistics at Wright-Pat, Yeager may have gained a few hours in the pilot's seat of C-124s, checking out maintenance. After the MiG flight evaluation, Yeager and Boyd flew back to the United States from Kadena AB at the controls of a C-124, crossing the Pacific with a 17-hour leg, which no doubt gave them ample time together in the cockpit talking about their experiences. Yeager flying a C-124 Globemaster at an airspeed of 185 knots, imagine that! In December 1953, Yeager flew to 80,000 feet and superseded Mach 2 in the X-1A, an improved rocket-propelled plane. During one run, the controls of the X-1A were affected adversely at 1,645 mph, causing Yeager to plummet 51,000 feet in 51 seconds, yawing, spinning, and tumbling toward the earth. He regained control at 29,000 feet. His fellow test pilots at Muroc marveled at his ability to pull out of that spin and land safely. A later model of a rocket-propelled airplane owned by the USAF still holds the world's speed record for airplanes at Mach 6.72, or expressed another way, the X-15 piloted by Pete Knight in 1967 flew at a speed of a mere 4,519 mph. NASA's unpowered space shuttles returning to earth reached speeds of 17,000 mph on reentry and were fully under the control of the pilot.

In 1962, President Kennedy, himself a *bona fide* war hero, told Congress and the American people, "We choose to go to the moon in this decade." Now that's a mission statement! The National Aeronautical and Space Administration, NASA, a civilian agency often employing civilian test pilots, had already been established in 1958 by President Eisenhower as a response to the USSR launch of Sputnik in 1957, but the Kennedy commitment brought bigger budgets and unlimited optimism to the space program.

The Air Force wanted to participate in aerospace as its natural jurisdiction and wanted to prove that a rocket-powered airplane could blast off, fly into orbit, and land safely on a runway. The U.S. Air Force and the U.S. Navy were bent on controlling space not only for this country, but for the military, and considered themselves jointly in the running not for just flying to the moon, but for missions far more important to the military mind, that is flying into space and linking to an orbiting station/laboratory.[5] The Air Force plan, the budget, the experiment itself went under the program name, Dyna-Soar, and for it, building on the X-1A, Boeing developed the X-20, a lifting body airplane that really was the forerunner of the space shuttle. Eight Air Force pilots were awarded astronaut wings, and one plane flew into space which, by international agreement,

7. "The Right Stuff"

begins at 100 kilometers, an altitude of 330,000 feet. More than $600 million was spent before the military gave way entirely to NASA's Mercury program and its one-man capsule, which of course, like the Gemini and Apollo spacecrafts after it, rode a rocket into orbit, returning to the earth not through a pilot's skill in landing, but by parachuting into the ocean. John Glenn and the astronauts were, however, cut of the Chuck Yeager cloth, an interpretation shared by author Tom Wolfe in his famous book, *The Right Stuff*. While modest in speech and cool in time of danger, most pilots obviously have large-size egos. Also obvious is that air crews kidded and jibbed themselves into a modest behavior.

The keep-calm attitude of two experienced pilots was tested on a night landing at Lajes AB, where cross winds are often a big factor. Their C-124 carried a cylindrical steel storage tank so large that it filled the cargo compartment. Going from aft to the rear, one had to squeeze between the tank and the cabin wall. The cylinder had been loaded in the C-124 at Dover and planned to fly non-stop to the Azores.

After a long and uneventful flight, the TACAN locked on and a straight-in approach to Lajes airport was initiated. The aircraft commander was a lieutenant colonel, as was the co-pilot who had just arrived at Dover, his new station, and who was getting a check ride. These old, brown-shoe types had spent most of the long overwater leg in the cockpit exchanging flying adventures which dated back to the 1940s, each just slightly trying to top the other. They had decided on a test of skill for the landing. The co-pilot would take the landing, and he placed an empty coke bottle on the radio console between the seats. He offered to buy the A/C dinner if his landing tipped over or even jostled the bottle. The approach went smoothly, with the runway in sight, gear down, and over the landing lights, when a sudden boom from the interior of the C-124 rocked the plane. At that time, the steady hand at the controls jerked and the A/C yelled into his headset mike, "What the hell was that!?" The landing was off-center line with a bounce or two, and as soon as all wheels were on the ground, the pilots reversed props full power and stood on the brakes. They plane screeched to a stop as though we were on a short field assault landing. The coke bottle was nowhere in sight, thrown under the seats. The boom mystery was soon solved when the loadmaster reported from the cabin that the sound came from an implosion of the storage tank. In flying 12 hours on the trans-oceanic route at 9,000 feet, we were up long enough for the ambient air in the unpressurized cabin to fill the space inside the tank. When the outside air pressure mounted during the approach to Lajes field, the tank walls collapsed abruptly with a huge boom. Scratch one storage tank and scratch two pilots' friendly dinner and drink wager. Nothing else was said about coke bottle-steady landings.

A C-124 pilot practicing approaches at Memphis International Airport lost an engine, feathered the propeller, and was diverted to Millington NAS, Tennessee, for an emergency landing. With fire trucks preparing to foam the runway, a crew comedian got on the intercom and asked the pilot to please put the emergency on standby radio and call him in a lunch order to McDonald's: "That would be," he chanted, "a Big Mac, lettuce, pickle, onion, special sauce on sesame-seed bun with fries and a large coke." With priorities thus established and tension broken, the pilot landed safely and smoothly without the foam.

During 1964 joint Army-Air Force training maneuvers, C-124s dropped paratroopers from Fort Bragg, using Pope AFB as a mustering and boarding venue. Paratroopers jumped from the side doors near the aft of the fuselage. Packages or pallets could be dropped from C-124s out the elevator shaft, 7'9" wide and 13' long, which could be configured by hoisting the platform to the rails at the top of the cabin, allowing an opening for drops, the bomb bay doors capable of opening in-flight. On one occasion, the plan called for a cargo drop and when completed, doors closed and buckled up, the plane would return to Dover. The A/C happened to be the squadron commander, a serious man with unquestioned ability who could make personnel evaluations and decisions that were respected because he was known to be fair if rigorous. This night, after releasing the package and turning to the outbound heading, gaining airspeed and altitude, the loadmaster crackled in on the headset with the news that the bomb bay doors were not closing and it was getting rather drafty back there in the cabin. Since the mission was over and the crew headed home, the alternative of landing meant declaring an emergency at Pope, which evidently the pilot preferred not to do. He decided to lower the airspeed of the C-124 to create a shudder in the airframe that just might jar the mechanism and close the doors. The Globemaster was empty except for crew and fuel, so with full flaps and nose slightly up, the air speed dropped from 140 to 120 to 100 knots. Still no closure and really no shudder. The pilot continued to back off the throttles until the air speed went to 80 knots, stall speed. The plane did shudder. So did the nav. It worked, however. With doors shaken free, now closed and locked, our pilot put on power, climbed to flight level, and continued to Dover. I marveled at the coolness of the colonel's hand, his confidence in maintaining control at that dangerous level, and the confidence all the crew had in him. But to think of 140,000 pounds of airplane right on the back of the

7. "The Right Stuff" 127

power curve, 2,000 feet above ground level (AGL) at a speed less than that being cruised by most cars on the divided highway below, had a surreal touch.

Surreal perhaps as well was the parachute drop over the reviewing stand at Fort Bragg, home of the famed 82nd Airborne Division. Brass, politicians, and a host of guests attended a precision delivery demonstration of cargo pallets to a target painted in the center of the post parade ground. The lead navigator in a formation of C-124s, due to a sudden wind shift, miscalculated the release point, and the pallets drifted toward the assemblage, sending the distinguished spectators scrambling out of their bleacher seats to safety. Naturally, there was a less-than-happy officer from headquarters awaiting the crew at its parking spot on the ramp.

One navigator had learned his no-bragging-unnecessarily-or-out-of-turn lessons during flying with men with far greater adventures. During the C-124 era, crew members passed through Wake Island and never saw a woman. The one and only and favorite bar, Drifter's Reef, featured half-priced drinks. Here with cigarette and beverage, a seldom washed flight suit seemed tolerable, even macho. Once after a happy hour, our aircraft commander suggested a movie, which was in a long room equipped with folding chairs, a screen affixed to a tripod, and a 16mm projector on a table at the rear. The film that night was *Man from U.N.C.L.E.*, starring Robert Vaughn and David McCallum. It was a movie-length episode introducing a new TV series, and we watched while pleasantly stewed from the effect of gin and tonics but secure in the knowledge that nothing else was happening on Wake anyway. About halfway through this cold war spy movie, a mysterious blonde wearing a miniskirt engaged McCallum in a Pullman car. She would have looked

David McCallum and Jennifer Billingsley in the pilot movie, *The Man from U.N.C.L.E.*, shown in 1965 on Wake Island. Image from studio picture in possession of author. Billingsley appeared on the May 1962 cover of *Esquire* magazine.

inviting anywhere, let alone to an aircrew on Wake Island. Naturally she got some whistles from the audience attending the movie. Hold on! The actress was Jennifer Billingsley, from my home town. This was one-upmanship on Wake Island. Indeed, Jennifer had been my date at the high school senior prom, and she let me drive her home afterwards, too, despite several offers from date hijackers. Her ticket into the theater and film industry was that she was a fabulous dancer and looked a bit like Brigitte Bardot. No one believed me, of course, and ribbed me for braggin' and lying. I was still happy about it, though, and even though I might have been bragging a bit, I wasn't lying.

Air crew members in each position had come through rigorous schooling to get where they were, that is aboard an operational flight, part of a military team with high responsibilities and a duty to God, country, and family. Experience was needed, of course, and especially at the pilot position. Most aircraft commanders were captains or majors with 5,000 hours flying time or more. By the time they were promoted to lieutenant colonel, pilots did not fly as much but commanded squadrons or above or had staff positions. Not that they stopped flying, they just did not "fly the line" as they once did. At the height of the Globemaster era, a number of MATS pilots had World War II service and were prop plane oriented. But the jet age was arriving rapidly, and in the transport field that age was led by the turboprop Lockheed C-130 Hercules. First operational with the Air Force in December 1956, the C-130 was only two-thirds the size of a C-124, but twice as fast and built for short field operations.

In 1957, the Air Force phased in a new primary pilot trainer T-37 Cessna-built jet, which replaced the venerable, propeller-driven T-6 Texan that had been used since World War II. Coming out of training jet-certified, new pilots may be excused for thinking that going into MATS transport, with its stable of piston engine, low-flying, low-speed—lumbering was a description they used—airplanes was a step in the wrong direction.

Pilot schools, like nav schools, distributed operational assignments—or advanced training options—in order of class standing. Those at the top of the list had the first choice, and many of them eagerly accepted choice assignments to TAC or ADC jet fighters. All young aviators wanted, at least outwardly, to be fighter pilots, although bomber assignments appealed to romantic musings for some out of a sense of duty, SAC propaganda, and the challenge of learning a complicated system on the cutting edge of aircraft technologies. What was left? Well, rescue, refueling, and transport. Transport pilots could be likened to bus drivers and were. After all, the official blue Air Force uniform that replaced the appealing Silver

7. "The Right Stuff"

Tans in 1955 was like that of a Greyhound bus driver.[6] For navs, a sort of reverse thinking took place. The gung-ho nav-bombs, who called themselves "SAC Trained Killers" at the top of the class, chose to serve their country mostly by spending time in alert shacks or on airborne alert and practice missions.

A few other assignments came down the pike for nav-bombs to TAC or ADC, where interceptors like the F-101 Voodoo had backseats for Electronic Warfare Officers, EWOs for short. More of these openings for navs were on the way with increased production of Republic's F-105J Thunderchief and McDonnell's F-4 Phantom. These all-weather fighter/interceptors relied on electronics and radar to find, fix, and destroy enemy planes and ground targets. Those instruments fell within the realm of the EWO or, as he was later termed, the Weapons System Officer (WSO). This modernity blurred the distinction of exactly to whom a kill from a dog fight engagement with the enemy belonged, pilot or nav, something the World War II aces in single seaters did not have to consider. In the Vietnam War, for example, the leading ace with six MiG kills was an F-4 Phantom Weapons System Officer, navigator Charles DeBellevue, flying in tandem behind two different pilots with whom he shared the "victories."

But often navs opted for MATS, and that meant for most of them, a C-124 assignment at Travis and Dover, the two bases equipped between them with six squadrons of Globemasters and thus with the most openings for new navigators. But a few transport navigator slots came from other MATS bases and TAC troop carrier wings at Greenville, South Carolina, Hill AFB, Utah, and Hunter AFB in

Navigator Charles DeBellevue's flight suit, with stars signifying his "kills" and his ace rating from the Vietnam War, is on display at the Air Force Museum of History at Wright-Patterson AFB, Ohio.

Savannah. Exotic base locations such as Charleston, South Carolina, McChord AFB, Washington, Hunter AFB in Savannah, Georgia, and Hickam AB near Honolulu were airlifter bases with preferred but rare opportunities for those just out of school.[7]

Once the pilot or navigator reported in to a MATS base, he was assigned to a flying squadron and began to forge those relationships that created effective crews. Competition between squadrons in intramural sports and in flying rodeo contests honed the identity. So did happy hours with dice games and O Club special nights. The air crews combined gentlemen from all geographical areas of the country, a true mix there, but the ethnic identity was pretty much white middle class, almost all being college graduates except for the occasional mustang who had earned wings at Aviation Cadet School.

Mike Radowski graduated from James Connelly and was assigned directly to MATS and C-124s at Hill AFB, Utah. He had wished for C-130s and had never heard of Ogden, Utah, but as he said, "it was luck of the draw." Like most navs when getting their first look at a Globemaster, Radowski was awed by what he saw—"it was huge"—and could hardly believe that he had to climb a ladder just to get to his crew position. On a trip across the ocean and on the return home from Hickam, a Nav Flight Examiner jumped aboard to give the instructor nav a check ride who, in turn, would be giving instruction to young Radowski. The flight, however, was anything but ordinary, but rather had high drama. The story of an adventurous flight in a Globemaster is told in Radowski's words:

> There were the two pilot seats up front, the engineer sat on the right-hand side with a full panel of gauges monitoring everything that plane did. The nav station was right behind the left-hand pilot seat with all the latest equipment, APN-9 Loran (which they told us in Nav School was no longer in line aircraft—Ha!), APS 42 radar, absolute altimeter and all manner of gauges and compasses. The drift meter was downstairs. Some aircraft had a hand-held sextant, others had the D1 sextant. One or two of the aircraft had the new-fangled APN-70 Loran. The unique thing about the APN-9 Loran set is the little switch just below it that let out the antenna, in the tail of the aircraft. What was nice about that switch was the fact that you could tune the antenna length for the different loran stations and get a better signal. The bad thing was if you forgot to reel it in on landing, you had a couple hundred feet of wire and a brass weight hanging off the tail of the aircraft. This trip was either my second or third and I was still flying with an instructor. We were departing Hickam AFB, Hawaii, for Travis, going home. Just our luck, a wandering Flight Evaluator Nav (FE) jumped on board to give my instructor a no notice check ride. Another ten-hour night flight. We went to the Airlift Command Post (ACP), picked up the computer flight plan, and I proceeded to put the charts together and can the first few lines of the nav log. We then got our weather briefing. Smooth flying with a plus 10 wind factor meant we had a ten mile per hour tail

7. "The Right Stuff"

wind, no turbulence and a clear morning at Travis. With that info, we gave the flight engineer the recommended fuel load and filed Beal AFB, just up the road from Travis as an alternate landing field. All the paperwork done, we were off.

At the aircraft and under the watchful eye of my instructor and the FE Nav all equipment was pre-flighted and found A-OK. The checklists were run, engines started, and we taxied out and took off. About thirty minutes after takeoff, I got my departure fix, on course, on time. The instructor gave me the thumbs up and the FE Nav took the top bunk.

In the C-124 we took fixes every hour to an hour and a half. Because of the FE Nav on board, my instructor asked if I would take the first few fixes every hour. I took my second fix, a three-station loran fix. It put us about three or four miles south of track and we had lost a few minutes on the flight plan. I made a slight adjustment to the heading, did some fuel log updates, and chatted with the instructor. Then he took the lower bunk and said wake me if you need me.

The next fix was a combination three-star celestial fix and loran and we were on course but had lost another few minutes on the flight plan. The aircraft commander (AC) didn't seem concerned. We pressed on. Third fix was again a three star and loran, but the loran was now sky waves and not really that good. On course but again lost a few minutes of the flight plan. Wind factor thus far was only about a plus five and seemed to be dropping. Four and a half hours out and approaching the equal time point (ETP) and my latest fix gave us a negative wind factor. I was afraid I had a bad fix, so I woke up the instructor and asked him to get a quick fix. My last fix was right on, and in the half hour it took to get another fix we lost more time. We discussed the slowdown with the AC and the engineer and decided we had enough fuel to press on.

The next fix showed a minus fifteen wind factor and we had lost even more time. I alerted the AC who got on the HF radio and contacted Travis weather, who replied that the weather pattern had shifted, and we would be getting up to a minus twenty-five wind factor. Plus, morning fog would meet us upon arrival. The FE had the instructor take the seat and the two of them started checking and rechecking all the fixes. The engineer alerted the AC that we would have just enough fuel for one pass at Travis. Two hours out and we now had the minus twenty-five wind factor. Travis was now "zero–zero" and the field was closed. As we now planned for the alternate, AC contacted Beal who informed us they were at a hundred and a quarter and going down and that the entire Bay area was covered in fog.

We were low on fuel, all Bay area airports were covered in fog, what to do next? Travis said to contact Castle AFB a hundred miles or so to the south. The FE Nav and the instructor quickly calculated that we would have just barely enough fuel to make it but could only make ONE approach.

The AC got clearance to fly directly to Castle and contacted Castle approach control. The news that they had for us was NOT good. They were currently at minimums and scheduled do go down within the next fifteen to twenty minutes. We were about twenty minutes out.

The engineer was transferring fuel around [when] one of the engines went lean and over sped—That got everybody wide eyed. A quick flip of a switch and the engine was back to normal. At ten minutes out of Castle they were holding at minimums. The AC contacted approach control for landing instructions and we were now under their control. As we turned on final, approach control said the field just went below minimums and for us to enter a holding pattern. The AC explained that we didn't have the fuel to do that, just get us down or we would be a big black hole in the ground. All eyes were looking for runway lights. Just as the lights showed through the fog, number three engine sputtered, leaned out and quit. As the pilot flared, the main gear touched the runway as number two engine sputtered and quit. As we cleared the active runway, the other two engines sputtered, leaned out and quit and we rolled to a stop. The AC called ground control for a tug and the entire crew breathed a sigh of relief, the mission from hell was over! Oh, by the way, my instructor passed his check.[8]

On long trips away from home, bonding took place in the constant togetherness, the confinement of the cockpit and airplane for long hours at a time, and sometimes because there was a moment of sheer terror where a crew may have had a glimpse of "fate" mixed in with the ho hum hours spent boring a hole through the sky. Landing after a long day of flying, crews did not go their separate ways, but rode in a bus to their bunking place, relaxed, maybe even changed into civvies, and then went looking for a drink and later something to eat. If at a typical base, the officers and enlisted men split up to find an on-base club or dining hall that catered to flight crews. Certainly not all aircrew members drank, probably about 30 to 40 percent did not, I would estimate, among those with whom I flew. Meeting at the bar of the O Club was common enough, and conversations usually ranged, as they do with men, about sports, gambling, carousing, and where to find the best steak. Most clubs had a dice cup sitting on the bar, and a popular game was Ship, Captain, and Crew. Two could play, but it was far more fun if five or six were anteing up. You could go broke for a night when the dice were cold for you, but that was part of the camaraderie, too. Passing through Travis AFB, a jump-off spot for the Pacific, was a hit with EASTAF crews because you got to look forward to gambling and drinking at the huge Officers' Club and then moseying over to order from a fantastic menu at the Beefeaters restaurant inside the club. And after that it was usually off to bed. While, to be sure, some historic hangovers were created in the Travis evenings, the 12 hours from bottle to throttle rule was religiously obeyed as crews anticipated the two weeks of over-water flights that loomed ahead of them.

With so much time on long legs in cramped quarters, at least part of the crew rest demanded physical activity for such athletically inclined men who made up aircrews, and were, indeed, selected in part for that reason. At Hickam and Lajes, there were gymnasiums near the VOQs, so young navs and co-pilots could shoot baskets, play some hoops. Clark AFB had a tropically lush golf course, and even Wake had its ping pong tables and snorkeling spots. At Mactan AB, literally carved out of the jungle during the Vietnam War to relieve congestion at Clark AB near Manila,

7. "The Right Stuff" 133

one nav, aware of Ferdinand Magellan's demise on the island which was just across the bay and a ferry ride from Cebu, a major city of the southern Philippines, and with some time, decided to hike in the countryside to explore people and places. He came across a shaded outdoor cement pad with grass growing over the edges but marked in fading paint, a basketball court relic in the jungle! It had been part of a church mission to the adjacent village, he was told. The mission and the court had been abandoned. In the village, there was a bar serving a favorite beer in the Philippines, San Miguel. Over a bottle in a shaded outdoor table served by an attractive middle-age woman, the nav was approached by a local artisan who said that for a certain price, very low, he would carve a memento of Mactan from a seashell for the nav. A deal was cut, and a few days later, the nav picked up the finished, hand-carved conch shell with the nav's name, his squadron, the MATS emblem, and two flags on staffs crossed at the top, the American and the Filipino. The American aviator felt closer to the village people.

In this hot, hot land, aircrews slept in mahogany-floored canvas tents on cots with heavy mosquito netting. Air conditioning was far into the future. Not even electric fans had arrived at Mactan, and no natural breeze wafted through the thick mesh, so one's bedding was soaked with sweat. Airmen lay there waiting for the heat to abate. Sometimes it did that just before sunrise, allowing a chance for a little rem sleep, but in a sort of perverted circumstance, that was exactly the time, sunrise, when village goats stirred and started incessant bleating, a din through which no one could ever sleep.

Mactan had its other miseries, too, with a mess hall serving food to a line of men holding metal plates. After the meal, usually eaten while standing or outdoors on picnic benches, the men washed their own plates in a shiny G.I. can full of scalding water. It was an easy way to get food poisoning. The USO did what it could to raise spirits, but troupes that came through, while doing their best to provide entertainment and diversion, had understandably less pizzazz in the 100-degree, 100 percent humidity weather in which they were performing. Their limply applauding audience stood during performances, since evidently there were no folding chairs on Mactan.

The stage system pulverized on crews at Mactan. A crew would be alerted by the duty officer of the 606th Military Airlift Support Squadron and accept the mission (the aircraft commander did have the right of refusal), at which point duty time started. Getting to base ops, flight planning, and going out to the airplane on the crew bus consumed an hour or so. Next order of business was loading gear and making the walk-around inspection on the C-124 we were about to take. The airplane may have just arrived with its engines still warm from a long leg. The plane's home base might be Charleston or Travis or McChord or some other base participating in the stage. We seldom encountered the airmen who brought it in. Our crew's loadmaster would arrive at the plane early to inspect his cargo and make sure all was properly secured and ready for a long flight. Loadmasters had physically demanding tasks, good that they had the strength, stamina, and energy of youth. During the stage at each air base stop, including Mactan, avionic and mechanical work on the C-124s by maintenance crews went on around the clock. They had few days off and often used flashlights or the lights of their vehicles to accomplish their mechanical miracles. Throughout the Vietnam War, airplanes were used violently in some of the worst conditions for machinery. Aircrews praised maintenance men, building an excellent relationship. The blogs posted today by former C-124 technicians reveal their experiences, their dedication, and their deep affection for the Globemaster and for those who flew it.[9]

After the ground crew had performed its inspections, and after refueling the airplane, some discrepancy might be noted that would require a little more service, a little more time from flight line guys who were working to capacity in support of the endless traffic coming through. So there might be a delay. That resulted in "pounding the ramp," hanging around until some specialist airman who could repair the radar or HF radio or an engine or some segment of the electrical system had a go at fixing a problem.

Here's our worry: basic crew duty time is 18 hours. Mactan lies due east from Saigon, and the flight from Mactan to Tan Son Nhut, on the outskirts of Saigon and the hub for South Vietnam operations, is 1,062 nautical miles, about five hours in a C-124. Air controllers in Vietnam direct C-124s into airports for cargo and passenger airlift duties. The leg from Tan Son Nhut to Da Nang 319 NM, north by northeast of Saigon, is two hours. Returning to Mactan from Da Nang is another five-hour flight. That adds up to, counting on-loading and off-loading ground time, to about 16 hours, meaning that our planes must get off from Mactan with not more than two hours after alert or go back into crew rest while a backup is alerted to take our place. Crew rest, not so bad at Tachikawa or Bangkok, is to be avoided here because we had rather fly back to the war zone than spend another fitful, sweaty night, with raucous bleating kids at sunup. Only Magellan had it worse on Mactan—he got killed.

7. "The Right Stuff"   135

When the ops officer calls, the first question an experienced aircraft commander asks is "what is the ETIC?" The estimated time in commission gives at least an idea of our risk. We are all wary of "sliding" ETICs.

Fighting wars has these downsides, as we all understood. But just as parades build morale, wars build camaraderie, and whatever hardship comes along seems bearable if faced along with trusted companions. Indeed, that was the hidden genius in the MATS system of interchangeable crew members, interchangeable C-124s, and universal ground support. By way of contrast, Strategic Support Squadrons in SAC treated C124 crew members as B-52 crews were, that is with a permanent make-up, same aircraft commander, same co-pilot, same navigator, and so on for each crew position. Those who served in both systems thought the transport crew members progressed in airmanship a bit faster because restrictions inherent in the SSS for upgrading often led to delays in promotions. Since each squadron had a set number of crews, a co-pilot could only advance when there was an aircraft commander vacancy and not otherwise. Same was true of navigators stuck without much hope of advancement even in the crew, let alone progressing toward a command position within SAC. Standardization boards, confidential flights (which included every cross-country trip, a clear overreaction to realities), on-board maintenance people on every cross-country and many local flights, inhibited full development of a professional system. The other side of the coin, however, was that officer advancement in SAC was most often tied up with precision results in bombing tests which needed full cooperation of pilots, navs and nav bombs, creating a respect and trust that interchangeable system like MATS sometimes lacked. However, trust between pilots and navs in MATS and their professionalism marked even the young crews of MATS. No shortcuts on safety rules and crew rest hours taken. It is difficult to see how Globemasters could have performed any better than they did, far exceeding what a cold-eyed analyst might predict for it. In fact, a modern sports recruiting rating metaphor might suggest that the C-124 was a two-and-a-half-star airplane that went into battle and came out with five-star results. That was due to the people who operated the machine; their attitudes and their coolness and their professionalism led to exceeding performance expectation. Expect a miracle![10]

On low-level flights in Vietnam, airmen in the Globemaster could clearly see the ground, the vegetation, and the people as the plane crossed their paths. We could see Vietnamese people in boats, in villages, and in fields trying to carry on their lives amidst a civil war. This bird's eye view of grassroot scenes appealed to me, and I wondered what it would be like to change places. Luckily, I couldn't, but those thoughts steered me toward a bucolic life in the Ozarks after the war.

Of course, the Vietnamese people were not much left in peace as American intervention intensified a war already two decades old, bringing deeper gulfs and extreme pain in the populations. LBJ's forecast of an easy time of it in Vietnam did not come to pass. Our "best and brightest" escalated the war, and our soldiers inserted into those grassroots were in extreme pain, too, held together and in some sanity by that camaraderie. Fear created cowardice. Brothers in arms created bravery.

Boats along the Vietnam coastline near Danang, August 1965.

To help relieve pain, the military branches relied on abundant and dirt-cheap legalized drugs: tobacco and alcohol. Not so much on liberty, entertainment, or good food, though there were a few exceptions. Cigarettes and whiskey can serve as both anesthetic and depressant, paradoxically leading to increased frustration. Airlift crews were not exempt from these cycles, just perhaps not as exposed as soldiers, marines, sailors, and fighter pilots. Nerves of all can become frayed by war, and our C-124 crew flew round-trip missions into Pleiku, overnighting at Da Nang. After a few days of short fields, engine-running off-loads, and contested air spaces, we had our duty day extended by base ops to fly six hours on to Kadena AB in Okinawa for crew rest. Anything to get the elephant out of town.

After landing at Kadena, boarding the crew bus (for these, the AF bought thousands of Bluebird school buses and painted them dark blue instead of yellow), passing around a crew bottle on the way in, and obtaining rooms at the BOQ, the exhausted C-124 pilots and nav, still in flight suits, opted for a nightcap at the Officer's Club. At Kadena, the O Club bar seemed to be 40 feet long, and hanging over the middle of it was a brass bell with a long cord attached. Our pilot and co-pilot had already seated themselves and ordered a round of drinks, when the C-124 nav walked in, naturally with his cap on. Instantly, a half-drunk fighter pilot scrambled. He grabbed the cord and began clanging the bell, which sig-

7. "The Right Stuff"

nified that the unfortunate soul who entered this bar room covered (with hat or cap on) would buy drinks for the house. When the nav declined the honor, the fighter pilot decided to enforce the tradition. Conflict approached as insults and threats erupted between fighter pilots and airlift crew. Calm was restored by a third table of airmen, crew members of a B-52, TDY from a SAC base in the United States, men who had spent the day in high-level bombing of targets in Vietnam. These fighter pilots and EWOs were in an F-105 Thunderchief squadron that operated in the skies over Vietnam, giving support and keeping air superiority so that ground troops as well as C-124s and B-52s could carry out their missions. Perhaps the background to the near-brawl was that all the airmen in that Kadena O Club bar realized, at some level, the mismatch of their airplanes to carry out their assigned aerial tasks insofar as winning the war was concerned. The F-105, built by Republic, was huge with a big engine that consumed kerosene like there was no tomorrow. The Thud, as it was nicknamed, was mostly a flying fuel tank able to break the sound barrier at straightaway speed but without sharp turning and rapid climbing capabilities needed in dogfights with the MiGs. Moreover, the Thud—a cynic said so-nicknamed because that was the sound it made when it hit the ground—had overly sensitive warning lights that burst on when a bullet struck the skin of the aircraft. The procedure when a fire warning light came on in the cockpit was pilot ejection. F-105s were lost thusly when barely damaged.

The B-52, nicknamed the Buff, was meant to carry nuclear bombs to Russia, covering vast distances with air refueling, precisely navigated, and equipped with counter-measure electronics and a nav to operate them for getting through air defense systems. Dropping TNT bombs over jungles probably never entered the mind of its Boeing designers. While some B-52 crew members might have preferred duty in southeast Asia to sitting in alert shacks waiting for a scramble that never comes, it still in retrospect seemed like a job for which the B-52 airplane and its crews were out of their element. In addition, a B-52 had just been lost in a mid-air collision with its KC-135 tanker.[11]

Slamming a C-124 into forward strips in a combat zone, utilizing short field landing techniques that included sharp approaches, late flare, hard landings, and immediate full throttle prop reverse in an aircraft weighing 180,000 pounds, might have been exhilarating at the time for crew members and awed, beleaguered G.I.s watching from outposts and bunkers, but certainly these maneuvers exceeded the design concept of the Globemaster and stressed the airplane.

So, at Kadena on one night, frustrations almost erupted into fist fights between the airmen of vastly different callings, training and recent assignments. Fortunately for the quieting down of that night, there were no swings on the C-124 aircraft commander, a Finnish-American who stood 6'2" and weighed 220 pounds. No gang fight. The navigator finally forked up the 12 bucks or so to buy a round of drinks for the house, songs were sung, and the detente, no doubt, helped everybody at the bar perform unimpaired in the next day's missions. War builds camaraderie.[12]

More such good feeling between airlift crews occurred in the Dominican Republic, near war three years after the Cuban missile crisis. Coincidental with the build-up in Vietnam was this other crisis, a two-hour flight from home. Bases over the United States were put on Defcon five alert, and there was a flash deployment of 82nd Airborne troops from Pope AB, embedded at Fort Bragg, North Carolina, into San Isrido Airport, Dominican Republic. The feeling among the crews deploying on out-and-back shuttles between Pope and Ramey and San Isrido was as macho as it gets because, perhaps, of the wearing of sidearms in quarters and even to the mess halls. The crisis wound down quickly, however, and the full attention of combat airlift turned again to southeast Asia.

Carrying out this task were the rated officers who flew the line, an adventurous, meaningful, and sometimes harrowing life. Plenty of work, and a few sacrifices, but with the energy of youth that matters little. Each officer thought of his future in the service. Going to flight school as a navigator meant a five-year commitment, the same as for pilot school. All aircraft commanders were pilots, not navs, and the same was true for squadron commanders, wing commanders, and base commanders. A few navs reached command and staff school, and some found a path to promotion in administration of non-flying areas or in navigator specialties. But pilots ran the Air Force. A nav, of course, could apply for pilot school, and as the war in Southeast Asia ballooned, more were accepted into that career-fostering channel.

Conversations among navigators turned to such choices after being a TN (transport navigator, AFSC 1545). Bright young men in this AFSC felt stymied in the Air Force and could see that major trans-oceanic airlines used jet carriers, thus dissolving the nav position on civilian crews (Qantas was the last to do so). So of all the crew positions, that one with the oldest tradition in overwater travel would be the first to go in the modern world.

That being the rule, there were exceptions. One, James Harry Bassham, started his career in the Air Force after being named a distinguished graduate of AFROTC at the University of Arkansas. Bassham

7. "The Right Stuff" 139

could not have been raised further from sailboats (and the navigation instincts that endeavor develops), being the son of a grocer in Mountainburg, Arkansas. Bassham was assigned for nav training at James Connally AFB and from there went to Mather, where he led the class in navigator-bombardier training and chose B-52s as his operational assignment at Blytheville AFB (later to be renamed Eaker AFB) in northeast Arkansas. Home on leave en route before reporting to his new station, Bassham heard the breaking news of the 1962 Cuban missile crisis. Newspapers blazed with headlines that the world was on the edge of nuclear war. An alarmed Bassham called his squadron commander at Blytheville, whom he had not yet met, and asked if he should break off his leave and report immediately for this serious military threat. The squadron commander

```
                    7TH AIR TRANSPORT SQUADRON, HEAVY
                    62D AIR TRANSPORT WING (HEAVY) (MATS)
                           United States Air Force
                      McChord Air Force Base, Washington 98438

FLIGHT ORDER
447                                                            30 April 1965

     The following named crew members, this unit, unless otherwise indicated will
proceed on or about  1 May 65   in C-124 Aircraft from McChord AFB, Wash to
"CLASSIFIED"            to perform an airlift mission and upon completion
will return to proper station on or about   1 Jun 65          . Variations
in itinerary authorized.  Personnel have Security Clearance of Secret unless
otherwise indicated.  62D Fragmentary Order Nr        . Trip Identification
Nr                  .  Mission symbol Log          .

                                     CREW      INST                 TIME  REM
          GRADE, NAME, AFSN         POS  QUAL   RAT     PHONE       MON   QTR

  *$CAPT      GUSTAVUS M SUPE JR 50275A    AC    AC    1   JU43722   125   214
   1STLT      HAVEN S HILL 62621A          CP    1STP  2   JU84597   125   157
   1STLT      BILLY D HIGGINS 74706A       NAV   NAV       LE15859   125   236
  **SSGT      ROBERT G PACHKOFSKY AF19487965 FET INST      GR28061   125   199
    SSGT      JOHN J NICOLE AF16478817     FET   FET       LE75275   125   166
   $SSGT      ROSCOE BOOZER AF16386762     LM    INST      EXT2084   125   244

  *  In command of aircraft and crew
  ** NCOIC of airmen while on this mission
  $  TOP SECRET Clearance

FOR THE COMMANDER

/signature/
HAROLD J HUSTEN                               DISTRIBUTION
Major, USAF                                   A
Crew Control Officer
```

Above and following page: Navigator record of flight mission to Dominican Republic in May 1965.

```
                                          Local
DEPT  McCHORD          30 APR    1450        2+10 APRIL
ARR   MYRTLE BEACH      1 MAY    0450        9+50 MAY
DEPT                    2 MAY    1420
ARR   RAMEY AFB, P.R.   2 MAY    2140        6+20      16+30
DEPT                    3 MAY    0030
ARR   SAN ISIDRO AB     3 MAY    0040        1+10      17+40
      DOMINICAN REPUBLIC
DEPT                    3 MAY    0105
ARR   HUNTER            3 MAY    0725        6+20      24+00
DEPT                    4 MAY    0045
ARR   POPE AFB          4 MAY    0235        1+50
DEPT                    4 MAY    0630
ARR   HUNTER            4 MAY    1130        5+00      30+50
DEPT                    5 MAY    0500        1+40      32+30
ARR   POPE              5 MAY    0640
DEPT                    5 MAY    0900        6+30      39+00
ARR   SAN ISIDRO        5 MAY    1530
DEPT                     "       1540        1+10      40+10
ARR   RAMEY              "       1750
DEPT                    7 MAY    0205
ARR   SAN ISIDRO         "       0225        1+20      41+10
DEPT                             0500
ARR   HUNTER                     1050        5+50      47+00
DEPT                   11 MAY    0400
ARR   McCHORD            "       1430       12+30      59+30
```

may have suppressed a smile as he replied, "No, don't do that, Lt. Bassham. We'll just manage to hold on until you finish the leave."

This kind of dedication to country and duty would manifest itself over and over for Bassham, who after years on the Buff at Blytheville, took a short break in service, landing a position with Kimberly-Clark in Memphis. Then he joined the 164th Airlift Wing, Tennessee Air National Guard. He entered this unit at the same time a squadron of C-124s arrived there from active duty units. So Bassham was able to take his navigation and leadership skills to the Globemaster and the Guard wing that flew them. He was first named chief navigation officer and then squadron commander. Promoted to full colonel, Bassham became commander of the wing, and then, as a general, commander of the Tennessee Air National Guard, headquartered in Nashville. He retired as a major general. The Air Force and the Air National Guard in some instances opened command of flying units to navigators.

8

"Fate Is the Hunter"
Mountains and Thunderstorms

A C-124C lifted off from Cannon AFB, near Clovis, New Mexico, on May 9, 1964, flight-planned non-stop 1,447 nautical miles to its home station, Dover AFB, a preflight en route time of seven hours 35 minutes. It never got there. Witnesses described the crash of MATS 52–1008 as spectacular, occurring in a "violent rain and hail storm," the looming of which had sent residents of Cooperton, a small southwest Oklahoma farming community, scurrying toward their storm cellars.[1] Forty-six years after the crash that killed six men from my squadron at Dover, I visited the site where the C-124 hit the ground. I wanted to see if anyone around there remembered it.

On Monday July 12, 2010, my wife Peggy and I drove through Hobart, Oklahoma. I visited the sheriff's office, and the dispatcher told me that Sheriff Leon Messick, mentioned in newspaper reports as a first responder in the articles, was dead, as was Don R. Gish, the funeral director who received the bodies from the crash site. The funeral home had been sold and turned into a Bread and Breakfast establishment. On the town square, we saw a sign pointing to the Tommy Franks museum. Oklahoma-born Franks, who was commander of the Afghanistan Theater following September 11, 2001, has retired in the area and built a museum in Hobart.

We drove on toward Cooperton, passing through Roosevelt, a small town consisting of a convenience store/gas station and a winery named after TR following his visit to the Wichita Mountains early in the 20th century. From there, Peggy and I drove on Oklahoma state highway 19 toward Cooperton, population 20 in the 2000 census, and turned onto a dirt street toward a small cluster of houses. We saw one man getting out of an ancient pickup and going inside a house that struck me like the one

Turbulence and Thunderstorms

Image from C-124C Dash 1.

in *To Kill a Mockingbird* that Boo Radley lived in. Peggy said, "Be careful."

I knocked on the door, and an older man looked at me through the screen, which was torn. He had on overalls with a strap over one shoulder. Me: "I am looking into an airplane crash that happened 46 years ago. He: "I have tie down chains from it. Go back a mile to a cobblestone house. That's Allen Moore. It was in his field." I thanked him and followed his directions. Allen Moore had been mentioned as an eyewitness in the *Daily Oklahoman* article reporting the incident.

We found Moore's mailbox and turned into a driveway that wound to the back of the house. I stopped in the shade of a tree and got out. A tall, broad-shouldered man about my age or more stepped out of the back door onto the patio and said hello. He said that if I were selling anything, I could get back in the car. I got past that—a greeting for which he later apologized—and at his invitation beckoned to Peggy to join me on the patio. Allen Moore called his wife out to sit with us, and I told him what I had come for. Before he launched into the story, he mentioned that he made cedar chests and rocking horses in his shop.

Getting around to the subject of my visit, Moore described the evening of the crash. A huge thunderstorm had rolled in, so threatening that he had taken his six young step-daughters to the storm cellar in the backyard, just a few feet from where we were sitting in a swing. This ferocious storm brought large hailstones, and Moore was worried about the damage to his wheat crop even though he had it insured. Losing a crop meant a rough year financially since that was what he depended on for a living. He had 40 acres in wheat and more acres in alfalfa.

As he tried to get his step-daughters down the steps, the wind roared, and he started pushing them. He and the last girl on the stairs happened to look back amidst all the ado, and the sky turned orange. Moore thought he was seeing a tornado, but later believed it was the airplane explosion that he saw.

8. "Fate Is the Hunter"

Within 15 minutes, the storm passed, and then the telephone started ringing. People who lived four or five miles away knew something out of the ordinary had happened and were trying to find out what it was. Moore and some of his step-daughters piled into the truck and drove northwest, where wreckage was aflame in his wheat field. He was amazed by the many colors in the fire. He reflected later that the magnesium and the aluminum were responsible for such a display. People began to converge, and Moore took his family home.

The Air Force came the next day, commandeered Moore's wheat field, and kept it for 24 days. They placed an armed guard on the perimeter, brought in heavy equipment, and laid a steel mesh flooring for their vehicles to get over. The investigation team hauled away the major pieces of the plane left from the fiery crash.

Rick Parr, twelve-year-old witness, reported that he was standing on the porch of a house five miles from Moore's field with his uncle when they saw two bright orange balls coming three or four seconds apart and heard an awesome boom. Later, after the military had left, Parr walked over the field and remembered seeing big holes filled with water and oil where the big Pratt and Whitney's had hit the ground.[2] Moore said they compensated him for damages to his field, but he went a long time without hearing from the government, and the check did not arrive in a timely fashion. In the meantime, Moore was strapped for cash, having lost his crop. Desperate, Moore found a number, called the Pentagon, and connected with an Air Force officer who happened to be from Wichita Falls and had some sympathy for the predicament. The major traced the claim and got the $1,900 settlement sent right away when Moore told him he was about to starve out over this.

Moore said that he had saved a pair of wing-tips with the shoe trees intact that he had found in his field. He and others in neighboring properties picked up items from the C-124 like the tie down chains that the mid-air explosion had scattered about over a wide area. He showed me a cinching tool used to tighten the chains on loads in the plane. He had taken crash artifacts that he had accumulated to Altus AFB to return them. The officer on base with whom he spoke was incredulous that he would do this and told Moore that the Air Force had gotten all they wanted from the site, and anything else that he found was his to keep or sell. Moore kept the wing-tips for 20 years, thinking that one day a relative of one of the airmen who perished in the crash might come there. He planned to give them the shoes. No one ever came.

Allen Moore went to college when in his 40s. He became a carpentry instructor at a community college. In later years, he went blind but figured out a system by which he could still do his woodworking, even operating a table saw and a band saw. While in school pursuing a Master's degree, he had given some documents and papers to Western Oklahoma College on the subject of the crash. He suggested that I see them. Peggy wanted to buy a rocking horse from him. We have it, a memento of that conversation and a reminder for us of six 31st Air Transport Squadron airmen lost that day in May 1964: pilot and aircraft commander 1st Lt. Monte Patrick Williams, 27, of Hondo, Texas; co-pilot 1st Lt. Jerry Don Bateman, 25, Olney, Illinois; navigator 2nd Lt. Vernon Keith Brandenburg, 22, Woodbury, New Jersey; flight engineer Tech Sgt. John J. Norstrom, 40, Minneapolis, Minnesota.; flight engineer Staff Sgt. Richard Tkatch, 32, Upland, California; loadmaster A1C Jackie White, 24, Ridgeville, South Carolina. All except for Williams and Brandenburg were married. A memorial service was held on Wednesday, May 13, 1964, at Dover AFB. The airplane had an excellent maintenance record. The plane was flying at 9,000 feet through a severe thunderstorm when contact was lost. The official cause of the accident was weather.

Pilots of low-flying airplanes are taught to be aware of and avoid cumulonimbus clouds that can top off in an anvil shape at altitudes of 50,000 feet or higher. The downdrafts and updrafts within can destroy an airplane, even a huge one like the Globemaster, as surely as contact with a mountain will. Ground radar and on-board APS 42 radar at the nav station can depict these dangerous formations, and flight directions for avoidance can be issued. But a possibility remains: that there is no safe way to turn. Pilot/author Bob Buck, in *North Star Over My Shoulder*, wrote that thunderstorms were aviation's last barrier, and even with sophisticated systems, airplanes always must bow to this awesome power.[3]

The trouble, as any Globemaster pilot and nav can attest, comes from the speed with which these formations can occur and spawn new cells. In most instances, the airplane can find a soft enough spot to fly through, although even that can mean rough air. Some crew members have had the experience of suddenly being tossed, rudely and suddenly, to the 13-foot-high cabin ceiling because the plane flew into a cell.[4]

From some spiritual rather than secular motivation, it would seem, many maintenance men professed in later years to have loved the C-124 and working on it. The Globemaster, with its thousands of moving parts, miles of wiring, shelves of black boxes, and long hours in the air, required a lot of attention, so maybe that was why. Avionics, hydraulic systems, engines, tires, landing gear and flight controls, all needed the knowing

8. "Fate Is the Hunter"

eye of mechanics and technicians who could adjust or supervise a change-out of equipment. In the Vietnam War and along its airlift supply routes, maintenance men found few if any days off and worked diligently, sometimes around the clock, using flashlight or vehicle headlights at night and improvising to "keep 'em flying." Aircrews, who were often punishing their planes with the missions, praised these men to the heavens, thankful of the competence and the dedication of aircraft maintenance crews.[5]

Black boxes on the blink in the crew compartment were sometimes treated in-flight with "brogan adjusts," that is a quick kick from nav or engineer. Surprisingly, that remedied some illnesses, and the needle responded again, or the blip moved, or the static disappeared. When changes had to be made at the way stations, replacement parts often were rebuilt in base shops. The C-124 had a huge appetite for liquids: oil, gasoline, hydraulic fluids, ADI mixture, water, coffee. An item on the engineer takeoff check list was "Quantities checked."

While, naturally, most of the maintenance took place on the ground, flight engineers and flight mechanics, or navs for that matter, could access the engines of a C-124 in-flight through the wing tunnel. The common repair aloft through the wing tunnel was padding a burnt-out generator to prevent a fire, but a Dover AFB mechanic related a story that might have been more typical of the Globemaster than of any other airplane. This mechanic wrote that he and 100 other maintenance guys were returning home aboard a C-124 from a TDY tour to Vietnam and were happy to be at the end of a long leg from Hickam to Carswell AFB, Texas. As landing approached, the left main gear stuck in the

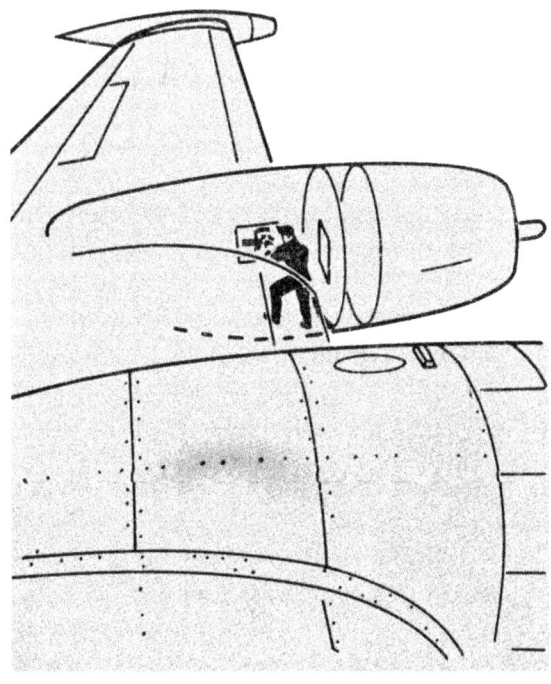

Dash 1 manual showing a flight engineer restoring service to an engine component while in flight.

up position. Unable to lower the main gear, the pilot declared an emergency. With fire trucks screaming to the rescue, ready to foam the runway, the situation looked grim. The mechanic "crawled out through the wing and got behind #2 engine, wrapped his legs around a spar, and used a screwdriver to pry the up lock to the center position." The gear then lowered and locked. The landing was smooth, and afterward the grateful crew treated the mechanic to a steak dinner and many "cold beverages" at the O-club.[6]

On at least one occasion, however, a C-124 pilot landed his plane with gear up, a belly landing. It happened sometimes with bombers in World War II, but they, four-engine of course, were nevertheless much smaller that the C-124. Aircraft Commander Jack Wofford successfully landed a SAC Strategic Support Squadron C-124 with gear up in 1956, coming into Mount Hope RCAF base near Hamilton, Ontario. En route from Columbus, Ohio, to Harmon AB, Newfoundland, with 96 souls aboard, copious fuel leakage out of two engines necessitated their shutdown. Heavy with no cargo to jettison, the Globemaster could not keep altitude. As Wofford said, "We were coming down somewhere." Nearby Mount Hope could serve as an emergency airport, but on final, the main gear would not free, remaining up and locked. Powered only by two engines, a missed approach and go-around procedure was impossible. Wofford made the decision to retract the nose gear and belly land. With Yeager–like, self-effacing humor, Wofford remembered it being a smoother landing that some he made with wheels down.[7] Fortunately, spark showers when the propellers hit the runway did not ignite any of the leaking fuel. Passengers and some of the 16 crew members exited through the troop doors in the rear of the fuselage, while pilots, the nav, and the flight engineers in the cockpit went out the observation hatch on top of the crew compartment, using the knotted escape rope to lower themselves to the ground. No one was injured. A few weeks later, a maintenance team showed up and mended the plane well enough to fly it out of Mount Hope and back to its home base in California. After further repairs, this hardy Globemaster returned to the flight line.[8]

Wofford's station, Castle AFB, in California, was a SAC base with a Strategic Support Squadron of 16 C-124s. There were SS squadrons at four SAC bases located in the United States. They were for logistic support of General Curt LeMay's Strategic Force. That meant the air transport of nuclear weapons, the size and configuration of such demanding a cargo capacity of the Globemaster. Jack Wofford went directly from Vance AFB and advanced pilot training into this transport wing of SAC.

8. "Fate Is the Hunter"

Jack Wofford of Sallisaw, Oklahoma, who crash landed a C-124 with 96 people aboard. Photograph taken in February 2014.

One of the C-124s that spent its career as a Strategic Support airlifter was on display at Offutt AFB, Nebraska, SAC headquarters until it was transferred to the Air Mobility Command Museum at Dover AFB, Delaware. These SAC Globemasters had their own special paint jobs and identifying markers. With 14 percent of the fleet, with special cargoes, and with a world-wide mission, it is little wonder that these C-124s would have experiences of odd or dangerous flights, witness:

> In Nov. of 1952 we flew in a C-124 from Travis AFB to Hickam AFB. The C-124 was stationed at Castle AFB. Going over was fine. Coming back # 2 caught on fire. The pilot turned the CO2 rings on. Cowling flew off and was hitting the tail. He kept dropping lower and lower. The bell rang, and we started putting on parachutes. We had a jeep, a big air compressor, and a B-36 (R-4360) engine on board plus about 100 tool boxes—the order was if the pilot gave the word, the tool boxes went first, the air compressor went second, the jeep (mine) went third. All of us would go next. We were 1500 miles out from Hickam AFB. No turning back. The C-124 kept dropping while those three old R-4360s were churning hard. #2 was feathered. We could see the white caps on the waves of the Pacific. Lucky for us the fire went out—the ice stopped coming off and hitting the tail, we landed safely at Travis only 45 minutes late. Prayers must a done it as all 100 of us were praying.[9]

Other flight mechanics, maintenance force, and crew members reminisce about fouling spark plugs and rattling rivets during engine run-ups, the number of times landing with three or even two engines in operation, or removing faulty generators in flight.

Some mishaps were almost fictional in character. Once I was aboard a Globemaster in a three-ship trail formation over the Kentucky countryside, with each plane carrying 60 paratroopers from the 101st Airborne headed to the jump zone, when a single-engine civilian airplane flew right through the formation, apparently without ever seeing the giants bearing down on it. Lucky. Not so lucky was an Arkansas pilot and his two passengers, who were killed instantly by a mid-air collision with Globemaster 52–942 in overcast conditions near Wagner, Oklahoma, on Sunday, November 7, 1965.[10] The C-124 was on a navigational flight to Birmingham, Alabama, flying at 9,000 feet, when the accident occurred. The Cessna wreckage lodged between the #3 and #4 engines on the starboard wing of the C-124. Incredibly, Captain Willis Beasley, the aircraft commander, with three engines operating flew 21 miles to Tulsa International Airport, landing the severely damaged plane safely. None of the Globemaster crew were injured.[11]

An experienced maintenance team was sent to Tulsa to change out the two engines and repair the leading edge and wing surface so that the Globemaster could be flown back to Hill AFB, Utah, its home base. One of those sergeants, John Hille, described to me the grisly remains found in the engine cowling and the blood stains on the fuselage left from the unfortunate occupants of the Cessna. Overcoming this revulsion, Hille and these maintenance pros put the C-124 back into shape, refitting the damaged engines and props where the Cessna had impacted and smoothing out the leading edges of the wing. With no small trepidation, these men boarded the Globemaster, and a Hill crew taxied it out for takeoff to return home. As Hille put it, "that entire episode was one that I would rather not have had to do, but also one that will be with me forever. We all, including the crew that came down to recover the aircraft, certainly had reservations about taking it for the first test flight and the return trip back to Hill, but the ol' bird held true to form and flew loud and proud back to Hill with the old engines and props in the back."[12]

That flight happened without incident, but in a tragic irony, four crew members who had stayed for the accident investigation were aboard a United Air Lines Boeing 727 returning to Hill when it descended too sharply and crashed on landing at Salt Lake City Airport. The two C-124 flight engineers and loadmaster were killed in the ensuing fire that engulfed the plane. There were 48 survivors of the crash including the C-124 navigator, 25-year-old, 1st Lt. John J. Sullivan.[13]

Remarkably, Globemaster 52–942 had a few more years of service, staying on active duty until November 25, 1969, when it was sent to the boneyard at Davis-Monthan AFB in Tucson, Arizona. So did Lt. Sullivan, who had a successful career in the air, afterward noting that "I went on to pilot training and had no bad events compared to the four days in November 1965."[14]

In his book *Douglas Jumbo's, The Globemaster* author Anthony J. Tambini, working from accident reports held at the Air University archives at Maxwell AFB, documented 36 Class A mishaps that occurred between March 1956 and May 1972. Class A mishap designates aircraft accidents that resulted in deaths of crew or passengers and/or the aircraft was destroyed or too badly damaged to be fixed. Twenty-five had loss of life. Mr. Tambini's fact-filled and useful book, however, does not include C-124 crashes that occurred before 1956, some of which were unusual in the annals of aviation history.[15]

A trans–Atlantic flight at the onset of the Cold War that ended in a deep mystery is a case example. On March 22, 1951, Strategic Support Squadron C-124 tail number 49-0244 departed Walker AFB, Roswell,

Number four engine damaged by the Globemaster-Cessna mid-air collision near Tulsa in 1965 (courtesy John Hille).

Hill AFB C-124 crew involved in mishap over Tulsa (1965): (*left to right*) Captain Beasley, co-pilot, Lt. John J. Sullivan, nav, FE, FE, LM (courtesy John Hille).

New Mexico, with a special group of passengers: pilots, bombardiers, and weapons specialists from SAC's 509 Bomb Group. After a landing at Barksdale AFB, Louisiana, the C-124 loadmaster added a distinguished name to the flight manifest, that of Brig. Gen. Paul Thomas Cullen, who was accompanied by several of his staff. This 50-man team of strategic bomb experts were on a mission to start up the 7th Air Division, a SAC unit that would spearhead strategic defense of Europe, i.e., provide a nuclear shield by basing SAC bombers in Britain. Cullen, and the men with him, had this kind of background expertise and consequently were chosen for such an important task.

After a refueling stop in Limestone AFB, Maine, the C-124 navigator most likely plotted a rhomb line route to Lakenheath RAF Station, UK, a distance of 2,963 nautical miles. The last message received by Aeradio Shannon, the air control center, was at 0106 GMT, giving a revised ETA. Shortly thereafter, a reported inflight explosion and fire occurred. The aircraft commander ditched the Globemaster in the Irish Sea. Evidently, the plane hit the water without breaking up, and persons exited safely into

8. "Fate Is the Hunter" 151

rubber rafts equipped with flares and Gibson Girl, hand-cranked emergency radios carried on the C-124. A RAF B-29 saw flares, circled the scene, and reported seeing rafts and receiving a voice from a radio that all were safe. Low fuel caused the B-29 pilot to return to base after radioing the coordinates of the survivors. No other signals were received, and it took rescue vessels 19 hours to reach the site of the ditching some 450 miles west of the Irish coast. By that time all had disappeared except for a torn, empty raft and inside it a burned briefcase. A massive air-sea search coordinated by the USS *Coral Sea* aircraft carrier extended over thousands of square miles but spotted not one other scrap of evidence.

Even though the sea was rough, it is hard to imagine that all the rafts would have been taken under or otherwise lost in less than a day. So what happened to them? One source stated: "Intelligence released in the decades that followed suggests there was some serious Soviet submarine activity in that area and speculated that Cullen and the other survivors were captured and taken to the Soviet Union ... a great mystery of the Cold War."[16] Sweden's 1953 official estimate of 72 Russian ocean-going submarines operating in Arctic and Baltic waters, with a range that would enable them a round-trip to New York without refueling, shows that the means to carry out the kidnapping of a down crew existed.[17]

Another C-124A disappeared 20 months later with all 52 people aboard lost. MATS serial number 52-107 from McChord AFB, Washington, with an 11-man crew and 41 passengers, was en route to Elmendorf AFB, Alaska, encountered heavy cloud cover, and commenced navigation by radio beacon and stopwatch. The plane struck 9,100-foot Mt. Gannet 45 miles east of Anchorage. Before the crash, a pilot of a commercial airliner in the area received a weak radio signal and heard a voice say, "As long as we have to land, we might as well land here." Nothing was heard beyond that. Although 32 search airplanes were in the air and with possible sightings of wreckage, not until November 28, 1952, did Thomas Sullivan and Terris Moore, experienced Alaska pilots, confirm what everyone had feared. After spotting the tail section, Sullivan and Moore landed on the ice, where they surveyed a grim scene. Moore was the president of Alaska University and included his remembrances of that day in the book, *College Hills Chronicles*. With location confirmed, search and rescue teams mounted efforts and established a base camp partway up the mountain, but the C-124 remained out of reach. Soon, heavy snowstorms and an avalanche buried the giant plane. Glaciers are defined as rivers of moving ice, and the glacier churned and slowly moved the wreckage to a new location. On June 10, 2012, a Blackhawk helicopter crew of the Alaska

National Guard flying a training mission saw signs of a downed airplane near the tip of Colony Glacier, 12 miles from the crash site. An eight-man military casualty search team from the POW/MIA Command got to the high mountain site this time but found only scant remains of humans who died in the crash.[18]

These disappearances, as well as two very deadly accidents, occurred during the Korean War era when the Globemaster was relatively up-to-date. In December 1952, afforded a goodwill gesture by the Air Force nicknamed "Operation Sleighride," airmen and servicemen with a mind to being home for Christmas boarded MATS 20-107 at Larson AFB near Moses Lake in the potholes area of central Washington, bound for Kelley AFB, Texas. Shortly after a 6:30 a.m. lift-off, the Globemaster slammed into the ground with 117 people on board. The crash and fire afterwards left 87 dead. Thirty people survived. The official accident report blamed locked elevator flaps specifically for the loss of control that had the left wing impacting the ground, causing a cartwheeling of the giant plane. At the time, it was the largest number of people killed in an airplane crash. That record was surpassed six months later on June 18, 1953, when C-124 tail number 50-137 went down just after takeoff from Tachikawa AB in Japan. The seven crew members and 122 passengers aboard, Korean War veterans returning home after their tour of duty, perished, making this the reigning deadliest single-plane aviation catastrophe until the jet liner age arrived and an Air France Boeing 707 crashed in 1962, killing 130 people.

With these incidents highlighting a list of 34 fatal crashes involving the Globemaster, one might reasonably argue that it was a dangerous airplane to fly. Appendix A lists each of the C-124s lost to accidents, mechanical malfunctions, navigator and pilot error, and weather-related causes. Moreover, as in the belly landing and mid-air collision accidents described above, several badly damaged C-124s, like others, recovered with patient repair work by dedicated maintenance men and returned to active flying duty. If nothing else, the C-124 proved itself surprisingly resilient. Accidents per 100,000 hours flown is an appropriate measurement of an aircraft's design and reliability and is computed by the military. In 2000, the rate for all military aircraft was 1.23 deaths per 100,000 miles. In the C-124s first 12 operational years, the plane's crews logged an estimated 2,000,000 flying hours. During that time, 522 crew and passengers were killed because of accidents, which comes to a fatal accident rate of 27 per 100,000 hours. In the operational life of the C-124, 1949–1974, 589 people were killed in crashes, including 222 crew members.[19]

Sixty-four class A mishaps out of 447 planes built by Douglas Aircraft

8. "Fate Is the Hunter"

Company and operated by the Air Force in one of the major commands meant that 15 percent of the fleet was destroyed either by crew error, adverse weather conditions, mechanical or structural failure, or mid-air collision.[20] Acting on operational and accident reports, Douglas made modifications to the systems and structures. At times, the Air Force would act. MATS in 1965, following the investigation of a fatal mishap which had revealed cracks in the wing spars of the involved airplane, grounded a portion of the C-124 fleet to make inspections. Some 40 Globemasters were documented with wing spar cracks, and restrictions were placed on operational use of these and the 160 others in MATS.[21] Globemaster crews, already accustomed to 185 knots top airspeed and gross takeoff weights of less than 180,000 pounds, did not see much difference with these 1965 restrictions as the Vietnam build-up began and with it a considerable increase in hours on the air frame. C-124 aircrew members often achieved their maximum of 330 flying hours per quarter and sometimes had authorization to exceed that heretofore strict limit.

Wear and tear on the air frame—in 1965 the newest C-124 had 12 years of service—pushed design capabilities to the limits, including the stated service life of the plane. Metal fatigue is mostly related to takeoff and landings, but any C-124 crew member can remember while in flight watching the wings of the plane flexing up and down, especially with the C models and the heavy heater pods at the very end of a 65-foot wing span, a bird-like flapping that had a sort of regal air to it. The wing tip on the C-124's moderately thick wing was designed to withstand deflection of up to 84 inches (seven feet) during flight. In static tests, a tip deflection of 100 inches (over eight feet) resulted in a broken wing.[22] All that flapping, the long hours in the air, the tossing created by weather, heavy cargos, violent short field landings, and lurching involved with para-drops from the elevator bay together exerted constant pressure on C-124 air frames and aircrews. If there is an irony or a surprise here, it is how well both stood up to this kind of dire use. Donald Douglas said of the Skyraider in 1944 to his protégé, engineer Ed Heinemann, that "Navy planes take a beating. They slam down on carriers and if we want them to buy our planes, we must build them rugged. They have to take punishment and still work."[23] Though the words were inspired by a different airplane, the same company philosophy applied to the C-124. It took the punishment and still worked.

Nevertheless, the condition of the metal caused concerns at headquarters, in the maintenance sheds, and among the flyers of the Globemaster. A McChord C-124 en route from Elemendorf to Sheyma Island Air Station in November 1965 had its number one engine wrenched off the airplane, probably because a prop blade broke, which in turn unbalanced the engine. With the sudden emergency, the aircrew reacted heroically, keeping the airplane aloft by jettisoning 26,000 pounds of cargo, an effort that took 20 minutes. During that time, the airplane lost almost 6,000 feet of altitude, stabilizing at 2,700 feet with max power on the three remaining engines. An emergency landing was made at Adak Naval Air Station. The mishap damaged the aircraft beyond repair, but the crew was unharmed.[24] Lasting on active duty until 1974 when enough C-141s, C-135s, and the C-5 could be delivered in a time of huge increases in the need for airlift and air mobility (and airlift budgets), the C-124, like the Eveready battery bunny, just kept on going, all the surviving fleet having 20-plus years of operational duty.

Even with exposure to enemy fire in combat zones during the Vietnam War, no Globemaster II, unlike its peer airlifters, was ever lost in that way. The documented targeting with gunfire of a C-124 in the Congo Airlift is one of the few such incidents ever recorded.

9

"Sorry 'bout that"
Korea and Vietnam

On November 20, 1953, in northern Vietnam eight miles from the Laotian border, 65 C-47 and C-119 aircraft of the French Air Force dropped two elite airborne battalions numbering 1,220 paratroopers. The planes, provided by the United States for our NATO ally, had taken off from Hanoi's Bach-Mai airport and flown 200 miles west to the drop zone approaches. This vanguard force of France's best troops in Indochina overcame light resistance from the small units of Communist Viet-Minh soldiers in the valley of the Nam Yum River. The French Indochina Army Command planned to place a string of "strong points" in this river valley around the provincial capital, Dien Bien Phu. The fully detailed and well-written account of the results of that decision can be found in Bernard Fall's book, *Hell in a Very Small Place*.[1] French strategy was to entice the Viet-Minh to attack the stronghold, as surely they would since it was in the middle of their territory. The French were correct in this judgment; it was an enticing target. Over the next three months, the Viet-Minh used "coolie" labor, carrying packs on their backs and on bicycles, to transport thousands of tons of material over a 600-mile distance from the Chinese border to support 50,000 Viet-Minh troops who were setting up around Dien Bien Phu.

Vietnam, the larger part of Indochina, had been a French colony since 1884. The Vichy government of France during World War II had condoned Japanese Imperial Army occupation of northern Vietnam in 1940 to prevent American supplies from reaching Chiang Kai-Shek's Chinese forces, with whom Japan was at war, through the port of Haiphong. Japanese invaders did encounter resistance on the ground, initially from Free French loyalists and throughout the interior by indigenous Communist forces, but Japan secured Indochina, replacing French hegemony with its own.

With Japan's surrender in September 1945 came withdrawal of its occupation forces, but struggle continued in Indochina as the French sought to re-colonize the land. France regarded Indochina as a key colony in their overseas empire, and indeed rubber and rice production from Vietnam had meant enormous profits for France prior to World War II. The postwar French government was ready to exert full diplomatic leverage and military force to regain the jewel.[2] Hanoi was in French hands by 1947, but the Viet Minh, while losing control of cities, remained popular and strong in the countryside, especially in the north. To restore profits in rubber and rice, French colonial officers set up large-scale plantations, re-directing hundreds of thousands of subsistence farmers into a new existence as plantation laborers. These once-independent farmers were integral parts of the village life in Vietnam.

Rocker patches popular in Vietnam.

Given a quantum change in circumstances, the loyalty of the countryside to the Communists might be understood as poor labor versus bad management. Merging this dissatisfaction in the countryside with guerrilla warfare methods of disruptive tactics and ambush attacks, the Communists peppered away, undermining post-war French colonial control of Indochina, a European term for the Southeast Asian peninsula which was and is occupied by three primary cultures and historic governments: Vietnam, Laos, and Cambodia. Within each of these countries are distinct ethnic, linguistic, and cultural minorities, including the T'ai tribal people of the Dien Bien Phu district. Often the French were able to recruit soldiers and loyalties from these groups, since minorities had the typical resentments toward majority people ruling the country. The French and the Americans after them would play on these resentments to make alliances. But the Communists in Vietnam won in rural areas where rice farming predominated, and the Viet-Minh turned village populations away from supporting the Saigon-based Diem government, which it portrayed as a colonial lackey of the French and Americans, the "aliens." Except in heavily Roman Catholic districts, grassroots backing for any Saigon government was difficult to muster if not, in the long run, impossible.[3]

Northern Vietnam borders China, where a civil war between Communist and Nationalists (Kuomintang) was placed on hold during the Sino-Chinese War and resumed with fury after Japan surrendered. The Communists won here, too, and the Chinese People's Republic came into being, a turn of events viewed with alarm by the United States but not with enough alarm to prompt intervention. A decision not to use an atomic bomb in 1949 against the Communist Chinese was, according to the John Birch Society, a shadowy, ultra-right-wing organization active at the time, a failure of will.

Failure of will or not, the United States had done enough for Chiang Kai-shek to insure lasting enmity from Mao Zedong, Red China's leader and mortal enemy of Chiang. Mao's government allied with the Soviet Union, adding to the seriousness of the Cold War. Reaching out, the Beijing government nurtured its relationships with North Korea and with the Viet-Minh, affording military training and, with the Soviet Union, providing material for these armies. In 1950, Kim Il Sung, head of government in the North, thought his army strong enough to invade South Korea, win the ensuing war, and unify the peninsula under his rule. There was some confidence among the Communists that the U.S. would not intervene here, either.

The invasion of the South began on June 25, 1950. The North Korean army pushed the Republic of Korea and its American ally to the tip of the peninsula, into an enclave around Pusan. The North Korean aggression may have succeeded but for a Douglas MacArthur-inspired landing behind lines at Inchon by an American force, a tactic that worked beyond expectations and, after hard fighting, led to a full-scale retreat of North Korean armies with American and ROK units in pursuit. Seoul was recaptured, Pyongyang was taken, and the Allies continued north toward the Yalu River, the boundary between North Korea and Red China.

An officer of the tough and cocky 5th Cav of the Eighth Army, stretching to reach the boundary with China, wrote home on Halloween that by the next day, his men would be peeing in the Yalu River.[4] What he did not know about, because Air Force reconnaissance planes could not reveal them, were the bridges being constructed to cross this one-mile-wide river. The photos did not show the bridges because they were being built a foot below the surface of the icy water by Chinese soldiers during a bitterly cold Korean winter.[5] Within a week, divisions were crossing those Yalu bridges in a deadly counterattack that deployed, according to some reports, up to a million troops.

The United Nations, with the Soviet Union boycotting the Security Council and so unable to use its veto, declared North Korea in violation of the UN Charter and sent a multi-national force to assist the South. These troops were welcomed but not large enough to stem the Chinese Red Army. The Allied (read American) armies and the Chinese army gave good accounts of themselves in the fierce battles that ensued down the peninsula. But the operative word here is down, as in southward. The Communists retook Pyongyang and Seoul. Around the original line of demarcation, the 38th parallel, the battle lines wavered, but in the end

C-124s scheduled for maintenance parked in a space-saving configuration at Tachikawa AB, Japan, during the Korean War, 1952 (courtesy Elio Argentati).

9. "Sorry 'bout that"

POWs returned in 1953 from Korea to Japan aboard a C-124 Globemaster II (Department of Defense).

became fixed. An armistice came in July 27, 1953, and at a small place called Panmunjom, peace talks began. While no treaty was agreed upon by the negotiators in the tent city in the Demilitarized Zone (aka DMZ, the only place in the Korean peninsula that appears not to have been deforested), much less signed and ratified, at least the truce has held for more than 60 years.

During the Korean War, aerial combat between jet fighters took place overhead, and B-29s and B-50s pounded enemy positions and supply lines. Helicopter technology had advanced, and good uses for them were found, as viewers of the movie or TV series *MASH* are aware. *And*, for the first time, C-124s entered a combat area.

With the truce came repatriation of American POWs, and Globemasters had the happy task of transporting the servicemen and sometimes their family members back to the United States.

The truce in Korea spelled good news in the United States, but bad news for the French in Indochina. Ho Chi Minh, a charismatic and determined leader for Vietnam independence had secured a large and loyal following among the Vietnamese people who had a tradition of fighting against domination by foreign powers. Ho tapped into that rich vein of resistance, found the Cold War the right time to amp-up anti-colonial battles and built an army to do that, the Viet-Minh which began to receive significant support from the Mao Zedong government in Beijing. By the end of 1953, the Viet-Minh was well on its way to becoming a powerful conventional military force under the command of a former history teacher, Vo Nguyen Giap, who became the invincible sword of Ho Chi Minh.

While the Viet-Minh had no Air Force or Navy, they did have ample manpower in well-outfitted infantry divisions, and they had artillery, 144 pieces including three batteries of 105-mm howitzers captured from the U.S. Army in Korea. Dug into the hilltops and hillsides around Dien Bien Phu, from November to May 8, these artillery pieces fired 103,000 shells supplied by China, except for 12,000 French rounds delivered by parachute, intended for the garrison but recovered by the Viet-Minh from misses to the drop zone during the battle. Heavy fire from the Communist batteries decimated the airstrips of Dien Bien Phu, eliminating air support and resupply or reinforcements coming in by transport airplanes. The few medical evacuation helicopters and light spotter planes that tried to sneak in at night or during diversions were usually destroyed.

C-47s dropped supplies, but with steadily increasing and accurate antiaircraft fire, drops were scheduled for night or from higher altitudes, resulting in a poor percentage reaching the besieged troops. Indeed, much of the parachuted cargo landed behind enemy lines. The Dien Bien Phu garrison, numbering 13,000 men, ten battalions at any one time, multicultural to be sure, consisted of elite French colonial units, a French airborne Battle Group, a battalion of loyal Vietnamese paratroopers, a T'ai battalion, two battalions of the fabled Foreign Legion (many of whom were Germans), Algerian and Moroccan battalions, all in the service of France, but included no units from NATO or any of France's Western allies. The U.S. had sent in a high-ranking officer to observe the position before the actual battle began (he thought it defensible) and had furnished C-119 Flying Boxcars for French aircrews. The Viet-Minh siege force totaled some 49,500 soldiers and 55,000 support personnel.

At first confident in the outcome of the battle, the French High Command realized by late April that without massive air strikes targeting the fixed Viet-Minh artillery that was systematically and daily shredding the fortress, little hope existed. With a tiny Air Force in Asia, the French were not capable of this kind of support and pled for assistance from the British and American governments. President Dwight Eisenhower, in considerations about relieving the French in Indochina, met at one point with Congressional leaders, including then-Speaker of the House Lyndon B. Johnson, who advised the president that without a stated American strategy for Southeast Asia, he would oppose any military commitment on behalf of Dien Bien Phu. Eisenhower declined to intervene with American combatants or combat aircraft. He did approve of use of C-124 Globemasters from the 322nd Air Division, based in Europe, to airlift from France to Hanoi the 7th Paratroop Battalion—in Operation Bali-Hai. The 62nd TCW from Larson AFB took the long air journey to Chateauroux AB in France and joined in the airlift of these French troops to Vietnam. Because of India's restrictions on use of its air space for this mission, the Globemasters had to refuel in Sri Lanka.[6] The 7th Paratroop Battalion was never air-dropped as a full unit which might have forestalled the fall of the fortress, but instead like other reinforcements was dribbled in piecemeal, not strong enough in that case to change anything on the ground.

The fall of Dien Bien Phu came on May 8, 1954. Later that year, France withdrew its forces and administrators from Southeast Asia. French Indochina would be no more. The Geneva Conference that had been in session to conclude a peace treaty for Korea switched its agenda to include a new configuration for the former French colony. North Vietnam became independent under the Viet-Minh government of Ho Chi Minh. The Geneva conferees divided the long, narrow country at the 17th parallel belt line, with South Vietnam remaining under the constitutional authority of Emperor Bao Dai. A plebiscite for all of Vietnam was to be held in July 1955, which would re-unite the country according to majority vote under one or the other of these governments. Those elections were never held, breaking the agreement made at Geneva. The Viet-Minh, which had been confident that it would win the elections, began a five-year campaign to reunify the country unilaterally through military force. The United States sent advisors to shore up the South Vietnamese army, and with the inauguration of John F. Kennedy in 1961 came a commitment to defend the government of Ngo Dinh Diem, who had replaced Bao Dai after a 1955 referendum to create a republic in South Vietnam.

The Kennedy administration's commitment to defend manifested as a steadily increasing stream of aid, military advisor assistance, civilian aircrews, and material supplies, but not combat troops. Many in the United States Army, beginning with Douglas MacArthur, had strenuously argued against a "land war in Asia." Nevertheless, in 1961, the first Army helicopter companies arrived in Vietnam. Soon after, Bell's newly developed gas turbine engine HU-1 began duty as a medevac carrier. These were the forerunners to a new concept of troop movements and maybe modified the warning against war in Asia. Air cavalry units would eventually deploy "Hueys" to carry U.S. combat troops into battle against the Viet-Minh and Viet Cong. The lesson seemingly learned at Dien Bien Phu was not to let the Vietnamese people establish their independence and settle their differences amongst themselves. No, it was rather to fight on but with much better airborne stuff than the French had.

Communist ground forces might have had a superiority in their weapons. The AK-47, for example, was considered more effective in most combat scenarios than the U.S. Army's standard rifle, the M-14. But in the air a different story was told. Not only were Huey's advanced machines coming off the production lines in Fort Worth, the C-130 Hercules, a racehorse compared to piston engine transports like the C-124, was ready for battle.

On August 7, 1964, the Vietnam conflict received an upgrade when the United States Congress approved a presidential initiative called the "Gulf of Tonkin Resolution." Waters of the Gulf of Tonkin, an arm of the South China Sea, lapped at the docks and quays of Haiphong, Hanoi's port city. Haiphong is to Hanoi as Piraeus is to Athens, and Portus was to Imperial Rome—that is, where the ships unloaded. In the deep waters of Tonkin, the U.S. Navy had stationed the Sixth Fleet to harass and perhaps prevent supply ships, some of which were carrying war material, from reaching their destination in North Vietnam.

While the North Vietnamese navy had nothing that could remove or even challenge this armada off their shore, they did have speedy PT boats which in 1964 engaged the USS *Maddox*, a U.S. destroyer, in an intense battle, and two days later may have fired torpedoes at another American warship. Both destroyers were gathering intelligence inside the 12-mile limit claimed as its waters by North Vietnam but unrecognized by the U.S. The torpedoes did no damage and could have been flying fish kicking up a white froth, but that mattered little as the incident would be used as *cause belli* by the administration. President Johnson persuaded Senator J. William Fulbright of Arkansas to lead the Gulf of Tonkin Resolution through Congress. A few peaceniks opposed the bill, but Fulbright and Johnson were overwhelming and the bill literally sailed through Congress without a single nay vote in the House. Fulbright garnered an 88–2 vote in its favor. Only Senators Wayne Morse of Oregon and Ernest Gruening of Alaska opposed it. The resolution empowered the president to commit U.S. Armed Forces to defend South Vietnam against attacks being mounted

9. "Sorry 'bout that" 163

by the Ho Chi Minh–led North Vietnam Republic. It must be supposed that many of the congressmen read the bill before voting for it and therefore knowingly approved of Johnson's authorization to send U.S. troops to an Asian war zone. The resolution was akin to a declaration of war, but not really that either. The ambiguity of it and the veiled way in which the resolution was used to create full-scale war led to a falling-out between Johnson and Fulbright, a pair of Southerners who had worked together amicably for years in the Senate before LBJ became president. Over this, they stopped speaking, and Fulbright wrote a book opposing the build-up in Southeast Asia entitled *Arrogance of Power*, thereupon becoming an iconic figure among Vietnam War protesters.

At Fort Benning, Georgia, the First Air Cavalry prepared to answer all questions about what American soldiers could do on the front lines, engaging in direct and pitched battle with the North Vietnam Army. Observers sent to Vietnam, civilian and military alike, thought our troops would make a difference. American advisors who had been in the field with South Vietnamese forces had been so critical of their resolve and abilities, and their arguments had convinced superiors on up the line that we could do the job that RVN soldiers were failing at, that is defeat a good North Vietnamese army. To accomplish this, of course, U.S. troops would have to be highly mobile.

Mobility was a U.S. Army specialty dating back to the 19th century. In a spectacular incident of this concept from the Civil War, the Union Army of the Frontier transported infantrymen to the battlefield in wagons, an innovation that sped coverage of the vast spaces in the western theater of the war, where there were no railroads. In summer 1863 from his base in Indian Territory, General James G. Blunt attacked Confederate-held Fort Smith, Arkansas, key to Union control of the southwest. As Confederate commander Brig. Gen. William Cabell abandoned the city in the face of superior numbers, Blunt's cavalry commander, Col. William F. Cloud, pursued the retreating garrison toward a Confederate trap 25 miles south of the city, touching off a battle that enabled federal forces to control of western Arkansas and Indian Territory for the duration of the war. Ironically, Cloud surprised the ambushers with his wagon-transported mobile infantry, which brought them into the engagement far sooner than they could have marched into position to support the cavalry in this crucial battle, and far sooner than the Confederate commander would have liked to see.

The victory and the tactics that brought it that day affirmed mobility for U.S. Army strategists, which pushed development of new transportation technologies to move troops quickly into position. A 1939 study recommended creating air infantry units to be deployed by parachute. By 1943, the U.S. Army had five airborne divisions capable of being parachuting in at the point of attack. This mobility proved decisive in some World War II battles. The mobile part of the Korean War depended on troops deployed in battle zones by armored personnel carriers. That ground-type mobility proved less useful in Vietnam for the French, as Bernard Fall's classic book, *Street without Joy*, documents. There, the roadless character, dense vegetation, and uneven terrain in the critical mountainous areas of the conflict presented an environment that seemed an ideal proving ground for the latest means of troop transport, the helicopter. "The genesis of air mobile operations came in 1957 from the Army Chief of Research and Development, the famous 82nd Airborne Division Commander, Lt. Gen. James Gavin. In an article entitled, 'Cavalry—and I Don't Mean Horses,' Gavin presented a vision of using the helicopter to transport soldiers to combat."[7] Secretary of Defense Robert McNamara took this vision of Gavin and turned it into reality with the creation of the 1st Air Cavalry Division (Air Mobile), which was operational by 1964, the year of the Gulf of Tonkin Resolution.

So what that Vietnam battlefields were some 8,000 miles (over the pole, 9,445 miles through Hawaii) from Fort Benning and the First Air Cavalry depended on helicopters for their raiding tactics? Airlift gave the capability needed to sustain this mobility by delivering helicopters, the new "steeds" of the new cavalry, to the forward areas. When the division was first deployed to Vietnam, ships carried the first three helicopter battalions to Da Nang, where they moved directly to the front.[8] But in determining logistics for the dependence on air mobility, a faster way, an expedient way existed with the C-124 transport that had sufficient cargo capacity to airlift the helicopters from the factories or U.S. staging areas straight to the battlefields of Vietnam. In 1965, Air Force inventoried 447 C-124 Globemasters, 283 in MATS alone, ready to transport helicopters and other bulky gear integral to the Gavin plan. C-124 crews were trained and standing ready after training and exercises of the previous three years. Swift Strikes I and II, Gold Fire, Jungle Strike, and Arctic Strike were in the book now, gigantic maneuvers spanning continents, involving all military branches closely cooperating. In 1965, C-124s supported helicopter warfare around Pleiku in the highlands of South Vietnam. President Johnson, at the time, "did not think winning the war in Vietnam would be inordinately difficult. The United States was the greatest military power in world history."[9]

9. "Sorry 'bout that"

Before the Gulf of Tonkin, John F. Kennedy's concept of meeting the enemy on the ground on his turf and playing by his rules—counter-insurgency or COIN—injected a new and thriving division of Pentagon budget planning that rivaled (and made uncomfortable) the Strategic Air Command—where the money was used to create and maintain a force to bomb the enemy into submission if not outright oblivion—and the U.S. Navy's program of building fleets of atomic-powered warships armed with nuclear-tipped missiles. The surface of the world was covered mostly by oceans of water, and unparalleled mastery of the seas had been the blueprint for empire and world dominance in the 19th century. World War II provided a concept of air power. Air and water, and now with counter-insurgency there would be a rollback to an emphasis on ground power—like the Romans crossing the Alps or the U.S. 7th and 9th Cavalry expanding American jurisdiction across the Great Plains.

The Globemaster did not represent any kind of power or anything new. At the time of the Gulf of Tonkin Resolution, the newest Globemaster was 13 years old. Globemaster A's, mostly built in 1949 and 1950, were in the inventory along with the C-124Cs, improved where power, wing heaters, interior arrangement, and nav equipment were involved. During the exercises, Globemaster pilots had practiced the techniques of short field landings and takeoffs and flew their giant planes in close, three-ship formations. Loadmasters had learned to configure the interior for paratroop drops and simulated cargo offloads with conditions of an air strip under enemy fire. The bottom of the fuselage doors, through which a platform could be lowered to heft loads into the ship, was used for engine-running offloads.

Navigators learned to guide a plane flying a low-level evasion route, using landmarks and visual references to home in on a drop zone, and once there, direct the pilot's pass over the zone and signal the jump to begin by turning on the green light. Sticks of paratroopers of the 82nd and 101st Airborne divisions jumped out of several types of Air Force transport planes. The twin-boom fuselage C-119 and the C-130 had ramps in the rear below the vertical stabilizer that opened wide, giving an unimpeded look at the space which paratroopers were about to enter. Troopers simply had to have the confidence to exit the plane from a height about the same as the Empire State Building's top floor. A C-124 had side doors with the horizontal stabilizer looking like an arm's length away, a breathtaking dimension. It may have been aeronautically impossible for a paratrooper to meet what must have seemed to be a huge meat cleaver coming right at him, but try telling him that the first time.

Although not exactly the plane of choice for troop drops or for short field landings in Vietnam, the C-124 was there when needed. All crew positions were primed for this duty, the pilots needing all that right stuff that they were supposed to be composed of. The flight engineers supervised, monitored, and maintained the engines and the airframe, both of which were subjected to stresses probably never dreamed of by the designers. A short field landing technique, for example, has the pilot diving the plane into a spot on the end of a 3,000-foot strip and flaring quickly, often banging hard into the runway. Then, he yanks back on the throttles, goes into full prop reverse, and orders max power from the engineer. Imagine in the summer of 1963, the cloud layer of dust kicked up when landing like that in a droughty area such as Walnut Ridge, Arkansas. Imagine the roar and groans of four 3,600 horsepower engines surging to their maximum. Imagine the bounce and flap of fuel tank pods weighing up to 3,000 pounds on the end of 70-foot wings. Imagine the awe of civilian witnesses to the spectacle of a monstrous airplane—half again the size of a C-130—slamming into an asphalt runway not even as wide as the plane's wingspan. Imagine the relief of the crew as the plane lurched to a stop with 200 feet of runway to spare! An eyewitness testified:

> A C-124 landed where I was in Udorn, Thailand in 1961. He landed OK, but when it came time to take off, they pushed the wing wheels to the absolute end of the tarmac. Every bit of the aircraft past that point was hanging over dirt. They set the brakes and revved those huge engines until there was a typhoon class wind behind the plane, flattening pop stands and hooches for a considerable distance before they released the brakes. When they did, big momma lurched and headed down the strip. It cleared the trees at the far end of the runway, but not by a heckuva lot. Later the runway was substantially improved and Phantoms, combat and recon, flew out of there to Viet Nam.[10]

In such missions, loadmasters had large responsibilities with configuring the airplane rapidly and securing the cabin, which could contain helicopters, tanks, bulldozers, troops, or other cargo that with the least bit of movement could jeopardize the operation and the airplane. Navs, of course, were flight planning, making en route adjustments, map reading, monitoring radar, working radios, giving headings, and assisting other crew members where needed.

Massive training operations were not enough, yet, to satisfy Gen. John P. McConnell, who on February 1, 1965, had followed Curt LeMay as the Air Force's top man. McConnell, an Arkansan, dissented to the Johnson administration's plan to deploy the 1st Air Cavalry Division in the interior of South Vietnam, citing the need to further test airmobile methods. Nevertheless, soon the discussions became not if but when and focused on air transportation and selection of suitable airstrips. Three brigades of Air Cav troops in forward positions needed 847 tons of supplies daily, which would have to come by the air link.[11]

In the crucial first year of America's combat commitment to Vietnam, the burden of supplying the forward strips fell to C-123s and C-130s, but C-124s "comprised the bulk of the airlift fleet at the start of the build-up" and were part of the forward base air link, too.[12] Unlike Provider and Hercules units, no Globemaster squadron was ever assigned to Vietnam. The Globemasters were, nevertheless, rotated into the supply lines on a temporary basis. The C-124 squadron based closest to Southeast Asia was at Tachikawa AB, Japan, where ramp space and large hangers, created for Globemaster use during the Korean War, accommodated the giants. From Japan to Vietnam, C-124s needed about an eight-hour flight time. Tachi became an airlift hub in the Pacific. One official history of airlift in Vietnam specified the invaluable contributions made by the C-124s in the war, and the author gave extra fuel drop tanks for fighters as an example: Old Shaky could carry six, the C-130, two. In 1968, C-124s airlifted 600 tons of cargo monthly, about a third of that between points in Vietnam, such as Song Be, where a news photo of a "gigantic C-124 on the ground at the primitive airstrip" was widely published.[13] In April 1970, four C-124s were assigned to Clark AB and would fly without accident for the next year while hauling cargo, troops, and foodstuffs into Vietnam. This presented exotic duty for planes designed for long overwater flights and heavy cargos. Not only the C-124s stationed in the Pacific participated, but planes and aircrews from CONUS flew supplies to troops in the trenches.

Another hub, Hickam AFB, Hawaii, adjacent to Pearl Harbor, supported Vietnam operations. A Hickam AFB nav, Barney Madden, flew 36 combat support missions in Vietnam. In 1969, as Old Shaky was being phased out to Air National Guard units, Madden, with 2,200 hours in C-124s (and 1,800 hours before that in B-52s) transferred to F-4s and a new AFSC, 1555, nav-weapons systems operator at George AFB.[14]

Prior to the Tonkin attacks, 48 Globemasters were based at Dover AFB, Delaware. After that, one squadron was transferred to McChord AFB in Washington to save time and miles in meeting growing concerns in the Pacific. McChord continued its airlift role in support of the Alaskan command while picking up new support commitments for the Commander-in-Chief, Pacific Fleet (CINCPAC), the military authority over Vietnam. Dover AFB Globemasters took on airlift assignments to Vietnam even while tending to Europe, Greenland, Canada, and the eastern half of the United States. Travis and Hill AFB Globemaster squadrons teamed with McChord in a new concept of faster delivery via the stage system.

The USAF was barely 20 years old as a separate branch, like most of its transport navigators. "Can do" and "gung ho" were the catch-phrases and the actuality of the era. As the build-up began, C-124s carried cargo from U.S. terminals and suppliers to Vietnam, an itinerary of some 42–50 hours flying time with 12 hours' crew rest between each leg. That meant a Globemaster loaded with a Huey from a Fort Worth plant could expect to deliver it within one week, perhaps six days. One crew, one airplane, one shipment bound for Vietnam, simple enough. Too simple, so it had, of course, to get more complicated. To speed up delivery time, MATS decided that crews were like sprinters and airplanes were the batons in a relay race to Vietnam to make more timely deliveries across the wide Pacific Ocean.

C-124s assigned to the stage would land at Hickam, Wake, Guam, Clark, or Mactan, and a crew coming off crew rest (12 hours minimum) would take over and plunge on to the next refueling stop, where another set of pilots, navs, engineers, and loadmaster, whose home base might be Travis, McChord, or Hill, would kick the tires, board, run the check lists, and fly the next leg. The Globemaster would be on the ground long enough for refueling and minor maintenance. Theoretically, a helicopter, a bulldozer, 20,000-gallon storage tanks, or a M41 Walker Tank replacement could arrive in Vietnam from Travis AFB in only two days. Cam Ranh Air Base came into service in 1966, and the C-141 Starlifter, which could transport material twice as fast, was in action then, but until the advent of the huge Lockheed-built C-5 Galaxy in 1970, only the Globemaster cargo bay dimensions, 77 feet in length, 13 feet wide, and 12-feet-eight-inches-high, provided the capacity for the largest heavy equipment and weapons.

Three thousand five hundred men of the 173rd Airborne Brigade, 1st Air Cav, landed in country May 3, 1965, the first U.S. combat unit to enter the fray but were not yet referred to as combatants. An advance cadre and material of the unit arrived via Globemasters.

These troops were paid $40 a month in combat pay, and the aircrews received the same boost to their paychecks plus an exemption on their income tax for service in a war zone. Hueys carried troops quickly and directly into the battlefield. Once a conventional infantry, the 1st Air Cav, like its namesakes from the 19th century that used horses for ranging over sparsely populated regions, now sought the enemy in a large, hostile land depending not on advancing battle lines, but on mobility to win the war.

Freed from the "march," U.S. soldiers armed with M16 rifles could attack the enemy suddenly.

Since technically, aircraft in the country were supporting the RVN in their battle to stay free of Hanoi (and remain in the clutches of the Saigon government, which was corrupt to the core), the Air Force came up with a new definition for what cargo-carrying airplanes and crews did in the war. Thus was born the designation, "Combat Support Flying Hours."[15]

The C-124 brought in replacement UH-1 Huey helicopters to Pleiku and frontline positions of the 1st Air Cavalry Division (Airmobile). And sometimes Caterpillars, as in the photo.[16]

As important as the giant airplane was to the supply of war material, it did not receive much red-carpet treatment. When unloaded and its job done, the Globemaster became a liability because of its size. Ramp space was at a premium in Vietnam, and maintaining the C-124 and refueling it required space for service, parts, and gasoline. The Globemaster participated in the re-supply of forward bases in Pleiku, Kham Duc, Song Be, where short field landings and quick turnarounds were the requirement.

C-124 based with the 22nd MAS at Tachikawa delivering a Caterpillar at Kham Duc on May 10, 1968 (USAF photograph mentioned in Ray Bowers, *Tactical Airlift*).

The ubiquitous C-123 Provider, the C-130s and helicopters saw to most of that, so the C-124 may have appeared as an out-of-place, prehistoric flying dragon to air traffic controllers and aerodrome managers. Once, when forced to RON (remain overnight) at Da Nang Air Base, an aircraft commander was awakened twice to come "move the elephant," taxi, that is, to a different spot so other airplanes could get by and operations proceed. In 1965, Da Nang and Tan Son Nhut came under mortar attacks by the Viet Cong, bad enough when a C-130 took incoming fire and burst into flames. Air Base command feared that a direct hit on a Globemaster might result in a towering inferno, a disaster that would drastically add chaos as well as ramp-up demands on firefighters and their equipment.

The C-124 seldom flew above 7,000 feet on in-country routes, and at that low level and with a ground speed of 150–180 knots, the plane must have seemed a tempting target for ground fire and especially for the Soviet-supplied surface-to-air missiles (SAMs) used in South Vietnam in 1965. That none were shot down in Vietnam gave credence to a remark made by an Air Force briefing officer to a crew departing Tan Son Nhut for the Highlands. When asked by the navigator why the route passed directly over a known SAM site, the young officer, in the way of wartime humor, replied, "You know, we have to expect losses." He quickly followed that assessment with something of a reassurance: "Stop worrying, they're not going to shoot you down. They know they'll eventually get everything you are carrying, anyway." On stops at Pleiku in 1965, cargo was unloaded via the freight elevator and the bomb bay doors with engines running. If the cargo happened to be large rolling stock, then the plane was parked, engines shut down—but not necessarily, as the engine running offload was practiced—the clam shell doors opened, and truck, tank, self-propelled howitzer, bulldozer, or helicopter were rolled down the ramps. This equipment was ready to start up and go to work or to war with little or no assembly required if hauled by a Globemaster.

Often, enemy activity in the vicinity shortened airlifter visits, giving not much time for onloading cargo. For the C-124, the return flight saw mainly personnel, live or sadly, in body bags. With a light load, the pilot revved engines and screamed down the runway rotating at 2,500 feet, more if the weather was really hot. With liftoff, gear came up, and the pilot put the plane into as steep a climb as regulations permitted and Old Shaky could stand, racking the rudder for a sharp turn. While to a ground observer, it might seem like a slow-motion film of an ungainly flying machine, to the crew inside it was different. Maximum effort on the part of man and machine created maximum excitement. Often in 1965, the

9. "Sorry 'bout that"

airplane and the crew could be scheduled for two of these round-trip deliveries, some crews stretching the limits for a third trip. On occasion, a flight examiner—who could choose to hop on—might augment the crew so that the flight day could be extended for another sortie.

This author was the navigator on one such flight, and the FE who came aboard introduced himself, Major Paul Beaulieu. Upon completing duties in Vietnam, we were routed to Clark Air Base in the Philippines, and Major Beaulieu rode with us, giving me a check ride over the South China Sea. Arriving at Clark late in the evening, a housing officer assigned us to a vacant colonial-style house raised off the ground with wood walls and floors and a screened-in veranda. A furniture-less living room had a large, slow-moving ceiling fan. These quarters had no beds, but we had pallets and a crew bottle that was passed around. A Motorola radio tuned to the Armed Forces Network gave us the background for relaxation as the pilot broke out cigars. We were happy with each other, the whiskey, the cigars, and the rock and roll music from the radio. No one worried about the next day right then, it seemed so far away. An Elvis Presley song came on and next to me, Paul said, "Do you like Elvis?" "Sure do," I replied. Paul said, "Glad to hear you say it since he's going be my son-in-law." I didn't know if he was kidding, but he explained that his daughter Priscilla (actually his adopted step-daughter) had come to know Elvis in Germany, where Paul had been stationed. Astounding.

For a couple of years, I stayed in touch with Paul, who was at Travis, and he once sent me a map from his collection since we had discovered a mutual interest. Elvis and Priscilla married two years later in 1967. The last time I saw Paul, the former navigator FE, he was sitting at a desk in the squadron office of the 155th Tennessee Air National Guard in Memphis in 1979. By then a colonel, he was visiting our squadron, part of an ORI team. He and I shared memories about our time in Southeast Asia. A limo arrived to take him to Graceland. After he retired from the USAF, Paul became a movie actor, playing himself in two film documentaries about the Presley family.

After a day of flying missions in South Vietnam, Globemasters were generally directed to bases outside the country for crew rest and maintenance, to Clark and Mactan, to Kadena AB in Okinawa, the Ryukyu archipelago being still under occupation as it is today. If the crew lucked out with a cargo destined for Thailand, then excitement awaited, and not just because of the occasional water buffalo on the runway (a C-47 hit one while landing in 1969). Bangkok's Don Muang International Airport had a U.S. Air Force presence for maintenance and support of our planes and

Top: Dwellings on a branch of the Chao Phraya River of Bangkok, 1965. *Bottom:* Floating markets of Bangkok in 1965.

9. "Sorry 'bout that"

leased the Grand Hotel for aircrews. The Grand was only a few blocks from the Erawan Hotel, *So mot*—Number one—in accommodations and entertainment with Balinese dancers nightly. If there was a delay in departure, say for waiting on a part to be delivered so the airplane could be fixed, then the crew might get an extra day or two in Bangkok.

The Bangkok zoo in 1965 was a transfer point for newly captured Southeast Asian tigers who were kept and displayed in 18-foot-high circular cages, diameter of about 60 feet and open at the top. Visitors were awed by the energy and leaping power of wild tigers as they constantly challenged the height of these roofless temporary cages, their bounds shaking and rattling the bars until it seemed the cage would collapse, and the fierce tigers would have freed themselves. The zoo operated a snake farm which included an Olympic-sized swimming pool populated by thousands of cobras. Attendants hand-caught cobras and, in a small concrete block laboratory building, milked the venom from dozens of cobras every day to produce antivenin. Cobras, like cottonmouth water moccasins, swim with body submerged and heads sticking out of the water, and like cottonmouths have no doubt that they are at the top of the food chain wherever they are.

A 1966 *Time* magazine featured King Bhumibol and Queen Sirikit of Thailand. Their Bangkok palace displayed the royal barge, and occasionally visitors were privileged to play golf at the Royal Golf and Country Club. Golfers enjoyed the services of not only a caddy, but a fore caddy, too. These young men dove into the canals lining the fairway to retrieve wayward balls from the water hazard. The water was not clear, muddy like in most Southeast Asia waterways, yet one fore caddy showed great skill in watching and finding any lost ball. Coming out of the canal with dripping wet hair, so black it was blue, with a huge grin, he handed it back, saying in pidgin, "please sir, the cobras become angry when you hit them." Asked if he was a caddy who played golf, he replied, "No sir, I am a kick boxer."

Chinese gem merchants cottoned on to visiting U.S. military and plied their prospects with amenities such as boat trips on the Chao Phraya River and to the floating markets, to the tourist Buddhist temples, to restaurants and their fabulous cuisine featuring jasmine rice, and, of course, to their own lapidaries, where the cutting of precious stones took place. Many crew members took sapphire, ruby, and gold jewelry home what with all this attention from the merchants. On their own, however, the aircrew visitors might roam the streets a bit, since Bangkok, like Manila and Cebu in those days, welcomed Americans. Marketplace bombers and kidnappers were in the distant future.

On one such adventure, I strolled the streets alone past store fronts, street musicians, and older gentlemen playing Thai chess, somewhat different that the western version, until I came upon an arena with kick boxing bouts that night. In 1965, this vicious sport had not been fully realized in the United States. Paying for a ticket, I went inside where the matches had already begun. The skill, athleticism, and courage of the boxers matched their bloodletting and as the bouts continued, this American visitor began to realize that almost everyone in attendance was Thai and was excited to point of frenzy—there was betting and drinking, too—begetting a frame of mind maybe best described as a blood lust. Growing uncomfortable, I made a move—watched, but unopposed—to the door, one of the few times in Southeast Asia that I felt uneasy as an outsider.

Yet Thailand was non–Communist, a staunch ally, and Bangkok was SEATO headquarters.[17] The pro–Western Thai government authorized the use of its air space and civilian airfields for military planes and allowed the U.S. Air Force to open air bases in northeast Thailand on the border with Laos. Thailand, in fact, was *the* domino U.S. foreign policy planners did not want to fall. Eisenhower, who denied meaningful aid to the French at Dien Bien Phu, had given presidential sanction to the concept that Southeast Asian countries would topple inevitably one after the other if the Communists in Vietnam were successful. He said this to House Majority Leader Lyndon Baines Johnson. Neither of these men, however, had wanted to help the French maintain its colonial presence in Indochina, so as president himself, Johnson was destined to devote himself to preventing this metaphor from actualizing itself, a devotion "that would make the presidency of Lyndon Johnson vivid in history."[18]

From Eisenhower's commitment of military advisors to South Vietnam in 1957 through the Gulf of Tonkin incident in 1964 to the evacuation of the U.S. embassy in 1974 and on to the surrender of South Vietnam in 1975, the U.S. lost 58,286 men and women. The names of each, so far as known, are inscribed on the Vietnam Memorial Wall in Washington, D.C. Of those casualties, 99 were navigators or navs who became pilots. No C-124s were lost in Vietnam, but other transport navigators aboard C-130s, C-123s, even a C-5 are listed. One navigator on the Wall is Paul Everett Getchell, my OTS roommate described earlier. He and his pilot went missing after bailing out of their disabled B-57 Canberra at night while on a mission over Laos on January 13, 1969. After relentless efforts by individuals as well as the Air Force, his remains were eventually recovered in 2007 and are buried at Arlington National Cemetery. He had one of the strongest hearts and the most accurate moral compass of anyone I ever knew.

9. "Sorry 'bout that"

Paul E. Getchell in back seat of B-57 Canberra, Vietnam, 1965 (courtesy Leigh Buttermore Lefaivre).

Another nav on the Wall is Richard Dean Smith, an aviation cadet at Harlingen who pinned on his nav wings in 1960 and, being good at the trade, was selected to stay in ATC as an instructor. Eventually he got the permanent change of station to an operational unit and by 1965 was flying as a nav-bombardier in a Canberra B-57 in South Vietnam. At Bien Hoa Air Base in March 1965, Smith bumped into Jimmy Pickens, a nav on a C-124 that had brought in fragmentation bombs. The two had grown close at Harlingen during navigator training. Scheduled for an offload and exit, maintenance found a problem with the C-124. The breakdown was fortunate for Smith and Pickens, as while Old Shaky had some of its parts changed, Pickens remained overnight and the two old friends dined together. They met again for breakfast the next morning before they went their separate ways, Pickens and the C-124 on to Tan Son Nhut, Smith on a combat mission. B-57s were susceptible to enemy fire, and flying over North Vietnam anywhere which had effective air defenses was very dangerous, especially where these boys went. When Pickens returned in April, he learned that Smith's B-57 was lost the day they last shook hands.

In July 1969, Neil Armstrong walked on the moon. NASA had, along with its Soviet counterpart, brought the world into the space age. Propulsion, computations, and navigation had entered whole new and brave worlds. The Tet Offensive in 1968 was a game changer, and directly affected was the Globemaster, as the C-141 became the major carrier of troops and war material across the Pacific. Combat pay was raised to $65 a month. Wars cost money. Johnson declined to seek a second term as president, remarking on television that he would spend all his remaining time and energy in office to concentrate on winning or ending the war in Vietnam. Bobby Kennedy campaigned for the office and was assassinated in the spring of 1968. The nervous country elected someone just as nervous, Richard M. Nixon. Nixon, discarding airlift and air mobility as strategies for winning the war, turned instead to air attack. Massive bombing had not exactly worked in World War II nor in Korea, nor would it work in Vietnam. Perhaps in the end, nothing would have worked. The only thing we can say in defense of the U.S. military campaign in Vietnam is "sorry 'bout that," a cynical, but accurate slogan of the Vietnam War. That, and as in China in 1948 and in North Korea in 1952, we can look back and say we were not cowardly enough to drop atomic bombs. *Do not*, however, say we lost our will!

10

"The backbone of airlift"
Epilogue

The Soviet blockade of Berlin in 1948–1949 sealed General William H. Tunner's convictions that airlift was the key to American military successes in the global age. Cut of the same determined visionary cloth as Billy Mitchell, Tunner had a golden opportunity to advance his agenda when Secretary of the Air Force and former Missouri Senator Stuart Symington visited Germany in December 1948. Duly impressed with the achievement and the charts that showed the drastic savings in round-trips, maintenance personnel, fuel expenses, and aircrews if 68 C-74s (Globemaster I) were deployed instead of the 178 C-54s or 899 C-47s it would take to fly in the same amount of cargo, Symington returned to Washington, where he added his considerable weight to the development of the C-124 Globemaster. The Tunner treatment impacted Secretary of Defense James V. Forrestal, whose response was to ask Air Force Chief of Staff General Hoyt Vandenberg for a briefing on the progress toward the larger cargo carriers. Vandenberg replied that the C-97 Stratocruiser, built by Boeing over the air frame of a B-29 with the same engines, was immediately available, and the Douglas C-124 was "waiting in the wings."[1]

Even with this kind of push, it seems astonishing that less than a year after Symington's *tete a tete* with Tunner on the front line of the Cold War, the first Globemaster II was in the air, being test flown by Douglas Aircraft Company pilots. Of course, Douglas engineers had an advantage with the designs and performance records of the C-54, and notably of the C-74—18 were built—in shaping the C-124. But materials, tooling, training, manufacturing space, and administrative strategies involved presented an enormous challenge as Douglas men and women set about producing the world's largest operational cargo airplane in quantities enough to make a huge difference in American airlift capabilities. For the next 15 years, through the Korean War, the Cold War, another threatened blockade of Berlin, and the beginning of the Vietnam War, the heavy lifting C-124 "served as the backbone of strategic air transport for the U.S. Air Force."[2]

Never in U.S. history had an instant global response to events of other powers been considered. Alfred Thayer Mahan, of course, had led the way in developing the American Century by blueprinting the global presence by the United States Navy, but the modernity of it was immediacy of response needed in the mid-20th century. That meant an airplane that could deliver unprecedented amounts of cargo and soldiers within hours if necessary.

World War I marked the first time that American combat soldiers had been transported in large numbers to another continent. Embarking in 1917–1918 from New York, Boston, Charleston, Baltimore, and other ports, the one million soldiers of the American Expeditionary Force (AEF) set foot "over there" after a 3,000-mile ocean voyage that took six days to complete. After the Armistice in 1918, our doughboys exited Europe by ship. Fifty years later, 1964–1973, 2½ million soldiers who served in Vietnam arrived and exited by airplane, a trip of about 9,500 nautical miles that took 24 hours of flight time.

While to be sure they and the tens of thousands of diplomats, civilian contractors, and consultants were transported not in C-124s (that would have taken three days) but by civilian contractors like Pan-Am and Continental flying jet-powered airliners, it was the C-124 that proved the feasibility of establishing and maintaining a military presence halfway around the world. The C-124 changed the air mobility game. Combat troops and their helicopters were airlifted by C-124s. Jet transports—the C-141, the C-5, and the C-17—soon followed the C-124, their powerful new engines improving every aspect of airlift. But in the 15 years the C-124 formed "the backbone of airlift" and was the plane on the ramp, America changed from its isolationist and its America First past into a global involvement role, put somewhat pejoratively in the 1950s as the "policeman of the world." This was indeed the work of diplomats and statesmen, but the concept rested on tools, the means to deploy the might of the empire quickly and to the far reaches. The C-124 afforded the nation's ability to take on this role, and as a good cop, the United States sought to be friends in the "hood." We were a good world neighbor, and the C-124 proved that, too, making delivery of not just troops and war material, but carrying U.S. largesse and support to people in literally every part of the world.

Before satellites and their wonderful navigation assistance, the time-hewn skills of celestial navigating across oceans, glaciers, deserts, and mountains had to be taught and practiced. As the "last great navigation platform," the C-124 stands as an awesome reminder of aircrews who navigated, piloted, and engineered a singular aircraft into and back from on-the-edge environments. Navigators of outlands Columbus, Magellan, Cook, Earhart, Roy Chapman Andrews, Meriwether Lewis, and Richard Byrd shared a star-trekking kinship with 20th-century C-124 Globemaster navigators.

Some historians have speculated that the acme of American world presence and influence came in the mid–'60s, in the middle of the Cold War, and at the height of the American Century.[3] That acme coincided with the vigorous and productive years of the U.S. Air Force Globemaster II fleet, which in 1962 numbered 396 aircraft based on four continents.

"Anything, Anywhere, Anytime" (mid–1960s) (courtesy George E. Price).

Postscript

There are no more flying C-124s. Nine are on static display, one in Korea, seven outdoors at USAF bases, and one indoors at the Museum of the United States Air Force on Wright-Patterson AFB, Ohio. Between 1969 and 1974, 323 decommissioned Globemasters were flown to Davis-Monthan AFB, the airplane graveyard in Tucson, Arizona. As happened to its peer, the B-52, the Globemaster's giant wings were lopped off by an enormous guillotine, sorted, and stacked for salvage, including the miles of copper wiring inside. Much of the aluminum went to make beer cans. The legacy of the Douglas-built Globemaster series continues with the C-17 Globemaster III.

Master navigator wings.

Appendix
C-124 Globemaster Accidents Involving Loss of Life or Loss of Airplane

> In 25 years of active duty and reserve unit service, 63 C-124 Globemaster II's were involved in Class A Mishaps out a total of 447 built. The accidents resulted in 222 lost crewmembers, an average of about nine per year of operation. In addition, 367 passengers were lost in Globemaster II mishaps for a total of 589 people who took their last ride in the C-124, an average of 23 people per year.

1. *Date*: February 7, 1951
   Serial Numbers: USAF 49–237; Douglas 43166A
   Home base: Rapid City AB
   Crew Lost: 0
   Passengers on board: 0
   Fatalities: 0
   Location of accident: Rapid City, South Dakota
   Details: Landing accident, plane destroyed.

2. *Date*: March 22/23, 1951
   Serial Numbers: USAF 49–244; Douglas 43173A
   Home base: Roswell, AFB
   Crew Lost: 9
   Passengers on board: 44
   Fatalities: 53
   Location of accident: Irish Sea
   Details: Spy novel type story that survivors of ditching were picked up by Soviet submarine in the area and never returned. Among those lost was General Paul Cullen, a nuclear weapons expert.

3. *Date*: May 23, 1951
   Serial Numbers: USAF 49–232; Douglas 43161A
   Home base: Wright-Patterson AFB
   Crew Lost: 3
   Passengers on board: 4
   Fatalities: 7
   Location of accident: New Castle, Indiana
   Details: Two engines went into reverse on experimental flight with four civilian techs on board. No nav. Emergency landing in a corn field attempted, but struck tree on descent.

4. *Date*: September 15, 1951
   Serial Numbers: USAF 50–092; Douglas 43230A
   Home base: Biggs AFB

Crew Lost: 0
   Passengers on board: 0
   Fatalities: 0
   Location of accident: Lajes, AB, Azores
   Details: Crosswind landing accident, plane destroyed.
5. *Date*: April 4, 1952
   Serial Numbers: USAF 50–1260; Douglas 43282A
   Home base: Brookley AFB
   Crew Lost: 6
   Passengers on board: 0
   Fatalities: 6
   Location of accident: near Mobile, Alabama
   Details: Night mid-air collision with USAF C-47. Both planes spun down and collided with parked railroad cars.
6. *Date*: November 22, 1952
   Serial Numbers: USAF 51–107; Douglas 43441A
   Home base: McChord AFB
   Crew Lost: 11
   Passengers on board: 41
   Fatalities: 52
   Location of accident: Mt. Gannet, Alaska
   Details: Buried in Colony Glacier until spotted June 10, 2012.
7. *Date*: December 20, 1952
   Serial Numbers: USAF 49–100; Douglas 43238A
   Home base: Larson AFB
   Crew Lost: 5
   Passengers on board: 105
   Fatalities: 87
   Location of accident: Larson AFB, Washington
   Details: Operation Sleighride to carry servicemen and veterans of the Korean War home for Christmas.
8. *Date*: June 8, 1953
   Serial Numbers: USAF 51–137; Douglas 43471A
   Home base: Tachikawa AFB, Japan
   Crew Lost: 7
   Passengers on board: 122
   Fatalities: 129
   Location of accident: Kodaira, Japan
   Details: Improper use of flaps and low take-off speed. Deadliest aircraft crash in history to that date.
9. *Date*: July 2, 1954
   Serial Numbers: USAF 51–5210 Douglas 43620C
   Home base: Donaldson AFB
   Crew Lost: 0
   Passengers on board: 0
   Fatalities: 0
   Location of accident: Fort Campbell, Kentucky
   Details: Damaged beyond repair.
10. *Date*: September 12, 1954
    Serial Numbers: USAF 52–1052; Douglas 43961C
    Home base: Westover AFB
    Crew Lost: 8
    Passengers on board: 7
    Fatalities: 11
    Location of accident: Thule, Greenland
    Details: Twelve minutes after take-off lost engine. Pilot radioed an emergency and turned around. The airplane crashed just short of Thule. Aboard were eight crew members and all perished. Seven Canadian contractors aboard, four of whom survived.
11. *Date*: April 27, 1955
    Serial Numbers: USAF 52991; Douglas 43900C
    Home base: Donaldson AFB
    Crew Lost: 0
    Passengers on board: 0
    Fatalities: 0
    Location of accident: Iqaluit-Frobisher Bay, Nunavut
    Details: Crashed on landing in Newfoundland. Berlin reported that one engine, control cables severed, ran for twenty-four hours after accident.

C-124 Globemaster Accidents

12. *Date*: May 29, 1955
    Serial Numbers: USAF 52–1016; Douglas 43925C
    Home base: Ellsworth AFB
    Crew Lost: 0
    Passengers on board: 0
    Fatalities: 0
    Location of accident: Killeen, Texas
    Details: Crash landed in a field. Plane repaired and flown out. In service for another 16 years.

13. *Date*: September 6, 1955
    Serial Numbers: USAF 50–097 Douglas 43235A
    Home base: March AFB
    Crew Lost: 0
    Passengers on board: 56
    Fatalities: 1
    Location of accident: Kirkland AFB, NM
    Details: Dust storm and strong winds on takeoff

14. *Date*: November 20, 1955
    Serial Numbers: USAF 51–149; Douglas 43282A
    Home base: Tachikawa AB
    Crew Lost: 8
    Passengers on board: 2
    Fatalities: 10
    Location of accident: Iwo Jima
    Details: Crashed after take-off.

15. *Date*: March 2, 1956
    Serial Numbers: USAF 53–021 Douglas 44316C
    Home base: Warner-Robbins AFB
    Crew Lost: 9
    Passengers on board: 8
    Fatalities: 17
    Location of accident: At sea, near Iceland
    Details: Ditched, no recoveries. En route from Keflavik, Iceland to Goose Bay, Labrador. Pilot reported losing #2.

16. *Date*: April 6, 1956
    Serial Numbers: USAF 52–1078; Douglas 43987C
    Home base: Travis AFB
    Crew Lost: 3
    Passengers on board: 0
    Fatalities: 3
    Location of accident: Travis AFB, California
    Details: On a routine test hop, climbed to 100' altitude and plunged back to runway. Four crew members survived.

17. *Date*: April 17, 1956
    Serial Numbers: USAF 50–090; Douglas 43227A
    Home base: Castle AFB
    Crew Lost: 0
    Passengers on board: 86
    Fatalities: 0
    Location of accident: Hamilton, Ontario
    Details: Fuel leak caused shut down of two engines. Main gear did not deploy, pilot raised nose gear and made a belly landing. No injuries.

18. *Date*: June 16, 1956
    Serial Numbers: USAF 51–5183 Douglas 43593A
    Home base: Hickam AFB
    Crew Lost: 0
    Passengers on board: 0
    Fatalities: 0
    Location of accident: Eniwetok, Marshall Island
    Details: Landed short of threshold on the atoll landing strip. Aircraft lost.

19. *Date*: August 16, 1956
    Serial Numbers: USAF 51–156; Douglas 43490A
    Home base: Kelley AFB
    Crew Lost: 0
    Passengers on board: 1
    Fatalities: 1
    Location of accident: San Salvador Island
    Details: Too low on approach, struck a 124' seawall with right gear, spun and slid down the runway. The crew and plane were on a humanitarian mission in relief of Hurricane Betsy.

20. *Date*: August 21, 1956
    Serial Numbers: USAF 52–1005
    Douglas 43914C
    Home base: Palm Beach AFB
    Crew Lost: 3
    Passengers on board: 0
    Fatalities: 3
    Location of accident: West Palm Beach, Florida
    Details: A training flight in which the airplane lost prop blade on engine #2, feathered. Engine #3 lost power on descent to runway, airplane stalled 50 feet AGL. Pilot banked away from residential area and crashed into a field.
21. *Date*: October 3, 1956
    Serial Numbers: USAF 53033
    Douglas 44328C
    Home base: Charleston AFB
    Crew Lost: 2
    Passengers on board: 1
    Fatalities: 3
    Location of accident: Charleston AFB, South Carolina
    Details: Clipped trees on approach that caused loss of power on #3 engine. Full USAF accident report in ASN.
22. *Date*: October 21, 1956
    Serial Numbers: USAF 52–982;
    Douglas 43891C
    Home base: Donaldson AFB
    Crew Lost: 0
    Passengers on board: 0
    Fatalities: 0
    Location of accident: McMurdo, Antarctica
    Details: C-124 christened "State of Washington" damaged in landing, see the McMurdo link for photo. Flown out after sixty days of repair work and returned to duty.
23. *Date*: November 28, 1956
    Serial Numbers: USAF 52–893
    Douglas 43892C
    Home base: Donaldson AFB
    Crew Lost: 0
    Passengers on board: 0
    Fatalities: 0
    Location of accident: McMurdo, Antarctica
    Details: Damaged in landing, part of Operation Deep Freeze, the 9 TCS from Donelson AFB. Plane was flown out with civilian technicians aboard who completed the repairs in New Zealand. It eventually made a flight to Norton with front landing gear in a fixed non-retractable position.
24. *Date*: November 29, 1956
    Serial Numbers: USAF 52–1015;
    Douglas 43924C
    Home base: Donaldson AFB
    Crew Lost: 0
    Passengers on board: 14
    Fatalities: 0
    Location of accident: McMurdo, Antarctica
    Details: Aircraft named, the "State of Oregon" carried volunteer civilian technicians from Norton. It was the third damaged-124 from Donaldson. Scrapped on site and cargo compartment used as a storage shed at McMurdo. Parts used to repair 982 and 983.
25. *Date*: January 15, 1957
    Serial Numbers: USAF 52–1027;
    Douglas 43936C
    Home base: McChord AFB
    Crew Lost: 0
    Passengers on board: 0
    Fatalities: 0
    Location of accident: McChord AFB, Washington
    Details: Destroyed in a hanger fire.
26. *Date*: January 27, 1957
    Serial Numbers: USAF 50–088
    Douglas 43226A
    Home base: Biggs AFB
    Crew Lost: 0
    Passengers on board: 1
    Fatalities: 0
    Location of accident: Cook Inlet, Alaska

Details: Engine caught fire after takeoff. Plane landed on an ice floe and could not be recovered.

27. Date: February 22, 1957
Serial Numbers: USAF 51–141; Douglas 43475A
Home base: Tachikawa AB
Crew Lost: 1
Passengers on board: 149
Fatalities: 21
Location of accident: Kimmo AB, South Korea
Details: Crashed on go around when #3 engine backfired, lost power on takeoff, disintegrated, causing a crash landing into the Han River.

28. Date: April 2, 1957
Serial Numbers: USAF 51–5176 Douglas 43586A
Home base: Donaldson AFB
Crew Lost: 0
Passengers on board: 0
Fatalities: 0
Location of accident: Cambridge Bay, Canada
Details: Landed short, both wings separated, plane destroyed but no serious injuries.

29. Date: August 31, 1957
Serial Numbers: USAF 52–1021; Douglas 43920C
Home base: Biggs AFB
Crew Lost: 5
Passengers on board: 5
Fatalities: 5
Location of accident: Biggs AAF. Texas
Details: Crashed on approach in bad weather. Airplane destroyed when it struck ground two miles from airport. Large ball of fire observed two miles from airport.

30. Date: September 4, 1957
Serial Numbers: USAF 51–5173 Douglas 43583A
Home base: Larson AFB
Crew Lost: 0
Passengers on board: 0
Fatalities: 0
Location of accident: Binghamton Airport, Texas
Details: Down draft on approach, landed short, broke in half, skidded down runway.

31. Date: November 28, 1957
Serial Numbers: USAF 52–995 Douglas 43904C
Home base: Dover AFB
Crew Lost: 3
Passengers on board: 0
Fatalities: 3
Location of accident: Ankara, Turkey
Details: Crashed on approach in foggy weather. Aircraft disintegrated with flight deck inverted. Villagers eye-witnessed the impact.

32. Date: January 8, 1958
Serial Numbers: USAF 53–0035; Douglas 44330C
Home base: Brookley AFB
Crew Lost: 0
Passengers on board: 0
Fatalities: 0
Location of accident: Mobile, Alabama
Details: Runaway prop on engine 2. Landed despite a yaw. Crew evacuated. Engine 3 continued to run for two hours. Airplane destroyed.

33. Date: March 27, 1958
Serial Numbers: USAF 52–981 Douglas 43890C
Home base: Hill AFB
Crew Lost: 10
Passengers on board: 5
Fatalities: 15
Location of accident: Fort Worth, Texas
Details: Mid-air collision with C-119. Both aircraft crashed, killing three crew on the Flying Boxcar.

34. Date: June 3, 1958
Serial Numbers: USAF 51–114 Douglas 43448A

Home base: Travis AFB
Crew Lost: 6
Passengers on board: 0
Fatalities: 6
Location of accident: Travis AFB, California
Details: Received overhaul at Douglas plant in Long Beach. On take-off bound for Tachikawa AB, Japan, the port wing dipped and hit the ground one-half mile from runway near HWY 12.

35. *Date*: July 4, 1958
Serial Numbers: USAF 50–107 Douglas 43245A
Home base: Travis AFB
Crew Lost: 4
Passengers on board: 2
Fatalities: 6
Location of accident: One hour from Johnson Island, north Pacific
Details: Prop separated, opened a hole in the fuselage, struck aileron, loss of control, ditched, three survived.

36. *Date*: September 2, 1958
Serial Numbers: USAF 52–1081 Douglas 43990C
Home base: Travis AFB
Crew Lost: 7
Passengers on board: 12
Fatalities: 19
Location of accident: Pacific Ocean near Guam
Details: En-route to Clark AB inflight fire occurred and contact lost after takeoff. Aircraft loss with rescue reporting an oil slick. Tambini lists seven crewmembers lost.

37. *Date*: September 17, 1958
Serial Numbers: USAF 51–0165; Douglas 43499A
Home base: Donaldson AFB
Crew Lost: 1
Passengers on board: 0
Fatalities: 1
Location of accident: Near Tulsa, Oklahoma
Details: Suspected fuel leak caused pilot to divert. Yaw occurred on approach, right wing struck the ground, aircraft destroyed.

38. *Date*: October 16, 1958
Serial Numbers: USAF 52–1017: Douglas 43890C
Home base: Donaldson AFB
Crew Lost: 3
Passengers on board: 3
Fatalities: 6
Location of accident: Cape Kellett Bay, Antarctica *Details*: Antarctic airdrop mission to supply timbers and mail for Camp Hellett. Navigation error cause plane to fly into a 3,200' mountain. Three crew members and three passengers lost but survivors rescued as teams battled a blizzard.

39. *Date*: January 11, 1959
Serial Numbers: USAF 50–111 Douglas 43249A
Home base: McChord AFB
Crew Lost: 9
Passengers on board: 0
Fatalities: 9
Location of accident: Homer, Alaska
Details: Two engines out cause diversion to emergency field. Airplane flew into a 5,224' mountain carrying 34,500 lbs. of cargo.

40. *Date*: March 31, 1959
Serial Numbers: USAF 51–5201 Douglas 43611C
Home base: Donaldson AFB, TDY to Wiesbaden AB, Germany
Crew Lost: 4
Passengers on board: 0
Fatalities: 4
Location of accident: Incirlik, Turkey
Details: Low take-off speed caused wing to drop and strike the ground. The plane disintegrated and burned.

41. *Date*: July 6, 1959
Serial Numbers: USAF 49–254 Douglas 43183A

Home base: Barksdale AFB
Crew Lost: 0
Passengers on board: 0
Fatalities: 0
Location of accident: Barksdale AFB, Louisiana
Details: Nuclear weapon aboard, backfiring engines failed to develop adequate airspeed on takeoff. Plane settled to ground and was destroyed. No fatalities.

42. *Date:* April 18, 1960
Serial Numbers: USAF 52–1062 Douglas 43971C
Home base: Dover AFB
Crew Lost: 9
Passengers on board: 0
Fatalities: 9
Location of accident: Harmon AB, Newfoundland
Details: Two minutes after takeoff aircraft struck a 450' mountain, crashed, and burned. All in the nine-man augmented crew perished.

43. *Date:* June 19, 1960
Serial Numbers: USAF 52–993 Douglas 43902C
Home base: Charleston AFB
Crew Lost: 3
Passengers on board: 0
Fatalities: 3
Location of accident: Paramaribo, Surinam
Details: En route to Recife, Brazil, low ceiling, airplane flew into large trees and disintegrated and burned. One crew member survived.

44. *Date:* January 8, 1961
Serial Numbers: USAF 52–969 Douglas 43878C
Home base: Hill AFB
Crew Lost: 0
Passengers on board: 0
Fatalities: 0
Location of accident: Spangdahlem AB, Germany
Details: Incorrect altimeter setting cause premature descent and on final, aircraft hit trees causing a wing to hit the ground and spin the plane 180 degrees causing a fire.

45. *Date:* May 24, 1961
Serial Numbers: USAF 51–174 Douglas 43508A
Home base: Donaldson AFB
Crew Lost: 6
Passengers on board: 16
Fatalities: 18
Location of accident: McChord AFB, Washington
Details: Crashed on takeoff 2 miles south of runway after 1 min 14 secs of flight.

46. *Date:* December 19, 1961
Serial Numbers: USAF 49–239 Douglas 43168A
Home base: Charleston AFB
Crew Lost: 7
Passengers on board: 0
Fatalities: 7
Location of accident: Richards-Gebaur AFB, Missouri
Details: Engine failed three minutes after take-off, crashed on attempt to return. Crewed by reservists called up for the Berlin crisis.

47. *Date:* May 24, 1962
Serial Numbers: USAF 51–147 Douglas 43481A
Home base: Tachikawa AB
Crew Lost: 7
Passengers on board: 0
Fatalities: 7
Location of accident: Yokota AB, Japan
Details: Night training flight. Plane crashed into Mt. Buko (4,278') after touch-and-go approach. Cause unknown. No navigator on board

48. *Date:* January 2, 1964
Serial Numbers: USAF 52968 Douglas 43877C
Home base: Hill AFB
Crew Lost: 8

Passengers on board: 1
Fatalities: 9
Location of accident: Pacific Ocean
Details: Disappeared after seven hours of flight Wake to Hickam. Cause unknown. Carrying one U.S. Navy passenger and eleven tons of cargo.

49. *Date*: May 9, 1964
Serial Numbers: USAF 52–1008 Douglas 43917C
Home base: Dover AFB
Crew Lost: 6
Passengers on board: 0
Fatalities: 6
Location of accident: Cooperton, Oklahoma
Details: En route direct to home base from Altus, AFB, flew into a violent thunderstorm. Airplane broke up, exploded, and crashed into a wheat field.

50. *Date*: January 22, 1965
Serial Numbers: USAF 52–1058 Douglas 43967C
Home base: Dover AFB
Crew Lost: 8
Passengers on board: 2
Fatalities: 10
Location of accident: Mt. Helmos, Turkey
Details: Navigation error probable cause. Plane impacted the snow-capped 7,726' mountain near Monastery of Holy Lavra, Kalavryta, Greece. Crew included two pilots, one nav, three FE's and two loadmasters. All lost along with two U.S. Army couriers on board.

51. *Date*: March 24, 1965
Serial Numbers: USAF 52–1075 Douglas 43984C
Home base: Dover AFB
Crew Lost: 6
Passengers on board: 0
Fatalities: 6
Location of accident: Cordova, Maryland
Details: On training flight, right wing separated outboard of engine #4 causing airplane to crash. No navigators on board.

52. *Date*: November 7, 1965
Serial Numbers: USAF 52–942 Douglas 43851C
Home base: Hill AFB
Crew Lost: 0
Passengers on board: 0
Fatalities: 0
Location of accident: Wagner, Oklahoma
Details: En route to Birmingham, Alabama, flying at 9,000' in overcast weather, endured a mid-air collision with a Cessna. Three people in the small plane perished instantly. The Globemaster landed at Tulsa International Airport where maintenance crew was flown in to replace two damaged engines and repair wing. C-124 returned to duty.

53. *Date*: November 18, 1965
Serial Numbers: USAF 50–114 Douglas 43252A
Home base: McChord AFB
Crew Lost: 0
Passengers on board: 0
Fatalities: 0
Location of accident: Adak NAS, Alaska
Details: En route to Shemya from Elmendorf with no warning engine #1 sheared off at an altitude of 8,000 feet. Crew jettisoned thirteen tons of cargo and airplane stabilized at 2,700 feet. Flying with maximum continuous power with three engines made a safe emergency landing at Adak.

54. *Date*: February 12, 1966
Serial Numbers: USAF 52–980 Douglas 43889C
Home base: Hunter AFB
Crew Lost: 8
Passengers on board: 0
Fatalities: 8

Location of accident: Moron AB, Spain
Details: Crashed in flight, last transmission nine minutes after takeoff. Cause unknown, wreckage found on side of 11,413' Mulhacén, the highest peak in the Iberian Peninsula.

55. Date: June 24, 1967
Serial Numbers: USAF 50-086 Douglas 43224A
Home base: Richards-Gebaur AFB
Crew Lost: 0
Passengers on board: 0
Fatalities: 0
Location of accident: Whiteman AFB, Missouri
Details: Crashed during go-around. No casualties reported but aircraft damaged beyond repair. Ground soften by recent rains cushioned the jolt.

56. Date: August 7, 1967
Serial Numbers: USAF 52-1012 Douglas 43921C
Home base: Clark AFB
Crew Lost: 0
Passengers on board: 0
Fatalities: 0
Location of accident: Mactan AB, Philippines
Details: Tested to extremes and damaged beyond repair.

57. Date: July 28, 1968
Serial Numbers: USAF 51-5178 Douglas 43588A
Home base: Dobbins AFB
Crew Lost: 10
Passengers on board: 0
Fatalities: 10
Location of accident: Fifty miles northwest Recife, Brazil
Details: Crashed into 1,890' hill fifty-one miles from Guararapes, Brazil, airport. The Globemaster was crewed by reservist called up for a crisis brought on by the capture of the U.S.S. *Pueblo* by the North Korean navy.

58. Date: March 6, 1968
Serial Numbers: USAF 51-5198 Douglas 43608C
Home base: Hill AFB
Crew Lost: 0
Passengers on board: 0
Fatalities: 0
Location of accident: Hickam AFB, Hawaii
Details: Ground accident caused loss of airplane.

59. Date: September 11, 1969
Serial Numbers: USAF 52-951 Douglas 43860C
Home base: Hill AFB
Crew Lost: 0
Passengers on board: 0
Fatalities: 0
Location of accident: Hill AFB, Utah
Details: Damaged beyond repair (only information accessible).

60. Date: August 26, 1970
Serial Numbers: USAF 52-1091 Douglas 43958C
Home base: McChord AFB
Crew Lost: 7
Passengers on board: 0
Fatalities: 7
Location of accident: Mount Pavlof, Alaska
Details: Aircraft hit the side of the 8,264' volcano near Cold Bay. Aircraft destroyed, crew lost. Carrying satellite observation equipment.

61. Date: June 6, 1971
Serial Numbers: USAF 51-0167 Douglas 43501A
Home base: March AFB
Crew Lost: 0
Passengers on board: 0
Fatalities: 0
Location of accident: March AFB, California
Details: Ground accident. Aircraft not returned to service.

62. Date: May 3, 1972
Serial Numbers: USAF 52-1055 Douglas 43964C

Home base: Memphis ANB
Crew Lost: 10
Passengers on board: 1
Fatalities: 11
Location of accident: Paramaribo-Zanderij Airport, Surinam
Details: Tennessee ANG aircraft impacted a 1,716' hill, forty miles from destination. Tennessee state flags flown at half-mast in memory.

63. *Date:* October 1, 1974
Serial Numbers: USAF 51–075 Douglas 43409A

Home base: Elmendorf AFB
Crew Lost: 0
Passengers on board: 0
Fatalities: 0
Location of accident: Elmendorf AFB, Alaska
Details: Damaged and written off.

Sources: Anthony J. Tambini, The Globemaster. Boston: Branden Publishing Company, 1999; Archives Branch Department, Air Force Historical Research Agency, Maxwell AFB, Alabama; Aviation Safety Network; Serial Numbers web site; Accidentreports.com; Newspapers.com.

Douglas C-214 Globemaster II A Model Production Numbers Involved in Class A Mishaps

Year	Model Production No	Manufactured	Accidents
1948	43160	1	0
1949	43161–43188	28	5
1950	43221–43256	36	9
1950	43227–43290	14	1
1951	43407–43516	110	11
1951	43583–43597	15	4
C-12A MODEL TOTAL		204	30

Douglas C-214 Globemaster II C Model Production Numbers Involved in Class A Mishaps

Year	Model production No	Manufactured	Accidents
1951	43598–43623	26	3
1951	43724–43737	14	0
1952	43848–43998	151	27
1952	43999 CX		
1953	44296–44347	52	3
C-124C MODEL TOTAL		243	32
1948–1953 ALL C-124 PRODUCTION TOTAL	447		

Major Accidents That Destroyed Aircraft

Total Class A Mishaps	63
Accidents with fatalities	38
Crashed planes that returned to service	4
Tulsa mid-air, Hamilton belly up landing, Texas cornfield, McMurdo, Antarctica	
Ground accidents	6

Chapter Notes

Introduction

1. Top Secret document declassified on October 24, 2013, ECJC-J, Headquarters United States European Command, 21 September 1961, To: Joint Chiefs of Staff, 23–25. Held in the National Archives.
2. Michael Burleigh, *Small Wars, Faraway Places: Global Insurrection and the Making of the Modern World, 1945–1965* (New York: Viking, 2013), 57.
3. In his book, *The American Century*, British-born author Harold Evans placed the 1960s as mid-point of what he considered a century of exceptional achievements by one nation, a presence accompanied by goodwill and genuine humanitarian concerns for the rest of the world.
4. Charles L. Mee, Jr., *Meeting at Potsdam* (New York: M. Evans, 1975), 112.
5. Quotation from Secretary of State George Marshall as printed in Robert H. Ferrell, *Harry S. Truman and the Cold War Revisionists* (Columbia: University of Missouri Press, 2006), 49. Bomb numbers as revealed by Truman are on page 51.
6. Ferrell's essay on the deplorable condition of the U.S. military in the period 1945–1947 is thorough and revealing as to reasons for that condition, reasons generally neglected by modern historians of the era and well documented.
7. Doughfoot was a World War II term for a U.S. Army infantryman.
8. *Greensboro Daily News*, November 7, 1956, 5.
9. SAC not only had its own C-124 airlift service; this unique and imperial command had fighter airplanes, mostly F-84s, used as escorts.
10. Interview with Major Marvin Franklin, USAF, retired, August 19, 2013. Interview in possession of author.

Chapter 1

1. John Gillespie Magee, Jr., *High Flight*.

Oh, I have slipped the surly bonds of earth,
And danced the skies on laughter-silvered wings;
Sunward I've climbed and joined the tumbling mirth of sun-split clouds
and done a hundred things You have not dreamed of—
wheeled and soared and swung high in the sunlit silence.
Hovering there I've chased the shouting wind along
and flung my eager craft through footless halls of air.
Up, up the long delirious burning blue
I've topped the wind-swept heights with easy grace,
where never lark, or even eagle, flew;
and, while with silent, lifting mind I've trod the high untrespassed sanctity of space,
put out my hand and touched the face of God.

Gillespie Magee wrote the poem in 1941 during the Battle for Britain. Magee, an American, enlisted in the Royal Canadian Air Force as a nineteen-year-old before the U. S. entered the war much like the "Air Ace of Arkansas," Pierce McKennon, did. Both were sent to England and engaged the enemy flying Spitfires in the Battle of Britain. Magee was killed in a flying accident three months after writing the verses sent in a letter to his parents. After the war, in the early age of television many stations signed on in early morning by showing a film clip of a jet plane as *High Flight* was recited with a music background. The poem version above is courtesy of the National Museum of the U.S. Air Force, which has an exhibit dedicated to Magee.

2. The term "cold war" was used by George Orwell in 1945, referring to the strange ideological struggle between Great Britain and the Soviet Union, the former World War II allies, and by U.S. diplomat Bernard Baruch in 1947. Walter Lippmann published *The Cold War: A Study in U.S. Foreign Policy* in 1947.

3. AFR 1 implements AFPD 11–2, Aircraft Rules and Procedures, by prescribing general flight rules that govern the operation of Air Force aircraft (manned and remotely operated) that are being flown by Air Force pilots or pilots of other services or foreign pilots or civilian pilots.

4. See David Halberstam, *The Coldest Winter: America and the Korean War* (New York: Hyperion, 2007), 103–105, for reference to the absolute power exercised by MacArthur after the Japanese surrender and during American occupation of Japan. LeMay commanded SAC from 1948 to 1957, at which time he moved to the Pentagon and, at age 44, received his fourth star. He was Pentagon Chief of Staff during the 1962 Cuban Missile Crisis and urged President John F. Kennedy to bomb Soviet installations in Cuba.

5. This third party, created by segregationist Alabama Governor George Wallace, gained voter support because of unrest springing from rapid change in racial patterns and perceived waffling in Cold War responses, and won electoral votes in five states.

6. Those were Greenville AFB, Mississippi; Webb AFB, Big Springs, Texas; and Williams AFB, Chandler, Arizona. All three are closed now. Vance AFB in Enid trains most Air Force pilots today.

7. Starfighter was the nickname of the Lockheed aircraft F-104. The Air Force fighter/interceptor inventory in 1962 included the F-100 Super Sabre, F-101 Voodoo, F-102 Delta Dagger, F-104, F-105 Thunderchief, and F-106 Delta Dart. Air National Guard units flew earlier jet fighters such as the F-86 Sabre jet and the F-84 Thunderjet.

8. United States and NATO countries assigned eastbound air traffic odd-number flight altitudes and westbound traffic even-number flight altitudes.

9. See Alan Gurney, *Compass: A Story of Exploration and Innovation* (New York: W.W. Norton, 2004), for the remarkable story of finding direction and its importance to world history.

10. Evan Thomas, *Ike's Bluff: President Eisenhower's Secret Battle to Save the World* (New York: Little, Brown, 2012), 372, 384. Khrushchev overreacted because he was embarrassed. The flights had been going on for two years and the Soviet Air Force, though sometimes knowing about the penetrations of their air space, were unable to do anything about it. Eisenhower, on the other hand, was highly reluctant to authorize the flights since, as a military commander, he knew the severity of reaction in cases of failure or a shoot down. Ike authorized far fewer missions than the swashbucklers at the CIA would have liked. For the strategic weapons comparison, see Neil Sheehan, *A Bright Shining Lie* (New York: Random House, 1988), 592.

11. Without the Amendment, passed in the aftermath of Franklin Delano Roosevelt's unmatched three presidential terms and four elections to the office, who knows if Ike would have declined to run again? He lived in relatively good health until 1969. A third term would have been within his physical capability and maybe within his personal philosophy.

12. Michael Burleigh, *Small Wars in Far Away Places: Global Insurrection and the Making of the Modern World, 1945–1965* (New York: Viking Press, 2013), 433.

13. Sheehan, *A Bright Shining Lie*, 43.

Chapter 2

1. Alfred H. Hurley, *Billy Mitchell: Crusader for Air Power* (Bloomington: Indiana University Press, 1975). The tests would eventually be made, and Mitchell, who had faced courts martial for his persistence, was vindicated in every way.

2. Bill Yenne, *McDonnell Douglas: A Tale of Two Giants* (Greenwich, CT: Bison Books, 1985), 12–15.

3. F. Robert van der Linden, *The Boeing 247: The First Modern Airliner* (Seattle: University of Washington Press, 1991).

4. Yenne, 92–93.

5. *Ibid.*, 95.

6. Magee, 153, 239.

7. Alexandra Richie, *Faust's Metropolis* (New York: Carroll and Graf, 1998).

8. Richard Reeves, *Daring Young Men: The Heroism and Triumph of the Berlin Airlift, June 1948-May 1949* (New York: Simon & Schuster, 2010), 19.

9. Berlin had an area of 355 square miles, about the same as New York City, and an overall population of 3.1 million, of whom 2.1 million lived in the West sector. About two-thirds of the population was female.

10. The Red Army had 20 divisions remaining in and around East German, compared to an allied troop count of 290,000, most of them in Military Police, engineers, mainte-

nance, and service units. Allies had only two combat brigades in Germany. Similarly, heavy weapons and airplane inventories greatly favored the Communist forces. In East Germany and Eastern Europe, the Soviets had 4,000 aircraft, many of them fighters and bombers, compared to 400 between the RAF and the USAAF. This imbalance did not dismay Major General Curtis LeMay, however. He thought his planes could destroy the Soviet air force on the ground in the first 12 hours and then claim air superiority over the battlefields. Although the United States was the only atomic power at the time, no one proposed using that weapon over Germany.

11. The twin engine DC-3, first flown in 1935, carried twice the payload and had twice the engine horsepower of its 1934 forerunner, the DC-2, though it was not much longer, and the cabin height was about the same. The DC-3, first ordered by American Airlines, was much wider to accommodate Pullman-type sleeping bays. The DC-3, some still in operation, has been called "the greatest airliner ever produced anywhere." The same airframe was used to produce 10,000 C-47s for the military during World War II. General Dwight David Eisenhower listed the C-47 as a piece of equipment "most vital to our success in Africa and Europe." Yenne, 96–97.

12. Jonathan Sutherland and Diane Canwell, *Berlin Airlift: The Salvation of a City* (Gretna, LA: Pelican, 2007), 187–188.

13. The C-74 Globemaster I was operational in 1948, with 14 delivered to the USAF by Douglas and deployed on two bases. Production stopped well short of the 50 aircraft originally ordered from Douglas. Instead, Douglas and the Air Force opted for constructing a larger cargo airplane, albeit on the design and test platform provided by the C-74.

14. Reeves, 221.

15. Frederick J. Shaw, editor, *Locating Air Force Base Sites: History's Legacy* (Washington, DC: Air Force History and Museums Program), 77–78.

16. So limited was the range of the six-engine *Gigant* that a navigator was not needed. The plane did cross the Mediterranean and supported the Nazi campaigns in North Africa. See the newspaper article, http://www.dailymail.co.uk/news/article-2203219/Found-70-years-Divers-discover-wreckage-Second-World-War-Giant-German-transport-plane-shot-British-fighter-flying-base-Sardinia.html.

17. The C-124 was a pet project of General Curtis LeMay because it could fly primary nuclear weapons (PNM). As the Globemaster came into active service, warheads were going from small, like the Davy Crockett, to the MK-17 bomb, which was so large it strained the airframe of the C-124 when being loaded. It strained it so much so that the Globemaster groaned as the weapon was slowly, tediously pulled into the cargo bay via the front-loading ramps. No mistakes were wanted for this heaviest U.S. nuclear weapon, which had a yield of 10–15 megatons, the second-most powerful the U.S. produced. Email exchange with Ronald P. Barrett dated December 20, 2015. Barrett is historian of the AFNOA.

18. Vance Quentin Alvis, "Arkansas and the Aluminum Industry" Master's thesis (Fayetteville, AR: College of Business Administration, 1952). Mark Harrison, *The Economics of World War II: Six Great Powers in International Comparison* (Cambridge: Cambridge University Press, 1998). At present, aluminum is used in the aviation industry everywhere in the world. From two-thirds to three-quarters of a passenger plane's dry weight, and from one-twentieth to half of a rocket's dry weight, is aluminum. In the Globemaster III built in the 21st century, aluminum constitutes 73 percent of the 213,000 pounds of total material weight, or 155,000 pounds of aluminum according to Boeing's historical site, http://www.boeing.com/boeing/defense-space/military/c17/c17numbers.page As of 2013, 256 of these giant transports had been built and delivered, 222 to the U.S. Air Force.

19. That would be $187,500,000 in annual payroll for C-124 workers, adjusted to 2010 dollars.

20. *Washington Evening Star*, December 20, 1952, 1.

21. Interview with former Douglas engineer Mike Crowly, January 3, 2015, in possession of author.

22. *Long Beach Press Telegram*, May 15, 1955, 1.

23. *Long Beach Press Telegram*, January 1, 1952, 12.

24. *New York Times*, April 12, 1951, 35.

25. *State Times Advocate* (Baton Rouge, LA), October 13, 1951, 16.

26. *The Plain Speaker* (Hazleton, PA), October 19, 1951, 13.

27. Douglas Aircraft Company, "Background Story—C-124 Globemaster," News Release, 1955. Document number K146.01–15B, 1949–1955, available from USAF AETC AFHRA/RS, Air University, Maxwell AFB, Alabama.

28. From the Air Mobility Command, C-

141 handbook, available online at this address: http://www.c141heaven.info/dotcom/manuals/c141_8999.pdf.

The navigation unit includes a precision, gyro-stabilized platform on which acceleration sensors (accelerometers) are mounted along with a digital computer which performs navigation computations. Each INS calculates and monitors track, ground speed, heading, drift angle, wind direction, velocity, and position (latitude and longitude). Insertion of the desired flight plan provides the system with information necessary to compute flight plan-related information, such as desired track, cross track distance, track angle error and distance and time to the next waypoint (a point on the earth to be overflown). This information can be called up and displayed on the control and display unit (CDU). In addition to performing primary navigation functions, an INS is a source for: en route steering signals for the automatic flight control system (AFCS) (autopilot), driving signals for flight instruments (HSI, ADI, BDHI), air drop calculations, and navigation information to FSAS for display on multifunction display(s).

29. Jay Spenser, *The Airplane: How Ideas Gave Us Wings* (New York: HarperCollins, 2008), 286–287. Tom Logsdon, *The Navstar Global Positioning System* (New York: Van Nostrand Reinhold, 1992), 153. Russia has worked on a similar infrastructure named GLONASS, and the European Union has its Galileo system, which essentially does the same thing as our GPS.

30. Yenne, 184–189.

31. Pat Maio, *Orange County Register*, September 13, 2013. http://www.ocregister.com/articles/boeing-526795-production-beach.html The cost of each C-17 Globemaster III was $202.3 million in 1998 dollars.

32. Yenne, 10.

Chapter 3

1. Laurence Bergreen, *Over the Edge of the World* (New York: HarperCollins, 2003), 13. A sailor who managed to bring back a small bag of cloves or nutmeg "could sell it for enough to buy a small house; he could live off the proceeds the rest of his life."

2. Gurney, *Compass*, 36–37.

3. Will Durant, *The Reformation* (New York: Simon & Schuster, 1957), 192–193.

4. Christopher Columbus, or Cristobal Colon in the Spanish spelling of his name, made four voyages to the New World, in 1492, 1493, 1498, and 1502. He refused to recognize that he had landed in islands other than the East Indies. Map makers never named new lands he had discovered after him. Instead, letters written by Amerigo Vespucci first used the term *novo mondo*, convincing scholars Martin Waldseemuller and Gerardus Mercator to label the Western Hemisphere *America* on maps that would become standard.

5. One nautical mile is officially 6,076.10 U.S. feet or 1,852 meters. Ten degrees of latitude separate, for example, Mexico City (N19° 20´) and Houston, Texas (N29°- 30´), thus the two great North American cities are but one hour 20 minutes of flying time apart in a Globemaster III at its cruise speed or about four hours in a Globemaster II.

6. Durant, 269. See also, Bergreen, *Over the Edge of the World*.

7. Per Collinder, *A History of Marine Navigation*. (London: B.T. Batsford, 1954), 19–20.

8. *Ibid.*, 135. Ty K. Botsford, "Finding Position at Sea: The Eighteenth Century Quest for Longitude," pamphlet accompanying a presentation to the National Collegiate Honors Council Conference, Washington, DC, October 18–22, 2003. For Cook's voyage, see Tony Horwitz, *Blue Latitudes*, New York: Henry Holt, 2002.

9. Charles A. Lindbergh, *The Spirit of St. Louis* (New York: Scribner & Sons, 1953), 103–104.

10. *Ibid.*, 295.

11. *Ibid.*, 401.

12. *Ibid.*, 459.

13. Collinder, 56.

14. Marilyn Bender and Selig Altschul, *The Chosen Instrument: Pan Am, Juan Trippe, The Rise and Fall of an American Entrepreneur* (New York: Simon & Schuster, 1982), 162–163.

15. *Ibid.*, 231–233.

16. http://tighar.org/Projects/Earhart/Archives/Research/ResearchPapers/Noonan.html. See *Popular Aviation* (May 1938).

17. Thomas A. Manning, et al, *History of Air Training Command, 1943–1993* (Randolph Air Force Base, TX: Office of History and Research, 1993), 6, 10.

18. Edgar D. Whitcomb, *On Celestial Wings* (Montgomery AL: Air University, 1995), 1.

19. Alan S. Milward, *War, Economy, and Society, 1939–1945* (Berkeley: University of California Press, 1954), 187. The war spurred an astonishing increase in production, both in quantity and quality, in this country. Milward mentions that "American armaments output exceeded that of the United Kingdom

in 1942 and by 1944 was six times greater," even though Britain had had a much longer period of effort.

20. In 1935, MGM filmed *West Point of the Air* on location at Randolph, a movie most remarkable for the quality of its cast: Wallace Beery, Robert Young, Maureen O'Sullivan, Rosalind Russell, Robert Taylor, and Lewis Stone.

21. Manning, et al, 15.

22. *Ibid.*, 90.

23. William H. McNeill, *Keeping Together in Time: Dance and Drill in Human History* (Cambridge, MA: Harvard University Press, 1995), 2. McNeill gathered considerable support for his hypothesis that, after Maurice of Orange introduced daily drill to the Dutch army in the 1590s, others quickly followed his lead and modern European superiority over other armies resulted.

24. Air Force Specialty Code. Transport navigator AFSC was 1535.

25. Interview with Mr. Robert Fox, October 2010, in possession of author.

26. Stanine (a military acronym from Standard Nine) scoring on a nine-point scale was used by the Army Air Force during World War II to categorize aviation aptitude test results in a simple and accurate manner.

27. Quotation from the movie *Dead Poets Society*, a movie about John Keating.

28. The Convair's two Pratt and Whitney R-2800 engines gave it a cruising speed of 200 knots. There is a static display of a "Flying Classroom" at the Strategic Air & Space Museum on I-80 near Ashland, Nebraska.

29. By the summer of 1945 the United States had produced two atomic bombs through the ultra-secret and ultra-expensive Manhattan project, under the supervision of Gen. Leslie R. Groves, Jr. The two bombs used on Japan in August 1945 made up the whole inventory. It might have been six months before another atomic bomb could be produced. The Imperial Japanese Government surrendered unconditionally on August 15, 1945. The formal ceremony took place on the deck of the U.S.S. *Missouri* in Tokyo Bay one month later.

30. Given is the year of first delivery to the Air Force. Bill Gunston, *American Warplanes* (New York: Crescent Books, 1986).

31. This tipi technique was used by the Stephen H. Long expedition to the Arkansas River source and is described in Edwin James, *Account of an Expedition from Pittsburgh to the Rocky Mountains in the Years 1819–1820* (London, 1823. Reprinted by University of Oklahoma Press), 109.

Chapter 4

1. *History of the 1607th Air Transport Wing, Heavy*, June 1964–December 1964. These figures typify unit strength from 1954 through 1964.

2. *The Daily Mail* (Hagerstown, MD), April 3, 1963, 22. The last man sentenced to a flogging was Franklin W. Cannon, Jr., who as sentenced to 20 lashes for stealing cigarettes in 1963. The punishment received authorization from the Delaware Supreme Court but was not carried out.

3. http://www.heritage.org/research/reports/2004/10/global-us-troop-deployment-1950-2003.

4. Frederick A. Johnsen, *Lockheed C-141 Starlifter*. (North Branch, MN: Specialty Press, 2005), 6.

5. In the campaign of 1960, Kennedy articulated his ideas of a new force to meet Soviet challenges other than what had been conventional wisdom, that is reliance on nuclear weapons to deter aggression. Some thinking during the later days of the Eisenhower administration concerned the option of limited nuclear warfare to confront limited-war situations. See General Frederic H. Smith, Jr., "Nuclear Weapons and Limited War," *Air University Quarterly Review* 12, no. 1 (Spring 1960): 3–27.

6. Dover AFB, *The Airlifter* 6, no. 1 (January 1961), 1.

7. Department of Defense, "Narrative Summaries of Accidents Involving U.S. Nuclear Weapons, 1950–1980," 9, 17, 20. http://www.dod.mil/pubs/foi/operation_and_plans/NuclearChemicalBiologicalMatters/635.pdf.

An incident involving a C-124 occurred on July 6, 1959, after the plane crashed on take-off from Barksdale AFB, Louisiana. The ensuing fire destroyed the airplane and the nuclear weapon that was aboard without its exploding. Safety devices prevented detonation, but the accident resulted in radioactive contamination in the immediate area. Another C-124 was involved in a nuclear accident at Wright-Patterson AFB, Ohio, on October 11, 1965. Contamination infused the airplane, but after normal cleaning, the Globemaster returned to service.

8. *Delaware State News*, January 9, 1961, 1.

9. A tradition started with C-17 Globemaster IIIs to name them after specific American people, as the U.S. Navy does with its aircraft carriers. One C-17 is named *The Spirit of Strom Thurmond* and is stationed with the 437th Airlift Wing, Charleston AFB.

10. The treaty was signed in Washington, DC, by Dean Acheson, Truman's Secretary of State, and ratified in July by the Republican majority U.S. Senate. The original NATO members were Belgium, Netherlands, Luxembourg, France, United Kingdom, Portugal, Italy, Norway, Denmark, Iceland, Canada, and the United States. Greece and Turkey joined in 1952. As in the Hegelian view, every thesis gets its antithesis, so the Soviet Union formed the Warsaw Pact in opposition to NATO.

11. An offhand remark by the Soviet premier on November 18, 1956, in Poland, was interpreted by the U.S. public as a threat to bury us under rubble with a nuclear bombardment. The wisecracking Nikita Khrushchev might have meant that. He never explained the remark, but more likely it was an ominous translation of indomitable peasant will more closely resembling "I will be at your funeral."

12. *New York Times*, January 27, 1961, 4.

13. *New York Times*, September 22, 1961, 5.

14. World copper production went from 4 million tons in 1960 to 7.2 million tons in 1980. From 1980 to 2010, production again doubled to 16 million tons. United States Geological Survey, *Minerals Yearbook*, 2012.

15. Harry Heist, "The Flying History of the 1607th Air Transport Wing (H), Dover Air Force Base." An undated pamphlet available through the Air Mobility Command Museum.

16. Col. David M. Sibbald, "Abandoning the Congo," *Hanger Digest* 3, no. 2 (April 2003): 6.

17. Cecil Brownlow, "Congo Airlift Provides Tough Support Test for USAF," *Aviation Week* 73, no. 7 (August 15, 1960): 32–34. Digitized by the International Studies Association, "Background on World Politics," 4, no. 3 (Autumn 1960): 95 and accessible through JSTOR using this link: http://www.jstor.org/stable/3013739.

18. Air Mobility Command Museum, *Hanger Digest* 3, no. 2 (April 2003): 4–8.

19. Sibbald, 6.

20. *New York Times*, December 8, 1961, 1. Elisabethville is now Lubumbashi.

21. The four-engine, piston-powered DC-6 was built in the Douglas plant at Santa Monica. The Air Force version was named the C-118 *Liftmaster*. Goran Bjorkdahl insists that Hammarskjold's plane was downed by enemy fire with intention. See newspaper articles such as Julian Borger, "Dag Hammarskjöld: evidence suggests UN chief's plane was shot down," *The Guardian*, August 17, 2011.

22. *Gadsden Times*, September 17, 1963, 1.

23. Ray L. Bowers, "USAF Airlift and the Airmobility Idea in Vietnam." *Air University Review* (November–December 1974).

24. Walt Rykiel, *Airlifter*, 1965, 1.

25. Heist, "The Flying History of the 1607th Air Transport Wing (H), Dover Air Force Base."

Chapter 5

1. The "crush" came from prolonged use of the headset over the hat.

2. So-called because it took 38 cuts going around the lid of a C-ration can to open it.

3. A gallon of high-octane gasoline weighs a little over six pounds, and 36,000 pounds of fuel comes to about 6,000 gallons of gasoline on a max load for a C-124. The four engines together consumed about 603 gallons of fuel per hour.

4. Salazar, a former economics professor, ruled Portugal from 1932 until his death in 1968. The July 29, 1940, issue of *Life* magazine said he was "the greatest Portuguese since Prince Henry the Navigator." In the years of his rule, the U.S. Air Force enjoyed unbridled use of Lajes AB.

5. The first five women to complete Undergraduate Navigator Training at the Air Force Academy received their wings in 1981. John C. Fredriksen, *The United States Air Force: A Chronology* (Santa Barbara, CA: ABC-CLIO, Inc. 2011), October 12, 1977.

6. Samuel Eliot Morrison, *The Great Explorers: The European Discovery of America* (New York: Oxford University Press, 1978), 509.

7. *Ibid.*, 695. A contemporary Spanish nobleman's description of Drake referred to him as one of the greatest celestial navigators.

8. Led by the brightest, Sirius, the other 18 first magnitude stars selected for astronavigation are: Achernar, Aldebaran, Altair, Antares, Arcturus, Betelgeuse, Canopus, Capella, Deneb, Fomalhaut, Hadar, Pollux, Procyon, Regulus, Rigel, Rigel, Kent, Spica, and Vega. Stars are selected for brightness and factors such as azimuth, altitude, and continuity. The most-used second magnitude stars for North Atlantic routes included the lip star of the Little Dipper, Kochab; the lip star of the Big Dipper, Dubhe; and the end of the handle, Alkaid. Polaris, the North Star, is not in the sight reduction tables, but is a useful star at the end of the Little Dipper handle. Four planets are used in celestial navigation, including the brightest body in the

heavens other than the Sun and the Moon, the planet Venus. The others are Mars, Jupiter, and Saturn. Of these, it is known that Meriwether Lewis, setting out from St. Louis in 1804 on the epic Corps of Discovery journey to the Pacific and back, used a sextant and was trained by Jefferson himself in the art of celestial navigation. Lewis knew by sight Antares, Altair, Regulus, Spica, Pollux, Aldebaran, and Fomalhaut. Stephen E. Ambrose, *Undaunted Courage: Meriwether Lewis, Thomas Jefferson, and the Opening of the American West* (New York: Simon & Schuster, 1996), 119.

9. R. P. Dinsmore "Ocean Weather Ships, 1940–1980." http://www.uscg.mil/history/webcutters/rpdinsmore_oceanstations.asp. In the Atlantic, the U.S. Coast Guard operated five vessels; the UK, Norway, and France operated four additional.

10. Telephone interview with Mike Radowski, March 23, 2014. Notes in possession of author.

11. Richard Reeves, *Daring Young Men: The Heroism and Triumph of the Berlin Airlift, June 1948–May 1949*. (New York: Simon & Schuster, 2010), 36.

12. Interview with Emory Dockery, C-124 pilot, dated April 29, 2014, and in possession of author.

13. *New York Times*, May 7, 1954, 3.

14. Organized by Nancy Love, 29 WASP female pilots, including Jacqueline Cochran, took part in flying aircraft to Europe. Over 1,500 female civilian pilots flew for the military, ferrying planes and supporting training and logistics.

15. Alfred Goldberg, ed., *A History of the United States Air Force* (New York: Arno Press, 1974), 191–92. A traditional Inuit village has been recognized in the modern name Pituffik Airfield, although SAC retains the name Thule AB for its permanent installation.

16. Douglas Larsen, *Abilene* (TX) *Reporter-News*, January 19, 1954, 19. Larsen was on the flight.

17. *New York Times*, October 11, 1956, 33.

18. For a modern look at McMurdo Sound, see *Encounters at the End of the World*, a 2007 documentary film by Werner Herzog. Herzog and his film crew arrived at McMurdo on a Globemaster III.

19. *Redlands* (CA) *Daily Facts*, Tuesday, January 22, 1957, 4.

20. *New York Times*, October 4, 1957, 6; November 2, 1957, 8.

21. J. A. Bender and A. J. Gow, *Deep Drilling in Antarctica*. International Association of Scientific Hydrology Publication 55 (Helsinki: Symposium on Antarctic Glaciology, 1960), 132–141.

22. John Caffin, "Value of South Pole," *United Press*, syndicated news report available from *Logansport (IN) Pharos-Tribune*, December 4, 1957, 37.

23. *New York Times*, February 13, 1958, 12.

24. Ricky DeRoo, http://www.connie survivors.com/1-1960_mcmurdo_article.htm.

25. Titian Peale, the son of early American painter Charles Willson Peale, had accompanied Major Stephen H. Long, the explorer who land-navigated his way across what he described as the Great American Desert (Kansas and Oklahoma) in 1820. Yale University's Beinecke Library has a collection of Titian Peale's artwork from these adventures.

26. Ernest K. Gann, *Fate is the Hunter* (New York: Simon & Schuster, 1961), 263.

27. The Code of Federal Regulations of the United States of America, Title 32, National Defense, paragraph 761.8. The arrangement began in the 1950s and was updated annually through the present.

28. Sponge rubber paddles, introduced by the Japanese in the 1950s, had the capacity to move the ball around in an almost magical way. http://www.athleticscholarships.net/history-of-table-tennis.htm.

29. Evan Thomas, *Ike's Bluff: President Eisenhower's Secret Battle to Save the World* (New York: Little, Brown, 2012), 313, 366. Ike feared escalating military budgets and the ever-rising costs of arms more than he feared Soviet nuclear strike abilities.

30. Dan Briody, *The Halliburton Agenda: The Politics of Oil and Money*. (Hoboken, NJ: John Wiley & Sons, 2004), 164.

Chapter 6

1. Gann, 312.

2. Samuel Eliot Morison, *Admiral of the Ocean Sea* (Boston: Little, Brown, 1942), 105. The descendants of Cristobol Colon are entitled to receive ten percent of Spanish government profits derived from Columbus' Great Enterprise.

3. The most recent referendum on November 6, 2012, resulted in discussions with the U.S. Senate and President Barack Obama about a statehood plan for Puerto Rico.

4. Caamano escaped with his life to England and then took up residence in Castro's Cuba. In 1973 he returned to the Dominican Republic to lead a movement to overthrow the Balaguer government. He died in the

effort but has martyr status among the DR's masses.

5. Operation Urgent Fury resulted in a U.S. victory that proofed the small island (132 square miles) from what President Ronald Reagan called "the Soviet-Cuban militarization" of the Caribbean. The U.S. Army deployed 7,300 troops that were met by the Grenadian army with small contingents of Cuban and North Korean military advisors. The airlifters were C-141 Starlifters and the C-130 Hercules. No Globemaster IIs or IIIs were involved.

6. The Aviation Zone at theaviationzone.com.

7. Operation Urgent Fury resulted in a U.S. victory that proofed the small island (132 square miles) from what President Ronald Reagan called "the Soviet-Cuban militarization" of the Caribbean. The U.S. Army deployed 7,300 troops that were met by the Grenadian army with small contingents of Cuban and North Korean military advisors. The airlifters were C-141 Starlifters and the C-130 Hercules. No Globemaster II's or III's were involved.

8. Designated the 62nd Troop Carrier Wing until January 1, 1965, the Wing was composed of the 7th and 8th Air Transport Squadrons.

9. Sparky Imeson, *Mountain Flying* (Long Beach, CA: Airguide, 1982), 56.

10. *Seattle Daily Times*, April 7, 1963, 105.

11. United International News, "Arctic Night: Troops Maneuver at 40 Below Zero."

12. Leverett G. Richards, Aviation Editor, *The Oregonian*, April 9, 1956, 36.

13. Although Denali, "the High One," is preferred by many purists today, the highest North American mountain is still officially Mount McKinley and has been since 1917. The official elevation changed though in 2013, from 20,320 feet above sea level to 20,237 feet, as did the name of the National Park of the surrounding area. The other five Union Army officers who ascended to the presidency (Grant, Hayes, Garfield, Arthur, and Benjamin Harrison) had all been generals. McKinley, much younger than the others during the Civil War, rose to the rank of major.

14. Mark Obmascik, *The Big Year: A Tale of Man, Nature, and Fowl Obsession* (New York: Free Press, 2004), 168–171. There are charter flights into Attu and private, but sparse, quarters available for bird watchers who are pursuing life lists.

15. http://ww2today.com/29th-may-1943-the-dead-mans-guard-after-banzai-suicide-charge. See Donald M. Goldstein and Katherine V. Dillon, *The Willawaw War: The Arkansas National Guard in the Aleutians in World War II* (Fayetteville: University of Arkansas Press, 1992).

16. The Delco (a division of General Motors) 1958 advertisement can be seen via the link: https://www.youtube.com/watch?v=Ipcjwq3e6U4. The film was made when Charles Wilson was Eisenhower's secretary of defense. Wilson, a former CEO of General Motors, said something like "What's good for General Motors is good for the country" in his Senate confirmation hearings of 1953.

17. January 22, 1965, a MATS plane (52–1058) from Dover AFB impacted Mount Helmos in Turkey. Snow and poor visibility contributed to the crash, which was tagged as "navigation error."

Chapter 7

1. Gann, 292.

2. General Chuck Yeager and Leo Janos, *Yeager* (New York: Bantam Books, 1985), 129–130. Yeager wrote that, at 42,000 feet, his Mach needle went off the scale and he realized that he was flying supersonic, and it was, "as smooth as a baby's bottom. After all the anxiety, breaking the sound barrier turned out to be a perfectly paved speedway." On the ground, men in the tracking van heard what sounded like a distant rumble of thunder, which was the first sonic boom by an airplane ever heard on earth. Yeager had broken two ribs earlier in the week when his galloping horse hit a closed gate after dark and threw him head over heels to the ground. Yeager did not consult the flight surgeon, who would have grounded him, thereby risking the whole experiment. The prior eight X-1 flights had all had Yeager at the controls. No one else had flown the X-1 or knew the plane anywhere near Yeager's understanding of it. Muroc Dry Lake Air Base was used for testing as early as 1944. Two early settlers, the Corum brothers, spelled their name backwards to christen their pioneer settlement Muroc in the Dry Lake. Now on Edwards Air Base, the locale affords extraordinary features of visibility, lack of obstructions, and surface area for high speed and experimental testing of aircraft. *Chronicle of Aviation* (London: Chronicle Communications, 1992), 424.

3. But not to the public because immediately after breaking the barrier, the program was classified as Top Secret and Yeager was kept under wraps.

4. *Yeager*, 319.

5. Military versus civilian control over the aerospace decisions was at stake. NASA, like the NACA before it, used mostly contract civilian test pilots who were paid far more for their risky work than were the military test pilots like Chuck Yeager and Richard Bong. Yeager, a captain in the Air Force when he broke the sound barrier, was making about $250 a month. Neil Armstrong, a civilian, made up to $100,000 a year testing planes for the National Advisory Committee on Aeronautics (NACA), NASA's predecessor.

6. Silver tans were phased out and could be worn through 1965.

7. C-124s at Charleston, for example, in addition to the regular lines of supply, flew uncommon missions all over the world in the years 1957–1969, examples being Chile, Antarctica, and flying space capsules to Cape Canaveral. There is a C-124 on static display today at Joint Base Charleston.

8. Mike Radowski in nav stories, www.usaf-nav-history.com

9. See Bowers, 126, for example.

10. William L. Farrar interview as recounted in Earl Berlin, *Douglas C-124 Globemaster II* (Simi Valley, CA: Ginter Books, 2000), 64–66.

11. The official count of B-52s lost in the Vietnam War is 15, most of them to SAMs in the concentrated 1972 Christmas bombing of Hanoi.

12. In his excellent account of navigating C-130s in the Vietnam theater at about the same time, Bill Barry describes an incident generated by the no hat/bell ringing custom. *A Trash Hauler in Vietnam* (Jefferson, NC: McFarland, 2008). The rules of the bar are generally posted on a wooden or engraved plaque in grandiose language. Infractions are self-policed; if someone observes a rule being broken, they "ring the bell."

Chapter 8

1. *Daily Oklahoman*, May 10, 1964, 1.

2. Telephone interview with Mr. Rick Parr, October 24, 2010, in possession of author.

3. Bob Buck, *North Star over my Shoulder* (New York: Simon & Schuster, 2002), 256.

4. Web-published statement by Loadmaster John Christy on August 30, 2010: "In 1964, we were on our way to Korea with hazardous cargo ... over mountains in California, the C-124 dropped 4,800 feet. I left the floor, hitting my head on the ceiling which was thirteen feet up. I grabbed the hoist cable and slid down to the floor." Johnjames79@live.com.

5. Ray L. Bowers, *Tactical Airlift: The United States Air Force in Southeast Asia* (Washington, DC: Office of Air Force History, 1983), 126.

6. Web-published statement by M/Sgt James Zeitler on August 30, 2010. Jnjzeitler 689@cox.net.

7. Interview with Jack Wofford, February 3, 2014, in possession of author.

8. *Ibid.* See the *Hamilton* (Ontario) *Spectator*, April 20, 1956.

9. Web-published statement by Fred Barber, July 29, 2013. derfb1@aol.com.

10. The Cessna was registered to Richard Gordon Warfield of Helena, Arkansas, with passengers Warren Witt, Jr., and James Chaddick. The plane was flight planned for Pine Bluff.

11. National Transportation Safety Board report FTW66A0043, available at http://www.ntsb.gov.

12. Email from John Hille dated April 12, 2014.

13. *Ogden Standard-Examiner*, November 12, 1965. Reported in this article are these C-124 crewmembers who perished, along with 40 others, in the crash: T/Sgt Robert Leo Burnis, M/Sgt Fred Hart, and Herman E. Caling, all of Hill Air Force Base, Ogden, Utah. Captain Beasley and co-pilot Lt. Donald B. Maestaz had taken leave and were not on the commercial flight. Lt. Sullivan had first and second degree burns and smoke inhalation.

14. Email from John J. Sullivan dated March 22, 2014, in possession of author.

15. Anthony J. Tambini, *Douglas Jumbo's—The Globemaster* (Brookline Village, MA: Branden, 1999), 134–144.

16. USAF Serial Number Search Results at http://cgibin.rcn.com/jeremy.k/cgi-bin/gzUsafSearch.pl?target=&content=Globemaster. Visited by author March 18, 2014. See also a recent article on this mystery at http://www.shreveporttimes.com/article/99999999/NEWS10/103230325/60-years-later-mystery-lingers-over-general-s-loss. First viewed by author March 19, 2014. Aviation Safely Network website, address on this accident is http://aviation-safety.net/database/record.php?id=19510323-0. Viewed March 22, 2014.

17. Sweden's 1953 *Naval Calendar*, the equivalent of Britain's *Janes' Fighting Ships*, estimated a total of 340 known Soviet submarines. See the *Washington Evening Star*, December 20, 1952, 1.

18. Casey Grove and Mike Dunham, *Anchorage Daily News*, June 28, 2012. See article at http://www.military.com/dailynews/2012/06/28/alaska-glacier-debris-idd-as-long-lost-af-c124.html.
19. http://abcnews.go.com/U.S./story?id=95521&page=1. See Appendix 1 for Class A Mishaps for the C-124 Globemaster II.
20. See Appendix 1.
21. Earl Berlin, *Douglas C-124 Globemaster II* (Simi Valley, CA: Ginter Books, 2000), 20.
22. Frederick O. Smetana, *Flight Vehicle Performance and Aerodynamic Control*. AIAA Educations Series (Wright-Patterson Air Force Base, OH: Air Force Institute of Technology, 2001), 45–46. In comparison, the B-52's wing was thinner in structure and was more flexible, capable of moving up 26 feet from its position on the ground during pull-up.
23. Rosario Rausa, *Skyraider, the Douglas A-1 "Flying Dump Truck"* (Baltimore, MD: Nautical and Aviation Publishing Company of America, 1987), 7.
24. Pamphlet entitled "History of the 62nd Air Transport Wing (H), 1 July–31 December 1965," 34 available from Air Force Historical Research Agency, Maxwell AFB, Alabama. The crew received decorations.

Chapter 9

1. Bernard B. Fall, *Hell in a Very Small Place: The Siege of Dien Bien Phu* (New York: J. B. Lippincott, 1966).
2. France insisted on allied recognition of her rights to Indochina and restoration of her control as a condition to joining the North Atlantic Treaty Organization in 1947.
3. Bernard B. Fall, *Street Without Joy* (Mechanicsburg, PA: Stackpole Books, 1994), 15–16. Fall, an Austrian by birth and a Frenchman by choice, with the rise of Nazi power and practices spent much of his adult life in Indochina, witnessing and interviewing participants in the wars after 1945. He was killed in Vietnam in 1967. This book was originally published in 1961, in time for American planners to read before the 1965 buildup of combat forces in Vietnam. That would have been a good idea.
4. Stanley Weintraub, *MacArthur's War: Korea and the Undoing of an American Hero* (New York: Free Press, 2000), 213.
5. *Ibid.*, 197.
6. *Corpus Christi Caller-Times*, May 5, 1954, 20. "Second U.S. Airlift leaves for Indochina ... C-124 Globemasters of the 322nd U.S. Air Division today took off from Istres Le Tube air base near Marseilles with French Union troops in the second such airlift to Indochina. It did not disclose how many of the giant Globemasters took part in the lift, but seven were in the first operation."
7. Tom Waller, "War on a Flying Cloud," *Journal of the Fort Smith Historical Society* 37, no. 2 (September 2013): 25. See also Lt. Gen. Harold G. Moore and Joseph L. Galloway, *We Were Soldiers Once and Young* (New York: Random House, 1992), 25.
8. J. D. Coleman, *Pleiku: The Dawn of Helicopter Warfare in Vietnam* (New York: St. Martin's, 1988), 43.
9. H. W. Brands, *American Dreams: The United States Since 1945* (New York: Penguin, 2010), 137.
10. Email from Joe Dempsey dated June 1, 2015, in possession of author.
11. Bowers, 207. McConnell was born in Booneville, Arkansas, and served as Chief of Staff of the U.S. Air Force from 1965–1969.
12. Office of History, *Anything, Anywhere, Anytime: An Illustrated History of the Military Airlift Command, 1941–1991* (Scott Air Force Base: Headquarters Military Airlift Command, 1991), 120.
13. Bowers, 384. Most of this large volume recounts performances of C-123s and C-130s in Vietnam, but the C-124 is noted for its contributions. Deactivating the Tachi squadron in December 1969 was strenuously opposed by WTO and CINCPAC. Air National Guard units from Georgia and Tennessee took up the slack in delivering oversized cargo to the war zone in reserve C-124s.
14. Barney Madden account. Referenced August 25, 2016, at http://www.aviastar.org/air/usa/douglas_globemaster.php?p=4
15. Robert J. Brandt, *Thunderbird Lounge: An aviator's story about one early transportation helicopter company, along with its sister companies as they paved the way in what was to become "a helicopter war."* (Bloomington, IN: Trafford, 2006), 46–47.
16. Photo and caption courtesy of Sam McGowan. See his online narrative at http://www.sammcgowan.com/c124.html.
17. SEATO, the Southeast Asia Treaty Organization, a defense alignment similar to NATO to resist Communism in this area of the world, was formed in 1954–1955 and included Australia, New Zealand, Thailand, Philippines, Pakistan and France. Next to the U.S., Australia sent more combat troops and suffered more losses in the Vietnam War than any other SEATO signer. Australia has its issues in properly recognizing and providing for its Vietnam veterans.

18. Robert A. Caro, *The Years of Lyndon Johnson: The Passage of Power* (New York: Knopf, 2012), 604.

Chapter 10

1. Roger G. Miller, *To Save a City: The Berlin Airlift, 1948–1949* (College Station: Texas A & M Press, 2000), 199.

2. *Ibid.*, 200.

3. "[By 1962] America had built the largest empire in history ... 850,000 military men and civilian officials serving overseas in 106 counties." Sheehan, *Bright Shining Lie*, 43.

Bibliography

"Air Navigation AF Manual 51–40 Vol. 1 and Vol. II." Department of the Air Force, 1954.
Alvis, Vance. "Arkansas and the Aluminum Industry." Master's Thesis, University of Arkansas, 1952.
Ambrose, Stephen E. *Undaunted Courage: Meriwether Lewis, Thomas Jefferson, and the Opening of the American West*. New York: Simon & Schuster, 1996.
Barry, Bill. *A Trash Hauler in Vietnam*. Jefferson, NC: McFarland, 2008.
Bender, J.A., and A.J. Gow. "Deep Drilling in Antarctica." *International Association of Scientific Hydrology*, Symposium on Antarctic Glaciology, Publication 55 (1960): 132–141.
Bender, Marilyn, and Selig Altschul. *The Chosen Instrument: Juan Trippe, Pan Am, and the Rise and Fall of an American Entrepreneur*. New York: Simon & Schuster, 1982.
Bennett, Jack O. "Reminiscences and Recollections of an Airlift Pilot." In *Concerning the History of the Berlin Crisis, 1948–49*. Berlin: Press and Information Office of the Land Berlin, 1985.
Bergreen, Laurence. *Over the Edge of the World*. New York: HarperCollins, 2003.
Berlin, Earl. *Douglas C-124 Globemaster II (Air Force Legends)*. California: Naval Fighters, 2000.
Bickers, Richard Townshend. *Military Air Transport Airlift: The Illustrated History*. London: Osprey, 1998.
Blum, Robert M. *Drawing the Line: The Origin of the American Containment Policy in East Asia*. New York: W.W. Norton, 1982.
Borowski, Harry R. "A Narrow Victory: The Berlin Blockade and the American Military Response." *Air University Review* 32, no. 5 (July–August 1981): 18–31.
Bowers, Jack S. et al. *The United States Air Force in Southeast Asia, 1961–1973*. Washington, D.C.: Office of Air Force History, 1984.
Brady, James. *The Coldest War*. New York: St. Martin's Press, 1990.
Brands, H.W. *American Dreams: The United States Since 1945*. New York: Penguin, 2010.
Brandt, Robert J. *Thunderbird Lounge: An Aviator's Story About One Transportation Helicopter Company Along with Its Sister Companies as They Paved the Way in What Was to Become a Helicopter War*. Bloomington, IN: Trafford, 2006.
Briody, Dan. *The Halliburton Agenda: The Politics of Oil and Money*. Hoboken, NJ: John Wiley & Sons, 2004.
Brownlow, Cecil. "Congo Airlift Provides Tough Support Test for USAF." *Aviation Week* 73, no. 7 (August 1960): 32–34.
Buck, Bob. *North Star Over My Shoulder*. New York: Simon & Schuster, 2002.
Burkard, Richard W. *Military Airlift Command: Historical Handbook, 1941–1984*. Scott Air Force Base, IL: Military Air Command Historical Office, 1984.

Burleigh, Michael. *Small Wars, Faraway Places: Global Insurrection and the Making of the Modern World, 1945–1965.* New York: Penguin, 2013.
Buzzanco, Robert. *Masters of War: Military Dissent and Politics in the Vietnam Era.* Cambridge, UK: Cambridge University Press, 1996.
Caro, Robert A. *The Years of Lyndon Johnson: The Passage of Power.* New York: Knopf, 2012.
Clark, Douglas Alan. *Aerospace Historian Cumulative Index by Author, Book Review, Title, and Subject, 1974–1983.* Manhattan, KS: Sunflower University Press, 1985.
Clinton, Bill. "Remarks to Employees of McDonnell Douglas in Long Beach, California." *Weekly Compilation of Presidential Documents* 32, no. 8 (February 26, 1996): 358.
Coleman, J. D. *Pleiku: The Dawn of Helicopter Warfare in Vietnam.* New York: St. Martin's, 1988.
Collinder, Per. *A History of Marine Navigation.* London: B.T. Batsford, 1954.
Cowles, Alfred. *The True Story of Aluminum.* Chicago: H. Regnery, 1958.
Dabney, Joseph Earl. *HERK: Hero of the Skies.* Lakemont, GA: Cobble House Books, 1979.
Donovan, Robert J. *Nemesis: Truman and Johnson in the Coils of War in Asia.* New York: St. Martin's-Marek, 1984.
Drendel, Lou. *Aircraft of the Vietnam War.* Fallbrook, CA: Aero, 1980.
Duncan, Scott. "The Combat History of the F-105." *Aerospace Historian* 22, no. 3 (Fall 1975): 121–128.
Dunn, Joe P. "In Search of Lessons: The Development of a Vietnam Historiography." *Parameters* 9, no. 4 (December 1979): 28–40.
Durant, Will. *The Reformation.* New York: Simon & Schuster, 1957.
Fall, Bernard B. *Hell in a Very Small Place: The Siege of Dien Bien Phu.* Philadelphia: Lippincott, 1967.
_____. *Street Without Joy: Indochina at War, 1946–54.* Harrisburg, PA: Stackpole, 1961.
Fay, Elton C. "Air Strength of the United States." *Annals of the American Academy of Political and Social Science* 299, no. 1 (May 1955): 30–37.
Ferrell, Robert H. *Harry S. Truman and the Cold War Revisionists.* Columbia: University of Missouri Press, 2006.
"Flight Manual Basic Book T.O. 1C-124C-1." Secretary of the Air Force, July 15, 1960.
Francillon, Rene J., Jim Dunn, and Carl E. Porter. *McDonnell Douglas Aircraft since 1920.* New York: Putnam, 1988.
Fredriksen, John C. *The United States Air Force: A Chronology.* Santa Barbara, CA: ABC-CLIO, 1977.
Gann, Ernest K. *Fate in the Hunter.* New York: Simon & Schuster, 1961.
Giangreco, D.M., and Robert E. Griffin. *Airbridge to Berlin: The Berlin Crisis of 1948, Its Origin and Aftermath.* Novato, CA: Presidio Press, 1988.
Gunston, Bill. *American War Planes.* New York: Crescent, 1986.
_____. *Chronicle of Aviation.* London: Chronicle Communication, 1992.
Gurney, Alan. *Compass: A Story of Exploration and Innovation.* New York: W.W. Norton, 2004.
Guston, Bill, and Mike Badrocke. *The Illustrated History of McDonnell Douglas: From Cloudster to Boeing.* Oxford, UK: Osprey, 1999.
Halberstam, David. *The Best and the Brightest.* New York: Random House, 1972.
_____. *The Coldest Winter: America and the Korean War.* New York: Hyperion, 2007.
Harber, B.B. *Logistical Support of Airmobile Operations Republic of Vietnam, 1961–1971.* St. Louis: U.S. Army Aviation Systems Command, 1971.
Harris, Mike. *Astro Navigation by Pocket Computer.* London: Adlard Coles, 1989.
Harrison, Mark. *The Economics of World War II: Six Great Powers in International Comparison.* Cambridge, UK: Cambridge University Press, 1998.
Heist, Harry. "The Flying History of the 1607th Air Transport Wing (H)." Air Mobility Command Museum, Dover AFB, Delaware, undated.

Hicks, Louis. "Normal Accidents in Military Operations." *Sociological Perspectives* 36, no. 4 (Winter 1993): 377–391.
Higham, Robin D.S. *Air Power: A Concise History*. London: Macdonald, 1972.
Hunt, Michael H. *Lyndon Johnson's War: America's Cold War Crusade in Vietnam, 1945–1968*. New York: Hill and Wang, 1996.
Hurley, Alfred H. *Billy Mitchell: Crusader for Air Power*. Bloomington: Indiana University Press, 1975.
Imeson, Sparky. *Mountain Flying*. Long Beach, CA: Airguide, 1982.
Johnsen, Frederick A. *Lockheed C-141 Starlifter*. North Branch, MN: Specialty Press, 2005.
Karnow, Stanley. *Vietnam: A History*. New York: Penguin, 1997.
Kurland, Gerald. *The Conflict in Vietnam*. Charlottesville, VA: SamHar Press, 1973.
Kyselka, Will, and Ray Lanterman. *North Star to Southern Cross*. Honolulu: University of Hawaii Press, 1976.
Launius, Roger D., and Coy F. Cross II. *MAC and the Legacy of the Berlin Airlift*. Scott Air Force Base: Military Airlift Command, Office of History, 1989.
Lindbergh, Charles A. *The Spirit of St. Louis*. New York: Scribner & Sons, 1953.
Logsdon, Tom. *The Navstar Global Positioning System*. New York: Van Nostrand Reinhold, 1992.
Maguire, Jon A. *Gooney Birds & Ferry Tales: The 27th Air Transport Group in World War II*. Atglen, PA: Schiffer Military History Publishing, 2004.
Manning, Thomas. *History of Air Training Command, 1943–1993*. Randolph AFB, TX: Office of History and Research, 1993.
Martin, Harold H. *StarLifter: The C-141: Lockheed's High-Speed Flying Truck*. Brattleboro, VT: Stephen Green Press, 1972.
McCullough, David. *Truman*. New York: Simon & Schuster, 1992.
Mee, Jr., Charles L. *Meeting at Potsdam*. New York: M. Evans, 1975.
Military Airlift Command, Office of History. *Anything, Anywhere, Anytime: An Illustrated History of the Military Airlift Command, 1941–1991*. Scott Air Force Base, IL: Headquarters Military Airlift Command, 1991.
Miller, Karen. "'Air Power Is Peace Power': The Aircraft Industry's Campaign for Public and Political Support, 1943–1949." *The Business History Review* 70, no. 3 (Autumn 1996): 297–327.
Miller, Roger G. *To Save a City: The Berlin Airlift, 1948–1949*. College Station, TX: Texas A & M Press, 2000.
Millward, Alan S. *War, Economy, and Society, 1939–1945*. Berkeley: University of California Press, 1954.
Moore, Lt. Gen. Harold G., and Joseph L. Galloway. *We Were Soldiers Once and Young*. New York: Random House, 1992.
Morison, Samuel Eliot. *Admiral of the Ocean Sea: A Life of Christopher Columbus*. Reissue. New York: Little, Brown, 1991.
_____. *The Great Explorers: The European Discovery of America*. New York: Oxford University Press, 1978.
Obmascik, Mark. *The Big Year: A Tale of Man, Nature, and Fowl Obsession*. New York: Free Press, 2004.
Owen, Robert C. *Air Mobility*. Lincoln, NB: Potomac Books, 2013.
Peake, Louis. *The United States in the Vietnam War, 1954–1975: A Selected, Annotated Bibliography*. New York: Garland, 1986.
Porter, Gareth, ed. *Vietnam: A History in Documents*. New York: New American Library, 1981.
Prochnau, William. *Upon a Distant War*. New York: Vintage Books, 1996.
Rausa, Rosario. *Skyraider: The Douglas A-1 "Flying Dump Truck."* Annapolis, MD: Nautical and Aviation Publishing, 1982.
Reeves, Richard. *Daring Young Men: The Heroism and Triumph of the Berlin Airlift, June 1948-May 1949*. New York: Simon & Schuster, 2010.

Richie, Alexandra. *Faust's Metropolis*. New York: Carroll and Graf, 1998.
Roberson, Patricia Q., and Naomi L. Mitchell, eds. *Aerospace Science: Frontiers of Aviation History*. Maxwell Air Force Base, AL: Air Force Reserve Officer Training Corps, 1997.
Rykiel, Walt. "Airlifter." *Airlifter*, 1965.
Shaw, Frederick J., ed. *Locating Air Force Base Sites: History's Legacy*. Washington, D.C.: Air Force History and Museum Program, 2004.
Sheehan, Neil. *A Bright Shining Lie: John Paul Vann and America in Vietnam*. New York: Random House, 1988.
Sibbald, David M. "Abandoning the Congo." *Hanger Digest* 3, no. 2 (April 2003): 6.
Slaughter, Frank G. *The Mapmaker: A Novel of the Days of Prince Henry, the Navigator*. New York: Doubleday, 1957.
Slayton, Robert A. *Master of the Air: William Tunner and the Success of Military Airlift*. Tuscaloosa: University of Alabama Press, 2010.
Spanier, John, and Steven W. Hook. *American Foreign Policy Since World War II*. Washington, D.C.: Congressional Quarterly, 1998.
Spenser, Jay. *The Airplane: How Ideas Gave Us Wings*. New York: HarperCollins, 2008.
Stanton, Shelby. *Anatomy of a Division: The 1st Air Cavalry in Vietnam*. New York: Presidio Press, 1987.
Sutherland, Jonathan, and Diane Canwell. *Berlin Airlift: The Salvation of a City*. Gretna, LA: Pelican, 2007.
Tambini, Anthony J. *Douglas Jumbo's The Globemaster*. Boston: Branden, 1999.
Taylor, Cal. *Remembering an Unsung Giant: The Douglas C-133 Cargomaster and Its People*. Olympia, WA: Firstfleet, 2015.
Thomas, Evan. *Ike's Bluff: President Eisenhower's Secret Battle to Save the World*. New York: Little, Brown, 2013.
Thompson, Leroy. *Uniforms of the Indo-China and Vietnam Wars*. London: Blandford Press, 1984.
Van der Linden, F. Robert. *The Boeing 247: The First Modern Airliner*. Seattle: University of Washington Press, 1991.
Waller, Jr., Thomas G. "War on a Flying Cloud." *Journal of the Fort Smith Historical Society* 37, no. 2 (September 2013): 20–26.
Wallwork, Ellery D., and Kathryn A. Wilcoxson. *Operation Deep Freeze: 50 Years of U.S. Air Force Airlift in Antarctica, 1956–2006*. Scott Air Force Base, IL: Office of History, Air Mobility Command, 2006.
Waterkeyn, Xavier. *Air and Space Disasters of the World*. Australia: New Holland, 2009.
Watson, Robert P., Robert J. Wolz, and Michael J. Devine, eds. *The National Security Legacy of Harry S. Truman*. Kirksville, MO: Truman State Press, 2005.
Weintraub, Stanley. *15 Stars: Eisenhower, MacArthur, and Marshall: Three Generals Who Saved the American Century*. New York: Simon & Schuster, 2008.
Whitcomb, Edgar D. *On Celestial Wings*. Montgomery, AL: Air University, 1995.
Williams, Nicholas M. "Globemaster: The Douglas C-74." *AAHS Journal* 25, no. 2 (Summer 1980): 82–106.
Williams, Robert E. "First Around the World by Air." *American Aviation Historical Society Journal* 59, no. 1 (Spring 2014): 41–59.
Wittel, Major E. G. "Interview, Mr. Airlift, Lieutenant General William H. Tunner." *Airlift Operations Review* 3, no. 2 (April 1981).
Woods, Randall. *LBJ: Architect of American Ambition*. Cambridge, MA: Harvard University Press, 2007.
Yeager, Chuck, and Leo Janos. *Yeager*. New York: Bantam Books, 1985.
Yenne, Bill. *McDonnell Douglas: A Tale of Two Giants*. Greenwich, CT: Bison Books, 1985.
Yergin, Daniel. *Shattered Peace: The Origins of the Cold War and the National Security State*. Boston: Houghton Mifflin, 1977.

Interviews

Fred Barber, July 29, 2013, available at derfb1@aol.com.
John Christy, dated August 30, 2010, available at Johnjames79@live.com.
Emory Dockery, C-124 pilot, interview dated April 29, 2014, in possession of author.
William L. Farrar, interview recounted in Earl Berlin, Douglas C-124 Globemaster II.
Robert Fox, navigator instructor, interview dated October 10, 2010, in possession of author.
John Hille, email dated April 12, 2014, in possession of author.
Marvin Franklin, USAF retired, interview dated August 19, 2013, in possession of author.
Alan Moore, interview dated July 11, 2010, in possession of author.
Rick Parr, October 24, 2010, telephone interview in possession of author.
John J. Sullivan, email dated March 22, 2014, in possession of author.
Jack Wofford, USAF pilot retired, interview dated February 3, 2014, in possession of author.
James Zeitler, dated August 30, 2010, available at Jnjzeitler689@cox.ne.

Index

Numbers in **_bold italics_** indicate pages with illustrations

Acheson, Dean 5
Adak Naval Air Station, Alaska 154
Adams, Jim **_58_**
Adana, Turkey 19
Aerial Navigation Platform 7
Air Cavalry, 1st, U.S. Army 71, 95, 164, 166–169
Air Defense Command (ADC) 13, 29
Air Material Command (AMC) 30–31
Air Mobility Command Museum 4, **_24_**, **_73_**, 147
aircraft: commercial development 23; comparisons 64; fighter aircraft in Vietnam 14; fighter planes 129, 136–138, 192ch1n7; propeller airplanes 14
albatross (gooney bird) 93
Al-Kemal 46
Altus AFB, Oklahoma 64, 143
Aluminum Company of America (Alcoa) 31
"Aluminum Overcast" 23, 31
American Airlines 25
"American Century" 4–6, 71, 86, 107 178–179, 191intro.n3
Argentati, Elio **_158_**
Armstrong, Neil 176, 199ch7n5
astrodome 17, 58
Athens International Airport **_2_**, 11, 14–15, 17
atomic bombs 4–6, 26, 31, 62, 72, 157, 175–176, 195ch3n29
Attu, Alaska 116–118
Aultman, Thomas O. 115
Azores *see* Lajes AB

B-52 *see* Boeing Aircraft Company
B-57 *see* Martin-General Dynamics
Balaguer, Joaquin 111
Bangkok, Thailand 134, 171, **_172_**, 173–174
Bao Dai, Emperor, 161

Barksdale AFB, Louisiana 53, 150
Bassham, James Harry 138–140
Bateman, Jerry Don 144
Beasley, Willis 148, **_150_**, 199ch8n13
Beaulieu, Paul 171
Bell HU-1 Huey 162, 169
Bell X-1 123–124
Benes, Edvard 74
Berlin Airlift 3, 28–29, 70, 74ch2n12, 199
Berlin Conference 74
Bibo, John J. **_122_**
Bien Hoa AB, South Vietnam 175
Billingsley, Jennifer **_127_**
Blackburn B-101 *Beverly* 30
Blytheville AFB, Arkansas (Eaker AFB) 139
Boeing Aircraft Company 25, 40; B-47 Stratojet 61; B-52 Stratofortress 6, 61–62, 67, 97, 137, 167, 180; Boeing 247 25; Boeing 747 40; C-97 Stratocruiser 30, 177; C-135 154; KC-135 37, 137; X-20 124
Bowditch, Nathaniel (*The American Practical Navigator*) 90
Boyd, Albert 123–124
Brandenburg, Vernon Keith 144
Brown, Pat 37
Brown and Root 105, 107
Buck, Bob (*North Star Over My Shoulder*) 144
Buys Ballot, C.H.D. and Buys Ballot law 90

C-5 *see* Lockheed
C-47 *see* Douglas Aircraft Company
C-123 *see* Fairchild
C-124 Globemaster II: Airborne Radar Approach (ARA) 119; airlift from Europe to Vietnam 161; airlift missions to Vietnam 167, 170; airplane graveyard 179; Aleutian flying conditions 116; Alliance

for Progress mission 95; in Antarctica 98; bunks in 87; celestial navigating 87–88; changed air mobility capability 178; crew captured 78; crews and equipment 83–85, 121, 132–136; deadly crash of 152; "Dewliner" press tour 114–115; ditching and crew disappearance of 150–151; at Dover 67–**68**, 81–82; drop zone techniques in Vietnam 165; embedded in Colony Glacier, Alaska 151; flying hours record of 152; formation flying **72 80**; gear up landing of 146; landing bet between pilots 125; loss of number one engine 154; metal fatigue of 153; mid-air collision with 148; mission to Congo 75–79; mountain wave 112; in newspaper datelines 96; 1965 inventory 111, 164; nuclear mishaps 72–73; operational temperature ranges 96; pallet dropping from 126; production 32–34, 36–38; range 85; stage system 133, 168; *State of Oregon* 184; *State of Washington* 184; Suez Canal 166; takeoff procedures 12; typical C-124 heavy lift round trip data 22; wing tunnel of 145

C-130 *see* Lockheed
C-141 *see* Lockheed
Caamano, Francisco 111
Cam Ranh AB, South Vietnam 168
Cannon AFB, New Mexico 141
Carswell AFB, Texas 145
Castle AFB, California 131, 146–147
Castro, Fidel 109
Chateauroux AB, France 77, 83, 85–86, 161
Chiang Kai-Shek 28, 155, 157
Churchill, Winston S. 4, 5, 18, 26
Cigli AB, Turkey 15, 17
Clark AB, Philippines 132, 167, 171
Clay, Lucious DuBignon 28
Cloud, William F. 163
Clover Field, California 24
Columbus, Christopher 1, 16, 38, 45–47, 50, 86, 88, 110, 179, 194*ch3n*4
Combat Survival Training 64–66
Congo 73, 74; airlift to 77, 81; Congo River 75; name change 78
Consol 89, 92
Consolan 92–93
Convair T-29 58, 61, 195*ch3n*28
Cook, Capt. James 1, 48, 179
Cooperton, Oklahoma 120, 141
Coriolis 41, 90
counter-insurgency (COIN) 21, 64, 66, 71, 81, 165
Cuba 108–111, 138–139
Cullen, Paul Thomas 150
Cypress, California 39

Dalhart, Texas 59

Da Nang, South Vietnam 134, **136**, 164, 170
Davis Monthan AFB, Arizona 179
de Gaulle, Charles 85
Delaware State News 73
Distant Early Warning (DEW) 96, 114
Dr. Strangelove 13, 63
Donaldson AFB, South Carolina 63
Douglas Aircraft Company 3, 6, 29, 31, **35**, 36–38, **39**, 40, 94, 96, 177; C-17 Globemaster III 31, 38, 41, 95, 180; C-47 Skytrain 26, 28, 87, 94, 155, 160, 177; C-54 Skymaster 28–29, 177; C-74 Globemaster I 3, 28–30; C-133 Cargomaster 37, **68**, **82**; Cloudster 24; DC-1 (Douglas Commercial) 24, 25; DC-2 25; DC-3 25–26, 94, 193*ch2n*11; DC-4 123; DC-8 36, 40; Douglas World Cruiser 24; MD-12 40
Douglas Park 38, **41**
Dover, Delaware 1, 68, 70, 72
Dover AFB, Delaware 22, **24**, 30, 38, 63, 66 **68**, 69–**72**, 73, 75–**76**, 77, 80–81, 83, 85, 96–97, 116, 125–126, 129, 141, 144–145, 147, 167
Driftmeter 38, 90, **91**
Dulles, John Foster Dulles 20–21, 73, 106
Durant, Will (*History of Civilization*) 47
Dutch Harbor, Alaska 117–118
Dyna-Soar program 124

Earhart, Amelia 1, 52, 179
Edwards AFB (Muroc), California 30, 123–124
Eisenhower, Dwight David 20, 116, 161, 170; foreign policy 21, 106, 109, 124, 174; Supreme Allied Commander 26
Ellington AFB, Texas 54
Elmendorf AFB, Alaska 112, 151, 153
Esenboga Airport, Turkey 19

Fairbanks, Alaska 113, 115
Fairchild C-123 Provider 37–38, 80, 167, 170, 174
Fall, Bernard (*Street Without Joy* and *Hell in a Very Small Place*) 155, 164
Feinsinger, Nat 35
Ferebee, Thomas Wilson 62
fighter pilots 21
flight rules, VFR, IFR 15, 19
Forrestal, James V. 29, 177
Fort Bragg, North Carolina 111, 114, 126–127, 138
Fortune Magazine 31
Forwood, William G. 98
Fox, Robert 57
Franklin, Benjamin 51
Franklin, Marvin 191*intro.n*10
Frye, Jack 25
Fulbright, J. William (*Arrogance of Power*) 162–163

Gann, Ernest K. (*Fate Is the Hunter*) 121
Gatow RAF Base, East Berlin 28
Gavin, James 164
Getchell, Paul Everett 55, 174, **175**
Glen Martin Company 24
Glenn, John 73, 125
Gish, Don R. 141
Gold Fire training exercise 79–80, 164
Goldwater, Barry 106–107
Gooney bird *see* Albatross
Goose Bay AB, Labrador 86, 96
Grand Coulee Dam 37
Greenland 2, 96–97, 114, 167
Greenwich Observatory and Greenwich Mean Time (GMT) 18, 48
Groves, Leslie 26
Gulf of Tonkin Resolution 121, 162, 165, 174

Hammarskjold, Dag 75–76, 78–79, 196*ch*4*n*25
Hanoi 161, 169; Bach-Mai airport 155; Haiphong 162
Harlingen AFB, Texas 54, 57–58, 175
Harmon Field, Newfoundland 85, 146
Harrison, John 48
Heinemann, Ed 153
Heller, Joseph (*Catch-22*) 53
Hickam AFB, Hawaii 34, 102–103, 130, 132, 145, 147, 167–168
Hill AFB, Utah 129–130, 148, 150, 168
Hille, John 148, **150**
Ho Chi Minh 159–160, 163
Humphrey, Hubert 37
Hunter AFB, Georgia 34, 129–130
Huntington Beach, California 39

Incirlik AB, Turkey 19–21
Inertial Navigation System (INS) 37–38
Intercontinental Ballistic Missile (ICBM) 7–8, 20

James Connally AFB, Texas 54, 57–58, 60, 139
Johnson, Lady Bird 107
Johnson, Lyndon Baines 107, 111, 136, 161–164, 166, 174, 176
Johnson Island 2, 52, 93, **94**

Kadena AB, Okinawa 124, 136–137, 171
Katanga province, Republic of Congo (Leopoldville) 73, 75, 78, 96
Kennedy, John F. 20–21, 60, 63, 66–67, 71, 79, 107, 109, 124, 161, 165
Kennedy, Robert (Bobby) 176
Kham Duc **169**
Khrushchev, Nikita 3–4, 20, 75, 196*ch*4*n*11
Kim Il Sung 6, 157
Knight, Pete 124

Lackland AFB, Texas 55, 57, 64
Lajes AB, Azores 22, 38, 85–87, 92, 125
Larson AFB, Washington 161
LeMay, Curt 6, 13, 27, 61, 146, 166, 192*ch*1*n*4, 192–193*ch*2*n*3
Lindbergh, Charles A. (*Spirit of St. Louis*) 1, 49–50
Lippmann, Walter 3
Lockheed Corporation 37, 40, 81; C-5 Galaxy 37–38, 81, 117, 168; C-130 Hercules 37, 71, 80–81, 111, 128, 165, 167; C-141 Starlifter 37–38, 81, 117; SR-71 Blackbird 116
Lockheed Martin 32
Long Beach, California 2, 30, 32, 34, 36, 38, 41
Long Beach Press Telegram 34
Long Range Navigation (Loran) 7, 58, 89, 91–92, 130–131
Luce, Henry 4
Lumumba, Patrick 75–78

MacArthur, Douglas 13, 81, 157, 161
Mactan AB, Philippines 47, 132–134, 168, 171
Madden, Barney 167
Magee, John Gillespie, Jr. (*High Flight*) 11, 191*ch*1*n*1
Magellan, Ferdinand 1, 47, 108, 133–134, 179
Mahan, Alfred Thayer (*The Influence of Sea Power Upon History, 1660–1783*) 23, 178
Maher, Richard **115**
Manhattan Project 26, 195*ch*3*n*29
Mao Zedong 27, 157
maps 7, 48, 51–52; grid maps 49; Operational Navigation Chart (ONC) 16–17, 59, 77, 87
Marshall Plan 73
Martin-General Dynamics B-57 Canberra 174, **175**, 176
Mather AFB, California 54, 61–63, 66
McCallum, David **127**
McCarty, Chester E. 98
McChord AFB, Washington 30, 70, 111–114, 117, 130, 134, 151, 153, 167–168
McConnell, John P. 166
McDonnell, James Smith 40
McDonnell Douglas Corporation 38
McGuire AFB, New Jersey 30, 67
McKennon, Pierce 191*ch*1*n*1
McMurdo, Alexander 98
McMurdo Sound 98–101
McNamara, Robert 164
Mercury space capsule, *Friendship VII* 73
Messerschmitt 323 *Gigant* 30
Messick, Sheriff Leon 141
Midway Island 51, 93–94
Military Airlift Command (MAC) 36

Index

Military Air Transport Service (MATS) 4, 6, 11–15, 22, 28, 30, 63, 67, 70, 75, 77, 79–84, 86, 96, 99–101, 104, 109, 111, 119, 121, 128–130, 133, 135, 141, 151–153, 168, 178
Milner, Chuck 33
Mitchell, Billy 23, 177
mobility: by airlift 6, 154, 178; need recognized by U.S. Army 163–164, 168
Mobutu Sese Seko 78
Moore, Allen 142–143
Moore, Terris 151
Morison, Samuel Eliot 88
Morrisey, William J. 34
Mount Hope RCAF, Ontario 146
Muroc AB, California *see* Edwards AFB
Museum of the United States Air Force at Wright-Patterson AFB *129*, 179

N-1 compass 15–16, 97; compared to "whiskey compass" 16
National Aeronautical and Space Administration (NASA) 98, 124–125, 176
Navigational radio system *see* radios
Navigator training *see* Undergraduate Navigator Training
Navstar Ground Positioning System 38
Newton, Sir Isaac 87
Ngo Dinh Diem 161
Nixon, Richard Milhaus 21, 37, 176
Non-Aligned Countries 20
Noonan, Fred 52
Norstrom, John J. 144
North American Air Defense (NORAD) 13, 71
North Atlantic Treaty Organization (NATO) 3, 5, 15, 18, 70–71, 74–75, 79, 85, 91, 97, 155, 160
North Vietnam 71, 161–163, 175

Ocean Station Vessel 93
Officer's Training School (OTS) 54–55, 57
Offutt AFB, Nebraska 13, 147
Operation New Tape 76–77

Pan American Airways (Pan Am) 26, 50–51, 53, 83, 86, 108–109
Parr, Rick 143
Pickens, Jimmy 175
pilot training 13, 53, 62, 128, 146, 149
Pleiku, South Vietnam 164, 169
Polaris (North Star) 46, 89, 196*ch5n*8
Pope AFB, North Carolina 126, 138
Pratt and Whitney engines 11, 17, 30, 32, 143
Price, George *56*, 66, *179*
Prince Henry (the Navigator) of Portugal 43–45, 47, 86
Ptolemy 48

radar 14, 36, 58, *92*, 93, 113, 119, 129, 134, 144, 166; Airborne Radar Approach (ARA) 119; APS-42 36, 119–120, 130, 113, 118, 130, 144; MA/6A 61, 119
radios, types of 15–16; beacons 77; navigational radio systems 15–16
Radowski, Mike 130–132
Ramey AFB, Puerto Rico 110, 138
Randolph Air Base, Texas 53, 195*ch3n*20
Reagan, Ronald W. 111–112
Red Elk, Sgt. 56
Rodney, Caesar 68
Roosevelt, Franklin 4, 25–27, 52
Rowlett, Cyrus 25
Rusk, Dean 110
Rykiel, Walt 81

Sahara Desert 77
Salazar, Antonio de Oliveiro 86
San Isrido Airport, Dominican Republic 138
Scott AFB, Illinois 2, 30, 53
sextant 17, 38, 40, *44*, 46, 52, 58–59, 64, 87–89, *90*, 130
Sheyma Air Station, Alaska 116–117, 153
Siple, Dr. Paul Allman 100–101
Smith, Richard Dean 175–176
Song Be, South Vietnam 1 67, 169
South Vietnam 70–71, 107, 134, 161–164, 166, 170–171, 174
Spaatz, Carl A. 29
Stead AFB, Nevada *see* Combat Survival Training
Stonecipher, Harry 40
Strategic Air Command (movie) 13
Strategic Air Command (SAC) 6, 13–14, 29, 36, 54, 61, 63–64, 66–67, 73, 95–97, 110, 119, 128–129, 135, 137, 146–147, 150
Sullivan, John J. 149, *150*
Sullivan, Thomas 151
Swift Strike training exercises 79, 164
Symington, W. Stuart 29, 177

TACAN/VOR 15, *16*, 17, 102–103, *113*, 125
Tachikawa AB, Japan 107, 130, 152, *158*, 167, *169*
Tactical Air Command (TAC) 13–14, 29, 36, 63, 98, 101, 128–129
Taft, Robert A. 5
Tambini, Anthony J. (*Douglas Jumbo's, The Globemaster*) 149
Tan Son Nhut AB, South Vietnam 38, 102, 134, 170, 175
Taylor, Maxwell 21
Tempelhof AB, Berlin *4*
Tennessee Air National Guard 1, 140, 171
Thomas, Evan (*Ike's Bluff*) 20
Thomas, James 100
Thule AB, Greenland 79, 96–97, 114
Thurmond, Strom 74

Index

Tibbets, Paul 62
Tkatch, Richard 144
Tommy Franks museum (Hobart, Oklahoma) 141
Torrejon AB, Spain 22
Trans World Airlines (TWA) 25
Travis AFB, California 30, 67, 147
Tripp, Juan 50, 52, 83, 86
Troske, Erwin E., Jr. 11, 14, 19–21
Trujillo, Rafael 111
Truman, Harry S. 3–6, 21, 26–29, 34–35, 73–74, 123; Executive Order 9981 29, 73; National Security Act 29; 1948 election 73; Potsdam decision 26; strike at Douglas plant 34
Truman Doctrine 73
Tshombe, Moise 75, 78
Tulsa, Oklahoma 25–26, 148–150
Tunner, William H. 28–29, 177

U-2 flights 20
Ulbricht, Walter 3
Undergraduate Navigation Training (UNT) 7, 57, 61

Vandenberg, Hoyt 177
Van Kirk, Theodore "Dutch" 62–63
Vaughn, Robert 127
Viet Cong 162
Viet-Minh 155–157, 160–162
Vietnam Memorial Wall 174
Vietnam War 107, 132, 134, 145, 154, 176, 178
Vo Nguyen Giap 160

Wage Stabilization Board (WSB) 34
Wake Island 51–52, 101–107, *103*, *104*, *106*, 127–128, 132
Weems, P.V.H. (*Air Navigation*) 52
Western Oklahoma College 144
Wheelus AB, Libya 77
White, Jackie 144
Wilkes, Charles 101
Williams, Monte Patrick 144
Wofford, Jack 146, *147*
Wolfe, Tom (*The Right Stuff*) 125
Wren, Christopher 48

Yeager, Chuck 57, 121, 123–125, 146, 198*ch*7*n*2
Yenne, Bill 39

www.ingramcontent.com/pod-product-compliance
Ingram Content Group UK Ltd.
Pitfield, Milton Keynes, MK11 3LW, UK
UKHW041959140426
5217IPUK00015B/889